Sentence Dynamics

An English Skills Workbook

Fourth Edition

Constance Immel

West Los Angeles College

and

Florence Sacks

West Los Angeles College

LONGMAN

An imprint of Addison Wesley Longman, Inc.

New York • Reading, Massachusetts • Menlo Park, California • Harlow, England
Don Mills, Ontario • Sydney • Mexico City • Madrid • Amsterdam

Editor-in-Chief: Patricia Rossi
Acquisitions Editor: Steven Rigolosi
Marketing Manager: Anne Stypuloski
Supplements Editor: Donna Campion
Project Coordination and Text Design: Ruttle, Shaw & Wetherill, Inc.
Cover Design Manager: Nancy Danahy
Cover Design/Illustration: Joe DePinho
Full Service Production Manager: Joseph Vella
Electronic Page Makeup: Ruttle, Shaw & Wetherill, Inc.
Senior Print Buyer: Hugh Crawford
Printer and Binder: Courier/Westford, Inc.
Cover Printer: Phoenix Color Corporation

Library of Congress Cataloging-in-Publication Data

Immel, Constance.
    Sentence dynamics: an English skills workbook / by Constance Immel and
  Florence Sacks.—4th ed.
        p.   cm.
    Instructor's manual to accompany Sentence dynamics.
    Includes index.
    ISBN 0-321-00343-8 (free copy). —ISBN 0-321-00342-X (pbk.)
    1. English language—Sentences—Problems, exercises, etc.
I. Sacks, Florence.   II. Title.
PE1441.I48   1998
428.2—dc21   98-13305
                                                               CIP

Copyright © 1999 by Addison-Wesley Educational Publishers Inc.

Please visit our website at http://longman.awl.com

ISBN 0-321-00342-X

12345678910—CRW—01009998

❋ *Brief Contents*

Detailed Contents

 *Preface*

The fourth edition of *Sentence Dynamics* retains many features of the previous edition. We have successfully used the material in the first three editions of *Sentence Dynamics* in our own writing classes, and we believe that the clearly worded definitions and examples, together with the variety of exercises, can help students in developmental writing courses, in English-as-a-second-language classes, and in writing laboratories and tutor-assisted classes.

To help students write clear, error-free sentences, the fourth edition of *Sentence Dynamics* features:

- **Thorough coverage** of key areas of grammar.
- **Clear explanations** with a minimum of grammatical terms.
- **Definitions** at the beginning of each chapter to serve as a reference guide.
- An **abundant variety of exercises**—multiple choice, sentence completion, sentence expansion, and original sentence generation.
- **Lesson reviews, practice tests, summaries,** and **sentence combining** in each chapter based on the skill presented in each chapter.
- An **answer key** at the end of each chapter to encourage students to work at their own pace and check their answers as they go.
- A comprehensive **instructor's manual** with a **test bank** and **additional writing assignments.**

New to This Edition

The changes we have made to the fourth edition of *Sentence Dynamics* are in keeping with our philosophy that students at this level learn best when they are actively engaged in the learning process. Therefore, we keep the explanatory material short, but we provide extensive examples and exercises that demonstrate the principle. Thus, the students are never faced with long, complicated explanations that are difficult to understand. New to this edition are **Group Activities** that encourage students to consult with one another as they work through some of the writing assignments.

Many of the exercises are in paragraph form or contain sentences all on one topic. They cover a wide range of subjects. The new topics we have supplied for writing assignments in each chapter should interest students, who then should be able to express opinions about them, based upon their own reading and observation. As in earlier editions of *Sentence Dynamics,* we have chosen expository topics rather than narrative or descriptive assignments. These topics include **material on public issues, popular culture, and matters of scientific interest.** We believe that students at this level should be learning how to write with the objectivity they must demonstrate in their college classes and in their careers.

Chapter 1, entitled "Writing a Paragraph," has been revised in response to instructors' requests for additional emphasis on the writing process, and it now includes **a new section on the writer's voice** as well as a section on keeping a **journal.** It has expanded coverage on the search for ideas, major and minor support, outlines, the topic sentence, methods used to develop paragraphs, unity, coherence, and the need to proofread and revise a draft before submitting an assignment.

The Teaching and Learning Package

A series of useful aids is available with *Sentence Dynamics*.

Instructor's Manual with Test Bank.   The Instructor's Manual with Test Bank contains material for the classroom in an easy-to-photocopy format. It includes teaching suggestions and an answer key to all text exercises, Group Activities, and tests. The authors have provided three different chapter tests for each of Chapters 2 through 10 (one of which is a shortened, multiple-choice format for instructors who prefer a briefer version), a midterm exam, a final exam, and additional suggested writing assignments (0-321-00344-6).

Longman's Grammar Software.   For computerized practice and tutorial, download Longman's free grammar software for our Web site. Organized by topic, the Longman Grammar Package is the ideal complement to *Sentence Dynamics*. Find the software at **http://longman.awl.com/basicskills/grammar.**

The Longman English Pages Web Site.   Both students and instructors can visit our free content-rich web site for additional reading selections and writing exercises. From the Longman English pages, visitors can conduct a simulated Web search, learn how to write a résumé and cover letter, or try poetry writing. Stop by and visit us at **http://longman.awl.com/englishpages.**

The Longman Basic Skills Package

In addition to our book-specific supplements discussed above, a series of other skills-based supplements are available for both instructors and students. All these supplements are available either free or at greatly reduced prices.

For Additional Reading and Reference

The Dictionary Deal.   Two dictionaries can be shrinkwrapped with any Longman Basic Skills title at a nominal fee. *The New American Webster Handy College Dictionary* (0-451-18166-2) is a paperback reference text with more than 100,000 entries. *Merriam Webster's Collegiate Dictionary,* tenth edition (0-87779-709-9), is a hardback reference with a citation file of more than 14.5 million examples of English words drawn from actual use.

Penguin Quality Paperback Titles.   A series of Penguin paperbacks is available at a significant discount when shrinkwrapped with any Longman Basic Skills title. Some titles are: Toni Morrison's *Beloved* (0-452-26446-4), Julia Alvarez's *How the Garcia Girls Lost Their Accents* (0-452-26806-0), Mark Twain's *Huckleberry Finn* (0-451-52650-3), *Narrative of the Life of Frederick Douglass* (0-451-52673-2), Harriet Beecher Stowe's *Uncle Tom's Cabin* (0-451-52302-4), Dr. Martin Luther King, Jr.'s *Why We Can't Wait* (0-451-62754-7), and plays by Shakespeare, Miller, and Albee. For more information, please contact your Addison Wesley Longman sales consultant.

80 Readings.   This inexpensive volume contains 80 brief readings (1 to 3 pages each) on a variety of themes: writers on writing, nature, women and men, customs and habits, politics, rights and obligations, and coming of age. Also included is an alternative rhetorical table of contents. (0-321-01648-3)

100 Things to Write About.   This 100-page book contains 100 individual assignments for writing on a variety of topics and in a wide range of formats, from expressive to analytical. Ask your AWL sales representative for a sample copy. (0-673-98239-4)

Electronic and Online Offerings

The Basic Skills Electronic Newsletter.   Twice a month during the spring and fall, instructors who have subscribed receive a free copy of the Longman Basic Skills Newsletter in their e-mailbox. Written by experienced classroom instructors, the newsletter offers teaching tips, classroom activities, book reviews, and more. To subscribe, visit the Longman Basic Skills Web site at **http://longman.awl.com/basicskills** or send an e-mail to **BasicSkills@awl.com.**

The Writer's Workshop.   The Writer's Workshop "pops up" over any commercial word processing program to provide writing prompts for students as they compose their papers. An online handbook provides instant reference. Available for a nominal fee when shrinkwrapped with any text. (IBM 0-321-04756-7; Mac 0-321-04757-5)

For Instructors

Competency Profile Test Bank.   This series of 60 objective tests covers ten general areas of English competency, including fragments, comma splices and run-ons, pronouns, commas, and capitalization. Each test is available in remedial, standard, and advanced versions. Available as reproducible sheets or in computerized versions. Free to instructors. (Paper version: 0-321-022246; Computerized IBM: 0-321-02633-0; Computerized Mac: 0-321-02632-2)

Diagnostic and Editing Tests.   This collection of diagnostic tests helps instructors assess students' competence in Standard Written English for the purpose of placement or to gauge progress. Available as reproducible sheets or in computerized versions, and free to instructors. (Paper: 0-321-02222-X; Computerized IBM: 0-321-02629-2; Computerized Mac: 0-321-02628-4)

ESL Worksheets.   These reproducible worksheets provide ESL students with extra practice in areas they find the most troublesome. A diagnostic test and post-test are provided, along with answer keys and suggested topics for writing. Free to adopters. (0-321-01955-5)

80 Practices.   A collection of reproducible, ten-item exercises that provide additional practices for specific grammatical usage problems, such as comma splices, capitalization, and pronouns. Includes an answer key, and free to adopters. (0-673-53422-7)

CLAST Test Package.   These two 40-item objective tests evaluate students' readiness for the CLAST exams. Strategies for teaching CLAST preparedness are included. Free with any Longman English title. (Reproducible sheets: 0-321-01950-4; Computerized IBM: 0-321-01982-2; Computerized Mac: 0-321-01983-0)

TASP Test Package.   These 12 practice pre-tests and post-tests assess the same reading and writing skills covered in the TASP examination. Free with any Longman English title. (Reproducible sheets: 0-321-01959-8; Computerized IBM: 0-321-01985-7; Computerized Mac: 0-321-01984-9)

Teaching Online.   Ideal for instructors who have never surfed the Net, this easy-to-follow guide offers basic definitions, numerous examples, and step-by-step information about finding and using Internet sources. Free to adopters. (0-321-01957-1)

Reading Critically.   For instructors who would like to emphasize critical thinking in their courses, this brief book (65 pages) provides additional critical thinking material to supplement coverage in the text. Free to instructors. (0-673-97365-4)

Teaching Writing to the Non-Native Speaker.   This booklet examines the issues that arise when non-native speakers enter the developmental classroom. Free to instructors, it includes profiles of international and permanent ESL students, factors influencing second-language acquisition, and tips on managing a multicultural classroom. (0-673-97452-9)

For Students

Researching Online, second edition.   A perfect companion for a new age, this indispensable new supplement helps students navigate the Internet. Adapted from *Teaching Online,* the instructor's Internet guide, *Researching Online,* speaks directly to students, giving them detailed step-by-step instructions for performing electronic services. Available at a nominal charge when shrinkwrapped with any Longman Basic Skills text. (0-321-02714-0)

Using Wordperfect in Composition and Using Microsoft Word in Composition.   These two brief guides assume no prior knowledge of WordPerfect or Word. Each guide begins with word processing basics and gradually leads into more sophisticated functions. Shrinkwrapped free with any Longman Basic Skills text. (WordPerfect: 0-673-52448-5; Word: 0-673-52449-3)

Learning Together.   This brief guide to the fundamentals of collaborative learning teaches students how to work effectively in groups, how to revise with peer response, and how to co-author a paper or report. Shrinkwrapped free with any Longman Basic Skills text. (0-673-46848-8)

A Guide for Peer Response.   This guide offers students forms for peer critiques, including general guidelines and specific forms for different stages in the writing process. Also appropriate for freshman-level courses. Free to adopters. (0-321-01948-2)

Acknowledgments

We greatly appreciate the assistance and understanding of Steven Rigolosi, our editor at Addison Wesley Longman. Special thanks to Jo Ellen Young, our colleague at West Los Angeles College.

In addition, we'd like to thank the following reviewers who provided us with many valuable suggestions: Cynthia S. Becerra, Humphreys College; Jessica Carroll, Miami-Dade Community College; Alice Cleveland, College of Marin; Mary Likely, Nassau Community College; Cecilia Lim, Arizona Western College; Kristina R. Michaluk, Community College of Beaver County; Linda Scholer, College of San Mateo; Gary D. Turner, Central Texas College; and Alfred J. Zucker, Los Angeles Valley College.

Constance Immel
Florence Sacks

1

❈ Writing a Paragraph

Lesson 1 ❈ *Planning a Paragraph*

You have registered in an English class, and you are eager to learn how to write clear, interesting paragraphs. Your first question is, "How do I start?" Let's assume that you have an assignment in front of you on the subject of protecting the environment, but so far you haven't written a word. You can continue to stare at the blank sheet of paper while waiting for inspiration; you can dash off whatever comes to mind and hope for the best; or you can begin by planning your paragraph before you write it.

Getting Started

Frequently the assigned topic will be broad enough to give each student an opportunity to draw on previous knowledge of the subject. For example, in the exercises that follow, you will be asked to discuss what you can do to protect the environment. Hardly a day goes by that you don't read or hear about the threat to life on our planet by the destruction of the environment, but what can you do about it? You have some general ideas about the problem, but what do you know specifically about it? Where do you find the information to write an entire paragraph on the subject?

First, look for ideas by exploring these five common sources of information:

1. Your own observation and experience
2. The observation and experience of people you know
3. Your college classes
4. Your reading
5. Radio and television programs

You probably have enough material for ten paragraphs if you can just take the first step. Begin by using the following techniques to start the writing process.

Listing Ideas

Make a list of your ideas on the subject by jotting down words and phrases in any order that they occur to you. Do not be concerned about anything except getting your thoughts down on paper. Here is an example of a list of ideas on the subject of protecting the environment:

> Keep my car in efficient operating condition.
> Don't use products made from polystyrene foam.
> Plant trees; landscape with shrubs that require little water.
> Recycle bottles, papers, etc.
> Carry cloth shopping bag to avoid using plastic bags at store.
> Use microwave for cooking small portions of food.
> Install a low-flow shower head.
> Contribute money to organizations working to save environment.
> Write letters to legislators on issues involving environment.
> Write letters to manufacturers to protest "overpackaging" of products.
> Join local groups that are working to save environment.
> Conserve energy in own home.
> Drive car as little as possible; use bike, walk to do errands.
> Check air conditioner to be sure it isn't leaking.
> Follow some of recommendations of gas, electric, water companies.
> Use cloth napkins instead of paper; don't use paper plates, etc.

You have completed a list of ideas; now you need to focus on one of them for your paragraph. Organize the material by grouping similar items. For example, from the list above, grouping the suggestions about cars could lead to the topic: acting responsibly as a car owner. You may want to start another list expanding on that idea. Your revised list might look something like this:

> Avoid making unnecessary sudden stops and starts.
> Keep engine tuned properly for efficient operation.
> Check air conditioner to be sure it isn't leaking.
> Reduce speed.
> Join car pool or use public transportation when possible.
> Bike or walk when doing errands.
> Drive a small or medium-sized fuel-efficient car.
> Keep tires properly inflated, check for wear periodically.

EXERCISE 1A

Make a list of your ideas on the topic "What Can I Do to Protect the Environment?" Discuss them with other students if you are working with a group in class.

_____

_____

_____

_____

_____

_____

_____

Freewriting

Instead of making a list, you may want to write in longer phrases and sentences in your search for a topic, producing a solid block of writing. Although your instructor has already provided some focus for your writing in an assignment such as this one, you still have plenty of scope to develop your own unique response. Here is an example of freewriting:

What can I do to save energy besides turn off the lights? In the kitchen, for instance. Both microwave ovens and stove-top cooking use less energy heating up a small meal than a conventional oven does. If you have a refrigerator over ten years old and can afford to, buy an energy-efficient one to save power. Use reusable plastic containers to pack lunches instead of using plastic bags that fill up landfills. Turn down thermostat ten degrees on water heater, put a jacket around it to save energy. In the bathroom, limit shower time to five minutes instead of almost draining tank of hot water. Can also put a water regulator on the shower head to save water. Turn off tap while brushing teeth or shaving. If you have an air conditioner, keep thermostat at 78 in the summer to cut down on use. In winter set thermostat between 65 and 68 and wear a sweater. Use biodegradable dishwashing liquid and laundry detergent. Don't buy products made of foam; choose cardboard instead of foam egg cartons, for example. Buying in bulk will cut down on packaging materials. Take plastics, aluminum cans, newspapers, glass to recycling centers.

EXERCISE 1B

Give yourself 15 or 20 minutes to record your thoughts as they occur to you on the topic, "What Can I Do to Protect the Environment?"

_____

_____

_____

_____

_____

_____

_____

_____

_____

After you have completed the exercise above, analyze what you have written to see if you have material for a paragraph by asking yourself some questions. How many possible topics do you have that you could develop? List them. What point is most important to you? If you choose the topic of greatest interest to you, you may find it easier to write your paragraph.

Clustering

Clustering should have a special appeal to those of you who like to sketch a diagram or make a map to explain a point. This technique will not only help you to put words on paper, but when you have finished, you may also discover connections among your thoughts that listing might not reveal. In the center of a blank sheet of paper, write the main word of your assignment and circle it. As you think of ideas, write them down, drawing lines to show the connections among them. Circle each word for easy reading. An example is shown on page 6.

The writer of the cluster on page 6 has a number of ideas that could be used as topics for a paragraph. "Protect the environment" is obviously too broad and complicated a subject for a single paragraph, but "recycling" and "reduce use of paper and plastics" are possibilities. Notice the connection the writer makes between "reduce the need for landfills" and "work on local problems." Some of the topics the writer thought of during the process of drawing the cluster, such as "save energy," led to ideas that would require some research and further limitation of the subject. However, the writer's interest in a local problem might be strong motivation for writing. Sometimes two clusters may lead to another approach more suited to a writer's purpose.

✳ *EXERCISE 1C* ✳

In the box on page 7 make your own cluster on how you can protect the environment and analyze it for possible topics.

Ask yourself which ideas interest you the most, which ones would require research, and which ones you already have material for. Can you add points to some of the clusters? Can you discover any relationship between two clusters of which you were unaware? Can you combine any of the clusters and come up with an even better idea?

By now you may have enough material to begin writing a paragraph, but consider the following method for developing additional ideas before you move on to the sections "Considering Your Readers" and "Outlining."

Keeping a Journal

Some professional writers keep a journal to record their observations of people, scenes, and events as well as their responses to their reading,

Example of Clustering

Your Own Cluster

including quotations and reactions to the writer's ideas. As a beginning writer, you may find that you enjoy writing in a journal for your own satisfaction instead of limiting your writing to class assignments. Some students say that after writing regularly in a journal, writing in class becomes easier.

How to Keep a Journal

1. Use a small spiral notebook you can carry with you in your purse or pocket along with a pencil or pen.
2. Write regularly, at least three or four times a week.
3. Date each entry.
4. Record the name of the author and the title of the book, magazine, or newspaper for reading notes.
5. Vary your entries by experimenting with freewriting, firsthand observations of your surroundings, and reading notes.

You cannot make a mistake in your journal. The notes you enter are to help you slow down and really look at the things around you. You might want to write about the first time you see a particular kind of flower each spring or about the first snowfall each winter. You could even use colored pencils to add a drawing of what you have described in words.

How to Get Started

Go outside. Walk around a parking lot, a patio, a porch. Find a brook or a pond, anything that is making a sound. If you live in the city, go to a neighborhood park and sit on a bench or under a tree. Ask yourself questions:

> What's different today?
> What sounds do I hear?
> What smells do I detect?

If you have a camera, you might want to take photos and paste the photos into your journal. Pay attention to detail such as size and color. You will soon find that your writing improves as you become a better observer of the world around you.

You may find that your journal can help you develop ideas for writing assignments in this class as well as others you are taking. Get in the habit of writing regularly.

Considering Your Readers

Another important point that you should consider after you have chosen your topic and are ready to begin the first draft of your paragraph is, "Who will your readers be?" If you can decide on a reader, real or imagined, you will sharpen the focus of the paragraph and generate additional ideas. Words may flow a little more easily as you gain a purpose other than writing to complete an assignment for class.

After you have decided on your readers, ask yourself what you might need to add to the material you have to attract, hold, and inform them. With your topic in mind, write down your answers to the following questions:

> Who exactly are your readers? What is their sex? Occupation? Educational background? Economic status?

What are their values? Their prejudices?

Why is this subject important to them?

What information can you expect them to know already about the subject?

What information must you supply?

Do you want to persuade them to take action? Or do you want to entertain them?

By the time you have answered these questions and any others you might think of, you should find not only that you have added some important details to your notes, but also that you have a better sense of what you want to do.

GROUP ACTIVITY

Suppose you have decided that the best place for an individual to begin protecting the environment is at home. You know that some communities require their citizens to separate trash. You have been separating yours and placing bottles, cans, and papers in separate recycling containers. Include some other activities you have begun to do at home, referring to the list you made in Exercise 1A, the Freewriting in Exercise 1B, and the cluster you have drawn in Exercise 1C. Don't forget to answer the questions about your intended readers before you begin to write.

Bring two things to class: the ideas generated for a paragraph through the listing, freewriting, and clustering exercises you have completed AND your list of answers to the questions about a reader. Your answers should give you a profile of your reader. Get together with a few classmates. Working together then, you can help each other out with your planning to this point. Concentrate on narrowing your focus to reach the best topic for your paragraph.

Outlining

Sometimes you will have a strong opinion about the topic before you begin making a list.

The author of the paragraph, "The Effects of the Oil-Drilling Project," was a student named Cathy. She knew who her intended readers were and what her opinion was, but she needed to get the reasons for her opinion down on paper before deciding on the exact wording of her topic sentence.

Cathy had read that an oil company was planning to drill for oil on a vacant lot near her house. On further investigation, she discovered that the company intended to erect a 135-foot derrick to begin with and then planned to drill up to 30 wells. Horrified, Cathy decided to write a letter to the city council members to dissuade them from approving the drilling project. She thought she knew what she wanted to say to her readers, so she drew up the following list as she sorted out her ideas in preparation for her letter:

Pollution of the air
Pollution of the ground water
Increased noise
Possible spills
Possible accidents
Waste disposal problems
Smells
Carcinogens
Loss of property values
Increased truck traffic

Making the list helped Cathy see that she had a lot of material to cover. She realized that making an outline would help her organize her material into a more manageable shape. She looked at the list and noticed that it could be broken down into three sections—the three major effects the oil project would have on her neighborhood:

1. Pollution
2. Increased noise
3. Increased traffic

Now she needed to fit in the other items on her list under these three major subjects:

1. Pollution
   a. Air
   b. Ground
   c. Water
2. Increased noise
   a. Babies sleeping
   b. People who work at home
   c. Interrupted conversations
3. Increased traffic
   a. Trucks bringing in equipment
   b. Trucks carrying away the oil
   c. Workers arriving and leaving

Cathy could now clearly see what her subject would cover and how she could develop her ideas. She began by writing her topic sentence:

> Increased noise, air pollution, and traffic will make life unpleasant for those of us who live near the oil-drilling project.

By "gathering up" her three major points from her outline, she was able to construct her topic sentence and to give shape to her paragraph.

Here is Cathy's paragraph as it looked when she was finished with the pre-writing and writing stages:

The Effects of the Oil-Drilling Project

Increased noise, air pollution, and traffic will make life unpleasant for people in the vicinity of the oil-drilling project. Drilling operations will be conducted from 8 A.M. to 7 P.M. Although many people are at work between those hours, many more are at home. Small children and babies nap during the day, as do elderly people who often do not sleep well at night. Most people leave their windows open to let in the breezes, and conducting conversations at a normal level will be impossible. And those people who earn their living by working at home will have a hard time concentrating because of the drilling noise. Furthermore, increased truck traffic will make the streets more noisy and dangerous. Pedestrians and drivers will have to be extra cautious to avoid encounters with large trucks bringing in equipment or hauling away oil and other products. The oil workers' cars and trucks will also contribute to the increased traffic in our quiet neighborhood. Finally, the problem of pollution will affect all those who live in the area surrounding the project. Site preparation, drilling, and production operations will pollute the air by emitting dust, odors, and hydrocarbons. Oil spills may contaminate the ground water. For all of these reasons, I urge the members of the City Council not to approve the oil-drilling project.

You probably noticed that Cathy decided to write about pollution last instead of first, as indicated in her outline. Why do you think she decided to do it that way?

Remember, the list and the outline are there to guide you in developing your paragraph. They should serve as an organizing method to put your ideas together coherently. It is not necessary to follow them exactly or to include everything in your paragraph. You are free to rearrange the order, omit certain ideas, or add other ideas as you are writing.

GROUP ACTIVITY

By now you should have an outline and at least one rough draft. Bring your outlines and rough draft to class. Form a group with several of your classmates to go over each other's work. You can help each other decide how the paragraph you are planning to write relates to your outline and which major points to stress. You may decide to change the order or leave out some parts of the outline altogether. Also, you can help each other to formulate a good topic sentence.

Lesson 2 ✳ *The Topic Sentence*

Composing the Topic Sentence

The topic sentence gives the writer's opinion about the topic, and it contains the main idea of the paragraph. Although a writer can place the topic sentence anywhere in the paragraph, it most commonly appears near the beginning. When you are writing a topic sentence, begin by looking at your list of ideas to determine how you can sum them up into one main point that will guide your discussion throughout the paragraph.

Example: Here is a list of Duke Ellington's contributions to jazz.

1. As a bandleader, Ellington was unique, creating his own jazz classification.
2. As a pianist, he was an original solo player and an imaginative accompanist.
3. He composed more than a thousand tunes.
4. He made over 2,000 arrangements, suiting them to individual players.
5. By the late 1970s, Ellington had recorded more than 150 albums.
6. He has had an important, lasting influence on musicians, composers, and arrangers.

Topic Sentence

Duke Ellington remains an outstanding figure in jazz.
OR
No one has made more contributions to jazz than Duke Ellington.

Judging the Topic Sentence

1. The topic sentence contains a *controlling idea.* It makes a judgment, gives an opinion about the topic.

    Examples: The Florida Keys have coral reefs. (No opinion is expressed about the subject.)

    Snorkelers love to explore the reefs near the Florida Keys because the coral offers hiding places for beautiful and unusual fish. (The controlling idea gives the writer's opinion about the subject.)

2. The topic sentence narrows and limits the subject.

    Examples: The grasses and other plants are dying. (too broad)

    As the turtle grasses have died off, large quantities of algae have formed and killed the sponges and corals. (limited)

3. The topic sentence is precise.

    Examples: Florida Bay water is polluted. (too general)

    The water in Florida Bay is becoming too salty because it is not getting enough fresh water. (specific)

4. The topic sentence is clear.

    Examples: The fish that used to live in the Florida Bay have disappeared. (vague)

    Fish such as the tarpon and the bonefish have left because they have nothing to feed on. (clear)

You can write better topic sentences if you follow these three rules:

1. Avoid dead end sentences or statements of fact or of intent.
    This paragraph will deal with the problems of the Florida Bay.

2. Avoid wild guesses.
    When the scientists can figure out why the algae bloom in the bay, they will be able to solve the problem of the dying reefs.

3. Avoid questions.
    What is the significance of the increased salinity of the Florida Bay?

EXERCISE 2A

For each group of sentences, write a topic sentence that could be used to develop a paragraph on the topic.

A.
1. The college bookstore was jammed with people.
2. It took me about 75 minutes to select and purchase books.
3. I could barely move through the aisles.
4. There were long lines at all the registers.
5. It was difficult to reach the books I needed on the shelves because of the huge crowd.
6. My feet were stepped on, and I was pushed and jostled rudely.
7. Furthermore, it was stuffy inside, about 85–90 degrees.
8. But the worst part was that the books were so expensive; I spent $268.20.

Topic Sentence: _____

_____

B.
1. Some fish make high-frequency sounds that are audible to other fish.
2. Fish use sound to keep schools of fish together.
3. Sounds give messages about mating, spawning, and fighting.
4. Changes in color and pattern tell a competitor that the fish will defend its territory and food.
5. Chemical signals probably involve taste and smell in mating rituals.
6. Ritualized movements are another means of relaying information.
7. Fish with electrical organs can give shocks as a warning to other fish.

Topic Sentence: _____

_____

C.
1. Gold miners of the 1850s faced a long, demanding journey to reach the gold fields.
2. They lived in primitive camps where tents or crude shelters provided minimum cover from the weather.
3. Miners spent hours working in the hot sun, mud, or icy water.
4. Health conditions were poor, and medicine was often nonexistent.
5. Saloon keepers, dance-hall women, gamblers, and merchants ultimately kept more of the gold than the miners did.

6. Within a few years, businessmen with capital to invest forced most of the individual miners from the gold fields.

Topic Sentence: _____

_____

D.
1. Albert Einstein was born in Germany in 1879.
2. He became a professor of physics in Berlin in 1914.
3. The Nazi government revoked his citizenship in 1934 because he was Jewish, and he fled to America where he worked at Princeton University until his death in 1955.
4. His famous Theory of Relativity dealt with systems or observers in uniform motion with respect to one another.
5. For his work in theoretical physics, he received the Nobel Prize in physics in 1921.

Topic Sentence: _____

_____

E.
1. Americans take 20,000 tons of aspirin a day.
2. We inhale the nicotine of 600 billion cigarettes a year.
3. We spend 10 billion dollars a year on alcoholic beverages.
4. Cola, cocoa, coffee, and tea that we drink daily contain caffeine and two other drugs.
5. Many people can't face the day without tranquilizers.

Topic Sentence: _____

_____

EXERCISE 2B

Write a topic sentence on the subject of protecting the environment.

_____

_____

_____

Supporting the Topic Sentence

By grouping the items on your list and writing the topic sentence, you now have a plan for your paragraph. You will be able to write the first draft after you take the next step—developing specific support for the main idea of the topic sentence. This material will come from your personal experience, your firsthand observation, and your reading.

General/Specific   A writer uses both general statements and specific words to get a point across to the reader. A term is general or specific only in relation to another term. For example, in the student's paragraph about the effects of the oil-drilling project, you can see that "trucks bringing in equipment" is more specific than the general description of "increased traffic."

Specific words explain a writer's meaning by giving details and creating pictures in the reader's mind. In the following example, the general statements on the left are explained in detail by the addition of specific support on the right. This writer describes the grounds at Monticello, Thomas Jefferson's home in Virginia.

General	Specific
Monticello had numerous flower gardens.	Twenty oval-shaped flower beds were located at the four corners of the house while long flower borders divided into 87 ten-foot compartments were placed on either side of a walkway that circled the front lawn.
The beds contained a variety of flowers.	In addition to tulips, sweet William, and Maltese cross, all newly imported from Europe, the garden included the cardinal flower native to the northeast and the "Columbian Lily" discovered by Lewis and Clark on their expedition.
Some of Monticello's original trees remain.	Five trees date from Jefferson's time: two tulip poplars, a sugar maple, a European larch, and a red cedar.
A "kitchen" garden provided vegetables for the family.	The garden had over 250 kinds of vegetables and herbs, such as sesame grown for its oil, sea kale, tomatoes, and twenty varieties of peas.

Three Kinds of Support   The three kinds of specific support that you will use most frequently in your writing assignments are *descriptive details, facts,* and *examples.* Although you could develop a paragraph with only one kind of support, generally you will use a combination of different types.

A. Descriptive Details: When you describe a subject in specific terms, you are appealing to the reader's five senses (sight, sound, smell, taste, and touch). If you are successful, the reader can see, hear, and feel vicariously what you experienced firsthand.

In the following example, a student uses specific descriptive details to describe the atmosphere and the food that contributed to her dining pleasure.

General Statement and Topic Sentence

We recently had a pleasant time in an Indonesian restaurant.

Specific Support

We recently had a pleasant time in an Indonesian restaurant. When we entered, the headwaiter seated us in a room with polished teak paneling and long, narrow, shuttered windows that extended from ceiling to floor. Large, slowly rotating ceiling fans hummed quietly and stirred the warm, moist evening air. Turbaned Malaysian waiters, dressed in short white cotton jackets and dark trousers draped with colorful, hand-printed batik sarongs, were serving the diners from hand-carved wooden Indonesian trays. Knowing nothing about Indonesian cuisine, we followed the waiter's recommendation and ordered rijsttafel (rice table) and a satay appetizer. After the satay of crisp, succulent charcoal-broiled lamb in a spicy peanut sauce, we ate the main course of curried chicken served with many different side dishes. These included salted, sliced duck eggs; spiced meats; fish fritters; fried cabbage and long beans; hot, spiced, paper-thin chilies; and many, many more. We wanted, of course, to sample as many of these delicacies as possible and still have room for the dessert, gulu malaca, a dish of native tapioca accompanied by sauces of coconut milk and molasses. Although the food may sound like a strange mixture, it makes, in fact, a delightful meal because the diners can "create" their dinners by selecting any number of dishes that they desire.

EXERCISE 2C

Write some specific descriptive details to support the following general statements.

General Statement

1. Robert was surprised by what he saw in the <u>courtroom</u> [or <u>classroom</u>]. (your choice)

_____

_____

General Statement

2. I have found the best place to study is the <u>school library</u> [or <u>my bedroom</u>]. (your choice)

_____

_____

B. Facts: Many times you will want to offer some evidence that can be verified. Facts provide exact details, for example, names, dates, places, and numbers. The following paragraph supports a general statement with factual details.

General Statement and Topic Sentence

Mrs. Pankhurst's activities, in fact, had an important influence on her American counterparts during those years.

Specific Support

The Seneca Falls Convention of 1848 is usually given as the event marking the beginning of the women's rights movement in the United States. Elizabeth Cady Stanton, Lucretia Mott, Susan B. Anthony, Lucy Stone, and Sojourner Truth are familiar names to most of us. Less well-known to Americans is Emmeline Pankhurst, who was one of the leaders of the British movement from 1903 to 1914. Mrs. Pankhurst's activities, in fact, had an important influence on her American counterparts during those years. Unable to move legislators by words, she founded the Women's Social and Political Union, whose motto was "Deeds not Words," and drew lower-class women into the movement. These British women used militant action as a new weapon, publicly heckling politicians and embarrassing police by provoking them to take violent action against women. When Mrs. Pankhurst arrived in the United States in 1913 to lecture at Madison Square Gardens, she was detained temporarily at Ellis Island as an undesirable alien. She was also arrested by the English at sea when she returned and imprisoned. By 1914 she had been arrested six times. The militancy of the British suffragettes gained international attention at a time when leaders of the American movement seemed to be marking time. Encouraged by Mrs. Pankhurst's success, the American movement took on new life as women sought public attention by parading, speaking at outdoor meetings, and picketing. This renewal of action would culminate after World War I in the passage of the 19th Amendment in 1919, followed by ratification in 1920 during Wilson's administration.

EXERCISE 2D

Write some specific factual details to support the following general statements.

General Statement

1. Jean planned her trip carefully.

_____

_____

_____

General Statement

2. If I could buy a new car, I would buy a _____.   (your choice)

_____

_____

_____

C. Examples: Another way to clarify your meaning is by giving your reader a short illustration with an example or two. The student writer of the following paragraph uses examples (and details) to define people who like to save things.

General Statement and Topic Sentence

"Squirrel people" will save just about anything.

Specific Support

My aunt "squirrels" away clothes among other things. Her closets are packed with boxes and bags of mothballed clothes from the 1960s, the 1970s, and the 1980s. Some women who are sentimental "to a fault" save all manner of romantic mementos. One friend has shoe boxes full of love letters and crackly dry, dusty old flowers. She saves matchbooks, napkins, ticket stubs, champagne corks, and even swizzle sticks from romantically memorable evenings. Another acquaintance keeps her souvenirs from the past ten years in marked files. She has a "Steve" file and a "Robert" file, among others. Parents are notoriously sentimental squirrel people. My parents' closet shelves have boxes with baby hair in envelopes, baby teeth in little boxes, bronzed baby shoes, bean and macaroni sculptures made in school, little plaster handprints, and, of course, mounds of photographs, report cards, and awards. My grandmother's files, drawers, and cupboards are full to the brim with string, coupons, business cards, glass jars, wine bottles, plastic containers, coffee tins, shopping bags with handles, empty egg cartons, buttons, rubber bands from newspapers, and scraps of material. She keeps small boxes to wrap presents in and gives me my presents in the same wrapping paper that I used to wrap her presents in. Don't laugh—every family has at least one squirrel.

❋   EXERCISE 2E   ❋

Write some specific examples to support the following general statements.

General Statement

1. Some advertisements use humor to sell a product.

_____

_____

General Statement

2. Tim was obviously suffering from stage fright.

_____

_____

Lesson 3 ❋ *Unity*

In Lesson 1 of this chapter, the student who wrote a paragraph on the effects of the oil-drilling project on the environment discarded three items from her list when she was planning her paragraph: waste disposal problems, carcinogens, and loss of property values. These items were of concern to her, but they did not support her topic—"the effect of increased noise, air pollution, and traffic on the quality of life." In fact, she might have developed these three items in separate paragraphs. The writer knew that *all* the sentences in a paragraph must support the main idea in a topic sentence if the paragraph is to have *unity*.

❋   **EXERCISE 3A**   ❋

Draw a line through the sentences that do not support the main idea in the topic sentence. For each item that you cross out, write a sentence of support on the lines that follow.

A. Topic Sentence: A dictionary is an indispensable tool for a student in a writing class.

1. It gives the origin and development of words.
2. A good hardback dictionary costs very little, considering its many uses.
3. This book is a good source of biographical information.
4. It tells the meaning of a word.
5. A dictionary should be required for most classes.
6. It lists both synonyms and antonyms.

_____

_____

_____

B. Topic Sentence: You don't have to join an expensive health club to keep fit.

1. Walk whenever possible, rather than drive your car.
2. You will find it easier to lose weight when dieting if you exercise.
3. Most park and recreation departments offer free or low-cost exercise classes.

4. You will sleep better at night if you exercise daily.
5. Exercise daily at a specific time.
6. Many television channels present daily exercise programs for you to do at home.

_____

_____

_____

C. Topic Sentence: Success in taking an essay exam depends on careful preparation.

1. Ask the instructor if he or she is going to give a multiple-choice test in addition to the essay exam.
2. Study your class notes to see what the instructor has emphasized.
3. Start studying well in advance of the test date, rather than the night before the exam.
4. Take along a candy bar to eat for quick energy during the exam.
5. If the instructor gives the class study guides, use them as a source of possible topics for essays.
6. Try to anticipate possible topics for essays; then outline answers.

_____

_____

_____

D. Topic Sentence: Good teachers have well-defined instructional methods.

1. They lecture clearly and slowly enough for students to take notes.
2. They participate in school functions.
3. They encourage students to ask questions in class.
4. They do not allow one student to monopolize class discussions.
5. They grade the work fairly and consistently.
6. They often attend teachers' conferences.

_____

_____

_____

EXERCISE 3B

Cross out the sentences that break the unity of the following paragraph. On the lines that follow, write sentences of your own that will fit into the paragraph and replace those you removed.

I have enjoyed this English class. We not only reviewed the basics of English grammar, spelling, and punctuation, but we also learned to expand sentences with the use of words, phrases, and clauses and to write well-developed paragraphs. The course theme might have been "taking a second look at what we know by reviewing the little things we take for granted but have forgotten." My physics class never reviewed any subject that we had already studied. The teacher expected us to know everything. The workbook that we used in this English class was well structured and clearly written. Our instructor gave us assignments from the workbook and explained any of the material that we had questions about. My math teacher ignored the textbook he had assigned and just lectured during class time. If we studied the practice tests ahead of time, the tests in this class were not difficult. My teachers in other classes made the tests too hard by not telling us what would be on them. I was discouraged by my low grades. The tests in this class were fun to take. As for the writing assignments, I found them interesting and helpful. All in all, I can honestly say that I learned a great deal in my English class this semester.

_____

_____

_____

_____

_____

_____

Lesson 4 ❈ *Organizing a Paragraph*

When you write a topic sentence stating the main idea that you plan to develop in your paragraph, you begin organizing it. When you cross out all the ideas in your list or cluster that do not directly support the topic sentence, you take another important step in that direction. If you also make an outline, even though you may alter it while writing your paragraph, you arrange your notes into a pattern that you can use to guide your first draft. Some writers feel limited by an outline and prefer to start writing without one, moving ideas around as they expand on their material. Whether you use an outline or not, keep in mind that each sentence of your paragraph should lead to the next one as logically and clearly as possible. Writers, of course, use many different ways to organize their paragraphs. For many of the assignments in this course, you may find the following three methods of organization useful.

Three Ways to Organize a Paragraph

1. General to Particular   State the topic sentence near the beginning of the paragraph and then provide enough specific support to explain your idea to the reader.

During the 1980s, basketball was transformed into a game that high-lighted running, quickness, and physical agility. For years, slow, deliberate play was the style in basketball, and teams required big centers and well-coordinated team effort. Teams passed the ball frequently to work it inside for a relatively short, easy shot. Player height was, of course, a valued physical trait. In the 1980s height was still a distinct advantage, but tall players, like Magic Johnson (6'9") of the Lakers and Larry Bird of the Celtics, added another dimension to the game by displaying the agility of six-foot athletes. The three-point basket contributed to the wide-open running game as teams quickly learned to push the ball up the court and take many shots, including the long three-pointer. Although team play was still important, the individual skills of running, dribbling, passing, and shooting attracted additional fans to the game. The popularity of this wide-open style resulted in increased revenues from both paid attendance and television. Subsequently, salaries rose for talented players with running-game skills. The Los Angeles Lakers, a winning team that captured nine NBA divisional titles and five world championships, typified that change.

2. *Particular to General*   Using this method, a reversal of the first one, get right down to specifics early in the paragraph. Lead up to the generalization contained in the topic sentence, which you place near the end of the paragraph.

The game of basketball has always placed a premium on the height of players. The franchise stars in the National Basketball League (NBA) are the giants, notably Shaquille O'Neal of the Lakers, Hakeem Olajuwon of the Rockets, and Dave Robinson of the Spurs. These men tower over all the other players on the court, who themselves stand at heights between 6 and 7 feet. Any knowledgeable fan, however, recognizes the skills of the talented, "smaller" men playing with the NBA's best teams. Topnotch point guards, for example, can dribble the length of the court, pass unerringly, shoot accurately from any range, and play aggressive and tenacious defense. Michael Jordan of the Bulls, rated by many experts as the greatest player of all time, John Stockton of the Jazz, and Nick Van Exel of the Lakers are prime examples of the importance of these key players. They contribute as much to team success as do the taller players, who figure so prominently in sports news. They play, in fact, a considerable role in making professional basketball of the '90s a fast-paced, exciting sport enjoyed by an increasing number of fans everywhere.

3. *Giving Reasons to Persuade*   You have a strong opinion to express and want to persuade your readers to share your point of view. Develop several valid reasons to support your position. State your main point in a topic sentence near the beginning of the paragraph, and if you wish, restate it in different words at the end of the paragraph as the student writer of the following one did.

A TV dinner, the instant meal in a throwaway pan, is one answer to the question, "What's for dinner?" The preparation of these frozen dinners requires no skill or thought other than the ability to read and to turn on the oven. They save the cook plenty of time, but they may deprive children of more than the flavor and nutrition of a home-cooked meal. First, our ever-increasing dependency on instant foods in throwaway containers may rob our children of a vital lesson. Because throwaway pans mean no table to set and no dishes to wash, children do not learn the responsibility of sharing these household chores. To have duties in a family assures them of being an integral part of the family. In addition, instant dinners require little or no preparation, so children are denied the valuable experience of learning to fix a meal. Moreover, they miss the praise they love to receive for a casserole they helped prepare or the cookies they baked "all by themselves." The child loses an opportunity to learn the value of giving and receiving in a family setting. Finally, families are often deprived of the intimacy that develops at the dinner table. Since TV dinners encourage us to eat in front of the television, we often forfeit this time together to watch a TV program. Gathered around the dinner table, the family can talk about the day's activities. Children and parents need this time to eat and talk together. When we hurry to heat and eat the food, and throw away the pan after dinner, we may also throw away the opportunity to develop lasting relationships that cannot be replaced by any instant, disposable product.

EXERCISE 4A

Write a paragraph on one of the following topics, using one of the methods in this lesson: general to particular, particular to general, or giving reasons to persuade.

1. A product that has remained popular for years
2. An important change in an activity or occupation
3. An important change in family values or relationships

Organizing with Transitional Words and Phrases

Arranging materials in a special pattern, such as general to particular, benefits both you as a writer and your reader. You have come a long way from your first tentative list of ideas to the carefully organized paragraph you now have in front of you.

If you read your paragraph aloud, however, your ears may tell you something that your eyes have overlooked. Although your discussion follows a logical order and does not stray from the path, the road may seem bumpy and not clearly marked. Therefore you need to provide some signposts to guide your reader—transitional words and phrases that will show the relationships among your ideas in the paragraph.

The following list contains the most commonly used transitional terms. Choose these useful expressions to fit the context of your sentences, or the result may be the opposite of what you intend. A careless choice can obscure what a writer is trying to make clear.

Addition—also, and, another, furthermore, moreover, too, in addition, in fact
Time—after, before, finally, first, second, meanwhile, next, then, while
Illustration—for example, for instance, such as, to illustrate
Contrast—but, however, instead, nevertheless, still, yet, in contrast, on the contrary, on the other hand
Conclusion—consequently, finally, thus, as a result, in conclusion, in general, in summary

EXERCISE 4B

Connect the following sentences by writing on each line an appropriate transitional word or phrase from the preceding list. Try to use a different word or phrase each time.

1. I am not against health foods in general. _____ I am opposed to the commercialization of certain foods known as "health foods."

2. Some T-shirt wearers have become walking billboards for a favorite product, while others display personal statements on their shirts. _____, many companies specialize in the personalization of T-shirts.

3. The automated bank teller is a convenience that I have found very useful. _____, with the automated teller, I never have to wait in line with more than two people. _____, the automated teller is

open twenty-four hours a day, on holidays, and weekends. _____, I don't have to deal with an unpleasant human bank teller or one who tries to rush me. _____, the automated teller makes banking more convenient for me.

4. How often have you, as a student, taken a test you felt was unsuitable for the material being covered? Have you ever been asked on a test, _____, to fit complex, detailed information into a framework of true-or-false questions?

5. Some kinds of "squirreling" or saving are considered acceptable, _____, stamp or coin collecting. _____, there are those wise people who save articles for future use. A true "squirrel" person, _____, pushes saving to an extreme.

6. The night before my final exam, I could not fall asleep until 3 A.M. My dog, _____, woke me up at 5 A.M., and I couldn't go back to sleep. _____, when I sat down at 8 A.M. to take my exam, I was very tired.

7. In my tight-knit community in England, everything was within a short bus ride or walking distance. In my American city, _____, everything is so spread out that I need a car to get around.

✳ EXERCISE 4C ✳

Read the following selection. Underline all the transitional words and phrases.

Pre-Columbian Art

Pre-Columbian Mexican art was collected extensively by the famous artist Diego Rivera. His collection of ceramic figures resulted in the first exhibit of the art of Western Mexico in 1946 in Mexico City. Since then, many exhibitions of these figures have been organized all over the world. Now, we recognize that West Mexican art consists mainly of ceramic figure sculpture that was found in tombs in the present Mexican states of Nayarit, Jalisco, and Colima. However, today these three names are used to describe pottery based on style rather than geography. It is clear, for example, that typical Nayarit figures can occur in the same tombs with figures of the Jalisco type. These artists of West Mexico made both large hollow and small solid tomb figures. Both have been found in the same burial chamber. To illustrate, the figures of Nayarit are characterized by their active forms, with clearly defined fingers and toes. Arms were usually long, thin ropes of clay. No attention was paid to anatomical details of the arms. Moreover, in the Nayarit figures, great attention was paid to the hair, which was incised in many straight lines. Figures of both sexes wore round earrings, nose ornaments, and facial markings that look like long slashes on the cheeks. Furthermore, these figures were usually painted red. On the other hand, Jalisco figures were usually gray or cream-colored. The heads of the Jalisco figures were elongated and decorated with an ornament that crisscrosses the head. In addition, they had enlarged, staring eyes, hatchet-shaped noses, and large, open mouths, with the teeth clearly defined. In contrast, the Colima figures were usually bright orange to deep red with spots of black scattered over their surface. The human figures of the Colima group were posed in a stiffly mannered style. It looks as though they were posing for the artist. No form of engraving or other decoration was used. The Colima figures were often animals, especially dogs. These dogs are thought to have been the gods that escorted the humans to the next world. In conclusion, these clay figures are only a small part of the artistic output of the ancient Mexican people. We can never know about their music, their oral literature, their wood sculpture, or their textiles. But the clay sculptures are beautiful works done by master artists.

Lesson 5 ✳ *Editing the Paragraph*

Revision

At last you have a paragraph in response to your first assignment. All you have to do is make a neat copy to turn in to your instructor. Right? Not quite. Now that your paragraph has taken form, you need to look at it as objectively as possible. Put it aside for at least an hour or two, preferably overnight, and then read it aloud or have someone in your class read it to you. Try to see it as though you were reading it for the first time. Just reading the paragraph, however, is not enough; you must take an active role in revision. Begin by asking questions that direct your attention to the topic sentence, development, unity, and organization of the paragraph. Here are a few you might consider:

1. Can you sum up the main point of the paragraph clearly and concisely in a few words? Does the topic sentence need rethinking and restating to clarify your meaning?
2. Does your ear catch any weak spots where the thought seems to falter? Is your discussion difficult to follow in places?
3. Was your voice strong and clear in the first supporting sentences only to become uncertain and fade away as you continued? Do you need to develop additional support or to clarify your ideas?
4. Did you stick to your subject? Does every sentence contribute an essential point or clarifying details?
5. Does it all hang together? Will the reader be able to see a guiding, shaping hand throughout the paragraph? Is there a plan, a logic in the order in which the supporting sentences are presented?
6. Does the thought flow smoothly? Should you arrange your sentences in a different sequence? Have you provided links between sentences? *Underline* the transitional words and phrases. Do you need to add or change any? Is each one the best choice in the context of the sentence?
7. Do you sound interested in your subject? Are you knowledgeable about it? Do you speak in a natural voice, or do you sound artificial and forced?
8. Have you been considerate of your readers and given them all the information they need to understand your ideas as clearly as possible?

Proofreading

After you have revised the paragraph to your satisfaction, you are ready to proofread it. The following chapters in this book and your instructor's guidance will help you gain the knowledge and expertise to edit your own work. Recognize your strengths and weaknesses early in the course. When your papers are returned to you, correct the mistakes and keep a record of them to help you avoid making them again and again all semester. Here is a partial checklist to guide your proofreading, but you should make your own list based on your own special problems:

1. spelling
2. punctuation and capitalization
3. use of the apostrophe in possessives
4. fragments
5. comma splices and run-on sentences
6. agreement of subject–verb and pronoun–antecedent

7. pronoun reference
8. faulty parallelism
9. sentence structure: rewrite unclear, awkwardly constructed sentences
10. diction: choose accurate, appropriate words
11. dangling and misplaced modifiers
12. wordiness

WRITING ASSIGNMENT

Write a paragraph of approximately 200 words about the different roles that people play every day. Before you begin to write, review the steps for planning and writing a paragraph described in this chapter.

We all play different roles every day. For example, as a woman, you may play the roles of a sister, a daughter, a daughter-in-law, and a mother just within your family. As a man or as a woman, you may play one role at church, one at a club you belong to, and still another at work. In school you play the roles of a student and a friend. You undoubtedly can think of many other roles.

Describe each role in detail. Is one role more difficult than another? Are these roles ever in conflict? As a man, for instance, do you have any problems playing the roles of husband and employee, or of son-in-law and father?

If you do not want to write about yourself, write about the roles of a person you know very well.

2

Nouns and Pronouns

In Chapter 2, you will learn about parts of speech called NOUNS and PRONOUNS.

Definitions of Terms

A NOUN names a person, place, thing, idea, or activity.

A PROPER NOUN names a specific person, place, thing, idea, or activity.

A COMMON NOUN names people, places, things, ideas, or activities in general.

A NOUN MARKER is an adjective that points to the NOUN that follows it (a, an, the).

A POSSESSIVE NOUN is a noun that changes spelling to indicate a belonging-to relationship.

A PRONOUN is used to take the place of a NOUN or to refer to a NOUN. A PERSONAL PRONOUN shows person, number, and gender.

PERSON indicates the person speaking, the person spoken to, or the person or thing spoken about.

NUMBER—PRONOUNS have singular and plural forms. SINGULAR means one person or thing. PLURAL means more than one person or thing.

GENDER—Third person PRONOUNS have masculine, feminine, and neuter gender.

Lesson 1 ✻ *Identifying Nouns*

If you were asked to give some examples of nouns, you probably would respond with words like <u>astronaut</u>, <u>Mars</u>, or <u>spaceship</u>. You would be right, of course, because a noun does name a <u>person</u>, a <u>place</u>, or a thing, but a noun can also refer to an idea such as <u>knowledge</u> or an activity such as <u>orbiting</u>. A noun, then, names a person, a place, a thing, an idea, or an <u>activity</u>. With this definition in mind, complete the exercise that follows.

✻   **EXERCISE 1A**   ✻

Write *one* word on each line, according to the instructions printed beneath each line.

Example: Did the <u>defendant</u> tell the <u>truth</u> at his <u>trial</u>?
                            (person)   (idea)   (place)

1. A _____ sat on the _____ .
          (person)   (thing)

2. I pledge _____ to the flag of the _____ _____
                      (idea)   (place)

    of _____ .
            (place)

3. _____ is one city that _____ would like to visit again.
          (place)   (person)

4. _____ is my favorite hobby.
          (activity)

5. _____ bought those _____ at a _____ .
          (person)   (things)   (place)

Study the Information in the Following Box:

Remember This Test for a Noun

To determine whether a word is a noun, place a noun marker such as a, an, or the before the word: a routine, an honor, the Washington Monument, the car keys. Note: In the last example, keys is the noun, not car.

Common and Proper Nouns

All of the examples in the box above except the Washington Monument are COMMON NOUNS. When we use common nouns, we refer to people, places, things, ideas, or activities in general terms. Notice that common nouns are usually not capitalized except at the beginning of a sentence.

However, when we refer to the name of a specific person, place, or thing, we use PROPER NOUNS. These nouns begin with capital letters. In general, we do not capitalize the names of ideas or activities. Using "the" as a noun test will not always help you identify proper nouns, but remembering that they are capitalized will help you pick them out.

Common Nouns	**Proper Nouns**
bridge	Golden Gate Bridge
woman	Eleanor Roosevelt
street	Main Street
college	Fairfax Community College

Before you go on to Exercise 1B, check your answers with the answer key at the end of Chapter 2. As you work in this book, check your answers after you complete each exercise.

EXERCISE 1B

Using the noun test, identify the underlined words.
a. If the word is a noun, write N above the word.
b. If it is not a noun, write X above the word.

Example: The clouds gathered before the storm.
                         N   X

1. The traffic on the highway stopped.

2. Rain fell last night.

3. Some <u>drivers</u> were <u>cautious.</u>

4. The <u>surface</u> of the <u>road</u> was slick.

5. John's <u>Buick</u> had good <u>brakes.</u>

6. <u>John</u> <u>tried</u> to stop suddenly.

7. His <u>foot</u> slipped <u>off</u> the pedal.

8. John's <u>car</u> skidded <u>across</u> the road.

9. The right <u>fender</u> hit the <u>bumper</u> of another car.

10. <u>Both</u> cars had to be towed <u>away.</u>

Do not be confused by other words in addition to the noun marker that may be in front of the noun. These words that describe or limit the noun are also called ADJECTIVES. For example:

Noun Marker	Adj.	Noun	Noun Marker	Adj.	Noun
the	car	keys	a	new	computer

Adjectives answer questions such as <u>which</u> or <u>how many</u> in reference to a noun.

Example: the car keys   Which keys?   The <u>car</u> keys.
                                            Adj.   N

EXERCISE 1C

In the following word groups, supply the missing noun.

1. science fiction _____

2. our blue _____

3. three pairs of _____

4. rusty metal _____

5. Monica's baby _____

EXERCISE 1D

Using the noun test, identify all the nouns in these sentences. Write N above each noun.

                  N   N   N

Example: Lori ate a large apple and a cheese sandwich.

Notice that the word cheese is not a noun in this sentence as it is in the sentence: Lori likes cheese. Lori is not eating plain cheese without any bread; she is eating a sandwich. Cheese tells us what kind of sandwich she is eating.

    Lori, a college junior, wanted a summer job. She noticed three listings on the bulletin board in the student center that matched her qualifications as a business major. She decided to apply to a large accounting firm that was listed on the board. Wanting to make a good impression, she wore a new green wool dress to the job interview. The office manager who interviewed her seemed impressed by her academic background and past work experience. As Lori left the interview, she felt confident that she would get the job.

Now write five sentences of your own. Use at least three nouns in each sentence. Use both common and proper nouns. Write N above each noun. You may use the sentences above as models if you wish.

1. _____

   _____

2. _____

   _____

3. _____

   _____

4. _____

_____

5. _____

_____

Lesson 2 ✳ *Singular and Plural Nouns*

Use a SINGULAR NOUN when you are referring to only one person, place, thing, idea, or activity and a PLURAL NOUN when you are referring to more than one.

	Singular Means One	Plural Means More Than One
Person	the astronaut	the astronauts
Place	a planet	planets
Thing	the rocket	the rockets
Activity	a flight	flights
Idea	achievement	achievements

Noun Markers for the Singular

These words indicate that a singular word usually follows:

one	each
a	every
an	a single

Note: The noun marker **a** is followed by a word beginning with a consonant, and the noun marker **an** is followed by a word beginning with a vowel or a silent **h**.

Examples: a shoe   a home   an orange   an honor

EXERCISE 2A

A. Write a singular noun after each of these noun markers.

1. every _____   4. one _____

2. each _____   5. a single _____

3. an _____

B. Write five sentences using the noun markers and nouns that you have written above.

1. _____

2. _____

3. _____

4. _____

5. _____

Plural nouns present a special problem: writing the singular form instead of the plural can change the meaning of your sentence. Study these basic rules for spelling the plural forms of nouns.

EXERCISE 2B

Most nouns form the plural by adding the letter **-s.**

bed, beds   pen, pens   pipe, pipes

Write the plural forms of these nouns.

1. dog _____   4. test _____

2. date _____   5. sale _____

3. trick _____

EXERCISE 2C

Words that end in **y,** preceded by a vowel **(a, e, i, o, u)** usually add **-s** to form the plural. Words that end in **y,** preceded by a consonant, form the plural by changing the **y** to **i** and adding **-es.**

city, cities   duty, duties   But note: bay, bays

Write the plural forms of these nouns.

1. sky _____

2. day _____

3. lady _____

4. turkey _____

5. county _____

EXERCISE 2D

Words that end in **sh, s, ch, x,** and **z** form the plural by adding **-es.**

wish, wishes   church, churches,   buzz, buzzes

Write the plural forms of these nouns.

1. brush _____

2. watch _____

3. bus _____

4. waltz _____

5. tax _____

EXERCISE 2E

Nouns that end in **f, ff,** or **fe** usually add **-s.** Certain nouns change the ending to **ve** and then add **-s.** Consult your dictionary to be sure.

knife, knives	loaf, loaves	calf, calves
thief, thieves	roof, roofs	belief, beliefs
proof, proofs	cliff, cliffs	staff, staffs

Write the plural forms of these nouns.

1. belief _____

2. half _____

3. hoof _____

4. shelf _____

5. wife _____

EXERCISE 2F

Most nouns ending in **o** form the plural by adding **-s.** Here are some commonly used words, however, that are exceptions: echo, hero, potato, tomato, torpedo, and veto. To these words, add **-es.**

echo, echoes   hero, heroes   potato, potatoes

Write the plural forms of these nouns.

1. soprano _____

2. veto _____

3. tomato _____

4. tornado _____

5. piano _____

EXERCISE 2G

Some nouns do not add -s or -es to form the plural. These nouns change their spelling.

woman, women   foot, feet   tooth, teeth
goose, geese   child, children mouse, mice

Fill in each blank with the plural form of the noun in parentheses.

1. The classroom had cages for three _____ (mouse) and two guinea pigs.

2. We should have our _____ (tooth) examined twice a year.

3. Many _____ (woman) watch Monday-night football on television.

4. All of the _____ (child) in Eric's family have gone to college.

5. There are five _____ (man) on the basketball court.

Noun Markers for the Plural

These words indicate that a plural noun usually follows:

all	two (or more)	many	several	one of (the)
a lot of (the)		both	few	some
each of (the)			most	

EXERCISE 2H

A. Write a plural noun after each of these noun markers.

1. two _____   4. all _____

2. both _____   5. many _____

3. several _____

B. Write five sentences using the noun markers and nouns that you have written above.

1. _____

2. _____

3. _____

4. _____

5. _____

EXERCISE 21

Fill the blanks with a correct form of the noun in parentheses.

1. Many (tutor) _____ were working in the computer lab when the power went out.   2. One of the (student) _____ had stepped on the cord and disconnected one of the (plug) _____ from the outlet, but nobody realized that at first.   3. Some (student) _____ lost their information because they had not saved all of the (page) _____ they had typed before the power failed.   4. Several (student) _____ were lucky.   5. They had remembered to save their data after five (minute) _____ of typing.   6. Each of the (tutor) _____ tried to figure out what was wrong. 7. Finally, one of the (instructor) _____ decided to check all three (outlet) _____ in the room.   8. Then several (tutor) _____ crawled around on their hands and knees in the dark until one of the (student) _____ heard a loud "Aha!" 9. Many (student) _____

were huddled in a corner of the darkened room until the computer screens were lighted again.   10. Both of the (instructor) _____ laughed when they saw the anxious faces of the baffled students.

GROUP ACTIVITY

To review the information in Lessons 1 and 2, check your answers to the exercise below with your classmates and your instructor. If you have any incorrect answers, go back over the material in the lessons. Be sure you correct any mistakes before going on to the next lesson.

Correct the following sentences by writing the correct plural form of each of the underlined nouns on the lines at the right. Check your dictionary for the spelling of irregular plurals.

1. One of the boy bought new shoe.   _____ _____

2. He built more shelf for the new dish.   _____ _____

3. Emergency supply were sent to several country.   _____ _____

4. Many of the model wore bikini.   _____ _____

5. This list includes the address of ten church.   _____ _____

6. All applicant must take a series of test.   _____ _____

7. Answer key are often included in language book.   _____ _____

8. Those box contain old photo.   _____ _____

9. Some of the tomato aren't ripe.   _____

10. Both of the secretary were assigned new duty.   _____ _____

Lesson 3 ✖ *Possessives*

Rules for Writing Possessive Nouns

1. Add an apostrophe and an **-s** to nouns that do NOT end in **-s**. This applies to both singular and plural nouns.

the girl	the men	Linda
the girl's scarf	the men's coats	Linda's pen

2. Add an apostrophe and an **-s** to singular nouns that end in **-s**.

Mr. Harris	my boss	the hostess
Mr. Harris's house	my boss's computer	the hostess's invitation

3. Add *only* an apostrophe to plural nouns that end in **-s**.

the Joneses	the students
the Joneses' vacation	the students' papers

4. Add an apostrophe and an **-s** to the final word in a compound noun.

my father-in-law's business	somebody else's mistake

5. Add an apostrophe and an **-s** to the second noun when two nouns are used to show common ownership.

John and Gina's mother	Smith and Lopez's market

    Note: Many writers add only an apostrophe to words ending in **-s** whether singular or plural.

✖   EXERCISE 3A   ✖

Rewrite the underlined words in the possessive form.

Example: The <u>claws of the cats</u> are sharp.   the cats' claws

1. The <u>names of the cats</u> are Ginny and Max. _____

2. They listen to the <u>commands of their owners.</u> _____

3. They like to sleep in the <u>bed of Christy.</u> _____

4. The <u>mother of Christy</u> chases them out of the bed. _____

5. Sometimes Max tries to eat the <u>food that belongs to Ginny.</u> _____

EXERCISE 3B

A. Rewrite each of the groups of words so that the underlined word is in the possessive form.

B. Use each group of words in a sentence.

Example: bicycles that belong to <u>children</u>

A. Change to: children's bicycles

B. Your sentence: <u>The children's bicycles</u> were parked in the driveway.

1. the shoes that belong to the <u>ladies</u> _____

   Your sentence: _____

   _____

2. the new car that belongs to <u>Juan</u> _____

   Your sentence: _____

   _____

3. the jokes that belong to the <u>comedian</u> _____

   Your sentence: _____

   _____

4. the wing of the <u>bird</u> _____

   Your sentence: _____

   _____

5. the medals of the <u>heroes</u> _____

   Your sentence: _____

   _____

EXERCISE 3C

Write five sentences using the possessive form of <u>singular</u> nouns.

Example: <u>Tanya's</u> workbook is complete.

1. _____

2. _____

3. _____

4. _____

5. _____

EXERCISE 3D

Write five sentences using the possessive form of <u>plural</u> nouns.

Example: The <u>tutors'</u> instructions were helpful.

1. _____

2. _____

3. _____

4. _____

5. _____

Review your sentences with a classmate. Check each other's use of possessive forms.

EXERCISE 3E

To improve your ability to proofread your own papers, underline and correct the mistakes in the possessive forms of the nouns in the following paragraph. Write the correct forms on the lines provided at the end of the paragraph.

My new job selling womens clothes in a small shop in the mall offers me a number of benefits. First, the companys policy on vacations is generous. After one years work, I will be given two weeks vacation with pay. Furthermore, I will be paid for all holidays and time and a half for overtime. In addition, I will receive a raise after the first six months work. Another one of the advantages is the 15 percent discount on any of the stores merchandise I wish to buy. Overall, I find the employers attitude very considerate.

1. _____   5. _____

2. _____   6. _____

3. _____   7. _____

4. _____

Special Forms of the Possessive

Relationships other than possession are also shown by using the apostrophe and the letter **-s.** Here are some examples:

time:	today's class	yesterday's visit
measure:	money's worth	two dollars' worth

EXERCISE 3F

Put the apostrophe in each underlined noun to make it a possessive form.

1. Rain caused a cancellation of <u>Saturdays</u> game.

2. Jenny will be paid for one <u>weeks</u> vacation.

3. That <u>countrys</u> flag is red, green, and white.

4. His beard was the result of one <u>months</u> growth.

5. The <u>planes</u> cargo bay will have fire detectors.

Plurals and Possessives

Not every word ending in **-s** requires an apostrophe. Most words ending in **-s** are not possessive; many of them are noun plurals. The following exercise will give you practice using the plural and possessive forms of nouns. If necessary, review the rules given in this chapter on forming noun plurals and possessives.

 EXERCISE 3G

Add apostrophes to the possessive forms of the nouns in the following sentences. Some of the nouns are plural but not possessive and do not require apostrophes.

1. I returned the students books to them.

2. Many customers were dissatisfied with the product.

3. Did the company refund the customers money?

4. My parents season tickets are on the 50-yard line.

5. Many parents of the athletes buy season tickets.

EXERCISE 3H

Complete the following sentences using the <u>singular possessive</u> or the <u>plural possessive</u> form of the noun in parentheses.

Example: (passenger) This _____ connecting flight has left without him.
You write: This <u>passenger's</u> connecting flight has left without him.

1. (traveler) A _____ arrival at the terminal of a large international airport can be a confusing experience.

2. (passenger) Fortunately, many airports have volunteers who have

   been trained to assist with these _____ problems.

3. (visitor) Foreign _____ lack of fluency in English, for example, can add to their confusion.

4. (aide) With an _____ help, these travelers can talk to telephone operators who speak to them in their own languages.

5. (volunteer) The _____ training also teaches them what to do in a medical emergency.

6. (worker) On the other hand, an airport _____ pleasant answer to a question simply may make the traveler feel welcome.

7. (tourist) And they can earn a _____ gratitude by recommending local places to visit during a layover.

8. (family) Or a volunteer may relieve a stranded _____ worries by booking a hotel room and another flight.

9. (motorist) They sometimes even find _____ cars when the tired vacationers can't remember where they are parked.

10. (Doris) But these troubleshooters really seem like heroes when they

    locate your Aunt _____ missing luggage after a long flight.

EXERCISE 31

Add apostrophes to the possessive forms of the nouns in the following paragraph.

My daughters boyfriend, Larry, drives a bright red Honda. On most

weekends, Larrys Honda is parked in front of my house. One morning,

I noticed the Hondas hubcaps were missing. Someone had stolen Larrys

car hubcaps during the night. Larry telephoned his insurance agent to

report the theft. The agents secretary mailed him two claim forms to fill
out. The claim forms arrived in the next days mail. Larry mailed both
forms back to the insurance company and waited. After a few days, the
insurance company paid Larry for his stolen hubcaps. Within two weeks
time, Larrys Honda had new hubcaps.

G R O U P   A C T I V I T Y

Review the information in Lesson 3 by completing the exercise that follows. Check your answers with your classmates and your instructor. If you
have any incorrect answers, go back over the material in the lesson. Be
sure you correct any mistakes before going on to the next lesson.

Rewrite each of the groups of words so that the underlined word is in the
possessive form.

1. the tools that belong to the <u>carpenter</u> _____

2. the motel that belongs to <u>Howard Johnson</u> _____

3. the pouch of the <u>kangaroo</u> _____

4. the briefcase that belongs to <u>Mr. Atlas</u> _____

5. a candidate of the <u>people</u> _____

6. the mother of the <u>twins</u> _____

7. the light of the <u>dawn</u> _____

8. the surfboard that belongs to my <u>brother-in-law</u> _____

9. the voices of the <u>sopranos</u> _____

10. the speech of the <u>Secretary of State</u> _____

Lesson 4 ✖ *Personal Pronouns*

PRONOUNS are words that take the place of nouns and noun phrases. SUBJECT and OBJECT PRONOUNS act as the subject or object of a verb just as nouns do. The use of pronouns avoids the unnecessary repetition of nouns. Although pronouns perform the same functions in sentences as nouns do, you do not make the same changes in their forms. Do not add **-s** for the plural and do not add an apostrophe in the possessive.

Person, Number, Gender

Personal pronouns show person, number, and gender. PERSON indicates the person speaking, the person spoken to, or the person or thing spoken about.

> **First person** shows the person speaking.
> I mailed the letter.
> We walked to the store.
>
> **Second person** shows the person spoken to.
> Did you mail the letter?
> You are both invited to the party.
>
> **Third person** shows the person or thing spoken about.
> She shopped all day.
> He wrapped and mailed the package.
> It should arrive soon.
> They enjoyed the play.

Avoiding Shifts in Person

Try to avoid unnecessary shifts from one person to another. These can confuse the reader. When writing about a person, choose one pronoun and stay with that pronoun.

The most common shift is to the pronoun you.

Incorrect: Most students can pass the tests my geology teacher gives if you study.

Correct: Most students can pass the tests my geology teacher gives if they study.

<u>Students</u> is third person; therefore, write <u>they</u> (third person) instead of <u>you</u> (second person). The pronoun should be in the same person as the noun it stands for.

Remember: Unless you are giving instructions to a specific person when you are writing, avoid using <u>you</u>. Write <u>you</u> when <u>you</u> means <u>the reader</u>.

Example: If <u>you</u> plan to camp in a national park this summer, make <u>your</u> reservations soon.

In this example, the writer is speaking directly to the reader, so the pronoun <u>you</u> is the appropriate choice.

 EXERCISE 4A

Some of the following sentences contain shifts in person. Identify each error by drawing a line under the pronoun; then write the correct form above the word. You may have to change the form of the verb.

 Example: Many commuters listen to tapes while driving. ^{They}<u>You</u> can hear stories or even learn a language.

1. I enjoy eating out instead of cooking at home. Living in Seattle, you

    have a choice of many different kinds of restaurants. My favorite

    restaurant is a Japanese one near my home. It is small and very pop-

    ular, so you usually have to wait for a table.

2. When drivers approach a yellow traffic light at the intersection, they

    should be prepared to stop. You should not try to "beat" the red light

    by increasing your speed. You hope to save a few minutes but you also

    may be risking an accident.

3. During the past year or two, most shoppers have found that the price

    of food has risen sharply. Every time you go to the market, you can see increases in several items. Not so long ago, twenty dollars bought quite a few bags of groceries, but now you can carry twenty dollars' worth of food home in one bag.

4. I received a camera for a graduation present last year. It worked fine at first, but after a few months, you could tell that something was wrong with it. The pictures were so blurry that you couldn't recognize the people in them. The repairman at the camera shop wanted so much money to repair it that I decided to buy a new one. You would be wasting your money to repair that camera.

5. My brother likes his job as a lifeguard at the beach. You don't have to wear a coat and tie to work, and you are out in the fresh air all day. During the summer, Steve conducts water-safety classes for elementary school children. You have to be patient to work with little kids. Lifeguards have an important job. You are responsible for the lives of all the people who come to enjoy the ocean.

NUMBER. Pronouns have singular and plural forms. Singular means one person or thing. Plural means more than one person or thing. Pronouns do not add **-s** or **-es** to form the plural.

Singular forms are used to refer to _one_ person, thing, or idea.
_I_ live in an apartment.
Don, have _you_ met Carole?
She sent _it_ to _her_ mother.

Plural forms are used to refer to _more than one_ person, thing, or idea.
Don't lose _them_ again.
Three of _you_ are tied for first place.
_We_ have never met _their_ son.

GENDER. Third person pronouns have masculine, feminine, and neuter gender.

Third Person Pronouns (Used as Subjects)

Singular	Plural
he	they
she	they
it	they

Study the pronouns in the neuter gender carefully. Notice that only the singular forms of this gender differ from those of the masculine and feminine. Subjects and objects will be discussed in the chapter on understanding the parts of the sentence.

In questions, use the pronoun <u>whose</u> unless you are writing the contraction of "who" and "is," for example, "Who's coming to the party?"

Never add apostrophes to possessive pronouns.

The long form of the possessive pronoun replaces the noun completely. We use the long form when the sentence follows another in which the noun is clearly stated.

> **Example:**   I washed my car. You didn't wash <u>yours</u>.

In these sentences, the reader should have no trouble understanding that <u>yours</u> replaces <u>your car</u> since the noun <u>car</u> is stated in the previous sentence.

The Pronoun <u>Who</u>

When used as the object of a verb or a preposition, the pronoun <u>who</u> has a special form—<u>whom</u>.

> **Examples:**   <u>Whom</u> do they recommend?
> For <u>whom</u> did the city council vote?

Informal English accepts <u>who</u> rather than <u>whom</u>, except after a preposition. In conversation, most people would say, "<u>Who</u> do they recommend?" Also, remember the possessive form <u>whose</u> is used before a noun. Do not confuse it with the contraction <u>who's</u>, which replaces <u>who is</u>.

Contractions

In conversation and informal writing, the pronoun is often joined with the verb that follows it. This is called a CONTRACTION. The two words are joined together with an apostrophe that takes the place of any missing letters.

Example: I am = I'm   you are = you're   it is = it's

Do not confuse the spelling of the possessive pronoun <u>your</u> with the contraction <u>you're</u>, or <u>its</u> with the contraction <u>it's</u>.

EXERCISE 4B

Correct the spelling errors in the underlined pronoun forms.

1. <u>Your</u> moving to Oregon in a new van.   _____

2. <u>Their</u> parked in a no-parking zone.   _____

3. <u>Whose</u> going to the restaurant with us?   _____

4. <u>Its</u> too late to register for this class.   _____

5. <u>Their</u> playing my favorite song on the radio.   _____

6. Joanne gave Marsha her house key because Marsha   _____
    lost <u>her's</u>.

7. The Yankees are leading in their division, and the   _____
    Dodgers are leading in <u>theirs'</u>.

8. My dog has learned to give me <u>it's</u> paw when I say,   _____
    "Give me <u>you're</u> paw."

9. <u>Who's</u> dictionary may I borrow?   _____

10. <u>Your</u> going to pass this test on the first try.   _____

Lesson 5 ⌘ *Reflexive Pronouns*

Pronouns that end in **-self** and **-selves** are called REFLEXIVE pronouns.

Reflexive Pronouns

Singular	I ←	myself
	you ←	yourself
	he ←	himself
	she ←	herself
	it ←	itself
Plural	we ←	ourselves
	you ←	yourselves
	they ←	themselves

Do not write *hisself, themself,* or *theirselves.* These words are nonstandard English.

The reflexive pronoun is used in two ways:

a. I cut myself.

In sentence a, myself is used to refer back to I.

b. The president himself shook my hand.

In sentence b, himself is used to emphasize the person named, the president.

Do not use reflexive pronouns instead of personal pronouns in this way:

c. Bill and myself distributed campaign leaflets Saturday.

You would not write: Myself distributed campaign leaflets Saturday. Use the subject form of the pronoun, I: Bill and I distributed campaign leaflets Saturday.

d. The precinct leader introduced the candidate to Bill and myself.

You would write: The precinct leader introduced the candidate to me, not myself. Use the object form of the pronoun, me: The precinct leader introduced the candidate to Bill and me. You can avoid making this error by using a reflexive pronoun only when it refers to another word in the sentence. Myself does not refer to any words in sentences c and d.

EXERCISE 5A

Write six sentences using reflexive pronouns.

1. (myself) _____

   _____

2. (yourself) _____

   _____

3. (himself, herself, or itself) _____

   _____

4. (ourselves) _____

   _____

5. (yourselves) _____

   _____

6. (themselves) _____

   _____

Below is a chart of the pronouns you have studied in this chapter. Use it to help you remember the different kinds of pronouns.

Person	Subject Pronouns		Object Pronouns		Possessive Pronouns (With Nouns)		-s Form Possessive Pronouns (Without Nouns)	
	Singular	*Plural*	*Singular*	*Plural*	*Singular*	*Plural*	*Singular*	*Plural*
First	I	we	me	us	my	our	mine	ours
Second	you	you	you	you	your	your	yours	yours
Third	he	they	him	them	his	their	his	theirs
	she	they	her	them	her	their	hers	theirs
	it	they	it	them	its	their		

Summary of Chapter 2

Complete these sentences by supplying the appropriate word selected from the box below.

1. _____ refer to people, places, things, ideas, or activities in general terms.

2. _____ refer to specific people, places, or things.

3. Add an apostrophe when the noun is in the _____ form.

4. Personal pronouns and the definitions of person, _____, and

   _____ were explained in Lesson 4.

| common nouns | proper nouns | possessive | gender | number |

Sentence Combining

Chapters 2–10 include sentence-combining exercises that ask you to rearrange the words, phrases, and clauses of five or six short sentences into one clearly written sentence. As you proceed through the book, these exercises should increase your writing fluency, add variety to your sentences, and give you practice in applying some of the grammatical principles you have been learning.

Example

Each of the following five sentences contains information about the writer's brother. When they are read one after the other, the sentences sound choppy and wordy, but when they are combined into a single sentence, the result is a direct, clear statement of the writer's ideas.

1. My brother was a pitcher once.
2. Tim was in high school then.
3. He was on the baseball team at the high school.
4. Tim was the best pitcher there.
5. It was during his senior year.

Combined Sentence

During his senior year in high school, my brother Tim was the best pitcher on the baseball team.

This model sentence is not the only possible way of combining these ideas. You will find that there is often more than one way of combining a group of sentences.

Here are some sentences for you to try.

A. Combine these six sentences into one sentence.

    1. Scott sat down.
    2. He read the instructions.
    3. The instructions were detailed.
    4. They were complicated.
    5. He read them carefully.
    6. He read them for the third time.

B. Combine these six sentences into one sentence.

    1. There was a windstorm last night.
    2. It was powerful.
    3. It knocked down several trees.
    4. They were beautiful.
    5. They were old.
    6. They were in our neighborhood.

C. Combine these five sentences into one sentence.

    1. Sumi rescued a nine-year-old boy.
    2. He was drowning.
    3. It happened last summer.
    4. She was at a camp.
    5. The camp was named Arrowhead Camp.

D. Combine these seven sentences into one sentence.

    1. The woman was tall.
    2. She was barefoot.
    3. She was dressed casually.
    4. She wore a tank top.
    5. Her tank top was red striped.

6. She wore pants.
7. Her pants were white cotton with a blue belt.

E. Combine these four sentences into one sentence.

1. I have always wanted to be an athlete.
2. I wanted to be like Jackie Robinson.
3. I wanted to be like Reggie Jackson.
4. I wanted to make a million dollars.

GROUP ACTIVITY

Combine several sentences from your own writing into one sentence. Bring the original sentences and the revised sentence to class for a group discussion. Decide in each case whether the revised sentence is an improvement. Is the meaning clearer now? Does the new version "sound" better when it is read aloud? Is there a second way to make the revision?

WRITING ASSIGNMENT

Write a paragraph about an important event that happened during the past five years of your life. This experience should be so important to you that you want to write it down for your grandchildren to read someday. Describe the event and explain why it was of such importance.

Step 1. Write down a few key words that come to mind about the event. Ask yourself questions to develop your list of words. (If you prefer, instead of making a list, begin by freewriting or by making a cluster, following the instructions in Chapter 1, pages 3–7.

WHAT?	What was the event?
WHO?	Who was involved?
WHEN?	When did it occur?
WHERE?	Where did the event occur?
HOW?	How did you find out about it? How did it occur?
WHY?	Why was it important to you? Why, many years later, would your grandchildren be interested to read about it?

Step 2. By the time you have tried to answer each of these questions, you should have several lines of notes. Reading them over, decide which of these ideas to develop in your paragraph. Don't feel that you must include every item in your list in your paragraph.

Step 3. Write a topic sentence that states the importance of your experience. You will probably have to write several versions of the topic sentence before it clearly summarizes what you plan to say. If necessary, review the material on the topic sentence in Chapter 1, pages 12–16.

Step 4. Write a rough draft of your paragraph. Use the answers to the questions in Step 1 to develop support for the topic sentence. Chapter 1, pages 16–19 discusses ways to develop specific support.

Step 5. Read the paragraph aloud. You do not need an audience, but if someone is willing to listen to your work, read it to him or her. Ask for comments. You may find that your first draft needs to be rewritten several times before you are satisfied with it. Use the guide to revision in Chapter 1, pages 30–31 to help you.

Step 6. If time permits, lay your composition aside for a few days. Then read it aloud again and try to imagine your grandchildren reading it many years from today. If everything you have written seems clear and orderly, you are ready to proofread it. (See Chapter 1, pages 31–32.) Then copy it over carefully and submit it to your instructor.

ALTERNATE WRITING ASSIGNMENT

Read the paragraph below about the radish festival in Oaxaca, Mexico. Write a paragraph about a festival, a celebration, or a special event you have attended. You don't have to travel out of the country to write an interesting account. If you plan to write about an event near you, imagine that your reader is someone who has never been to your area.

When was the last time that you gave any serious thought to the radish? Oh, you relish a few slices of radish in a tossed green salad, and you may glance appreciatively at the rosettes that decorate the platter of meat you are served, but confess: radishes are not important in your life. Visiting Oaxaca (wah-HAH-kah), Mexico, during the end of December would give you a fresh look at an old friend. On December 23, people gather to celebrate the Night of the Radishes. Booths that display large, specially grown radishes, imaginatively carved in the shapes of people, animals, plants, and buildings, fill the town square. People chat happily in line for an hour as they wait to file slowly past the stalls to see the winners and to decide if they agree with the judges' choices. This competition is part of a week of celebration filled with parades, fireworks, music, dancing, and all the activities that make a colorful fiesta. Do not think that this event is entirely a local enthusiasm. If you want to visit Oaxaca at Christmas, make your reservations six months in advance. You will compete for a room with visitors from the United States and Europe who have come to honor the lowly radish. The radish is truly king for a night. It reigns over a folk festival celebrated by those whose possessions may be few, but whose ingenuity is unlimited. Long live the Night of the Radishes!

Your paragraph should be more than just a description of sights and sounds; focus on one dominant impression, as the writer did in the paragraph above: "Visiting Oaxaca, Mexico, during the end of December would give you a fresh look at an old friend, the radish." If you can, conclude by showing what you find significant in your experience, for example: "It reigns over a folk festival celebrated by those whose possessions may be few, but whose ingenuity is unlimited." Follow the steps above as you develop this topic.

✍ Chapter 2 Practice Test: Nouns and Pronouns

Take this practice test to see how well you understand the forms of nouns and pronouns. Then show your work to your instructor before you ask to take the Chapter 2 test.

Name _____

Date _____ Class Time _____

Instructor _____

I. Using the noun test and your dictionary, identify each word as a noun or some other part of a sentence.
    a. If the word is a noun, place a check under the column headed Noun.
    b. If it is not a noun, place a check under the column headed Other.

	Noun	**Other**			**Noun**	**Other**
1. avenue	_____	_____	6. and		_____	_____
2. if	_____	_____	7. briefcase		_____	_____
3. what	_____	_____	8. dynamic		_____	_____
4. tigers	_____	_____	9. week		_____	_____
5. opened	_____	_____	10. Atlanta		_____	_____

II. Write N above each noun. Use the noun test and your dictionary.

1. Mrs. Tracy bought a bus ticket to Kansas City.

2. The doctor's nurse canceled his appointments for the day.

3. At the end of eight innings, we led by one run.

4. Before class many students study in the college library.

5. The wet poodle shook water on the sunbathers.

Chapter 2 Practice Test: Nouns and Pronouns (cont.)

III.   Each of the following sentences contains an error in the possessive form of a noun. Underline each error. Write the correct form on the line at the right.

1. The striking workers lost a weeks pay.   _____

2. What are Chris and Terrys plans for the summer?   _____

3. The kittens were playing in my sisters room.   _____

4. They waved to attract the bus drivers attention.   _____

5. The audiences response to the concert was
    enthusiastic.   _____

IV.   Change the underlined nouns to the possessive form. Write the possessive form on the line at the right.

1. the speeches of the <u>debaters</u>   _____

2. the addresses of the <u>senators</u>   _____

3. The backpacks that belong to my <u>children</u>   _____

4. the rights of the <u>consumers</u>   _____

5. the collars that belong to the two <u>puppies</u>   _____

V.   The following sentences contain shifts in person.
     a. Identify each error by drawing a line under the incorrect pronoun.
     b. Write the correct form on the line at the right.

1. Maya doesn't mind waiting in line because you can
    read a book or talk to people.   _____

2. When a person diets, they should not skip breakfast.   _____

3. A television newscaster is usually not a journalist.
    Their job is to present the news to the audience.   _____

✍ Chapter 2 Practice Test: Nouns and Pronouns (cont.)

4. I want to own a restaurant someday. Being in
   business for yourself will be a challenge.   _____

5. Motorcycles are economical to ride, but it can
   have disadvantages.   _____

VI. Correct the spelling errors in the underlined pronoun forms.

1. They brought their tickets, but we forgot <u>ours'</u>.   _____

2. <u>Who's</u> car is blocking the driveway entrance?   _____

3. How do you like <u>you're</u> new job?   _____

4. Although classes began last week, they haven't
   attended any of <u>theirs'</u>.   _____

5. The cat sharpened <u>it's</u> claws on the tree.   _____

VII. Write <u>two</u> sentences using the possessive forms of <u>singular</u> nouns.
     Write <u>three</u> sentences using the possessive forms of <u>plural</u> nouns.

1. _____

2. _____

3. _____

4. _____

5. _____

VIII. Write the plural forms of the following nouns.

1. match   _____

2. test   _____

3. knife   _____

4. silver   _____

5. boss   _____

Chapter 2 Practice Test: Nouns and Pronouns (cont.)

IX. If the use of the underlined pronoun is correct, write C on the line. If the use of the pronoun is incorrect, write the correct pronoun on the line.

1. She asked <u>herself</u> why the teacher had chosen her. _____

2. Babies cannot dress <u>theirselves</u>. _____

3. My husband and <u>myself</u> enjoy bowling. _____

4. Senator Boxer <u>herself</u> spoke at our graduation. _____

5. My parakeets like to look at <u>itselves</u> in a mirror. _____

Chapter 2 Answer Key

Exercise 1A
Your instructor will check your answers.

Exercise 1B

    X   N   N   X   N   X   N   N   N   N
1. on, highway   2. Rain, last   3. drivers, cautious   4. surface, road   5. Buick, brakes

    N   X   N X   N   X   N   N   X   X
6. John, tried   7. foot, off   8. car, across   9. fender, bumper   10. Both, away

Exercise 1C
Your instructor will check your answers.

Exercise 1D

   N   N   N   N
Lori, a college junior, wanted a summer job. She noticed three listings on the

        N   N   N   N
bulletin board in the student center that matched her qualifications as a business major.

                        N   N
She decided to apply to a large accounting firm that was listed on the board. Wanting to

         N   N   N
make a good impression, she wore a new green wool dress to the job interview. The

   N   N   N
office manager who interviewed Lori seemed impressed by her academic background

          N   N   N
and her past work experience. As Lori left the interview, she felt confident she would

    N
get the job.

Exercise 2A
Your instructor will check your answers.

Exercise 2B
1. dogs   2. dates   3. tricks   4. tests   5. sales

Exercise 2C
1. skies   2. days   3. ladies   4. turkeys   5. counties

Exercise 2D
1. brushes   2. watches   3. buses   4. waltzes   5. taxes

Exercise 2E
1. beliefs   2. halves   3. hooves or hoofs   4. shelves   5. wives

Exercise 2F
1. sopranos   2. vetoes   3. tomatoes   4. tornadoes (tornados)   5. pianos

Exercise 2G
1. mice   2. teeth   3. women   4. children   5. men

Exercise 2H
Your instructor will check your answers.

Exercise 2I
1. tutors   2. students, plugs   3. students, pages   4. students   5. minutes   6. tutors
7. instructors, outlets   8. tutors, students   9. students   10. instructors

Exercise 3A
1. the cats' names   2. their owners' commands   3. Christy's bed   4. Christy's mother
5. Ginny's food

Exercise 3B
Your instructor will check your sentences.
1. ladies' shoes   2. Juan's new car   3. comedian's jokes   4. bird's wing
5. heroes' medals

Exercises 3C and 3D
Your instructor will check your answers.

Exercise 3E
1. women's   2. company's   3. year's   4. weeks'   5. months'   6. store's
7. employer's or employers'

Exercise 3F
1. Saturday's   2. week's   3. country's   4. month's   5. plane's

Exercise 3G
1. students'   2. no apostrophe   3. customer's or customers'   4. parents'
5. no apostrophe

Exercise 3H
1. traveler's   2. passengers'   3. visitors'   4. aide's   5. volunteers'   6. worker's
7. tourist's   8. family's   9. motorists'   10. Doris's

Exercise 3I
1. daughter's   2. Larry's   3. Honda's   4. Larry's   5. agent's   6. day's   7. weeks'
8. Larry's

Exercise 4A
Your instructor will check your answers.

Exercise 4B
1. You're   2. They're   3. Who's   4. It's   5. They're   6. hers   7. theirs   8. its, your
9. Whose   10. You're

Exercise 5A
Your instructor will check your sentences.

Summary of Chapter 2
1. common nouns   2. proper nouns   3. possessive   4. number, gender

 # Verbs

In Chapter 3 you will learn about parts of speech called VERBS.

Definitions of Terms

An ACTION VERB tells what the subject does, did, or will do.

A LINKING VERB shows a relationship between the subject and a completer.

A REGULAR VERB adds **-d** or **-ed** to form the past tense.

An IRREGULAR VERB does not follow any spelling rules to form the past tense.

An AUXILIARY VERB is a helping verb used with the main verb to form a verb phrase.

The BASE FORM of the verb is the present form of the verb with no **-s** at the end.

The PAST PARTICIPLE is formed by adding **-d** or **-ed** to the base form of a regular verb.

The PRESENT PARTICIPLE is formed by adding **-ing** to the base form of the verb.

A COMPLETER follows the LINKING VERB to describe or rename the subject.

TENSE is the change of verb form to indicate when the action occurred.

PERFECT TENSES are formed by using a form of the auxiliary verb **have** and the past participle of the main verb.

VERB PHRASE is the combination of an auxiliary verb and one of the principal forms of the verb. It is used as the verb of the sentence.

Lesson 1 ❉ *Present and Past Tenses: Regular Verbs*

Every sentence must have a VERB. Let's review <u>three characteristics of verbs</u> that help to identify them.

1. The verb tells what the subject does, did, or will do (action), is, was, or will be (linking).

   Example: Reggie caught the fly ball.
   What did Reggie do?
   He caught. Therefore, <u>caught</u> is the verb.

2. The verb changes its form to show time (tense).

   Example: Reggie catches the fly ball. (The time is the present.)
   Reggie caught the fly ball. (The time is the past.)
   Reggie will catch the fly ball. (The time is the future.)

3. The verb changes its form in the third person singular, present tense to agree with the subject.

   Example: I catch the fly ball. (first person)
   She/He cat<u>ch</u>es the fly ball. (third person)

In Chapter 3 we will introduce two kinds of verbs: action verbs and linking verbs.

Action Verbs

Most verbs tell what the subject (someone or something) does, did, or will do. These verbs are usually easy to identify, especially when the action is a familiar one, such as *swim, talk, buy, chew, study,* or *explode.*

Linking Verbs

You may find linking verbs more difficult to identify than the action verbs above. These verbs show a relationship between the subject and a completer. The completer describes or renames the subject, and the linking verb links the subject to this completer.

Subject	Linking Verb	Completer
Mr. Lopez	is	my Spanish teacher. (renames the subject)
The exam	seemed	easy. (describes the subject)

The linking verb used most frequently is some form of the verb *be (am, is, are, was, were)*. Some other linking verbs are *seem, grow, look, sound, taste,* and *appear.* Linking verbs will be discussed in greater detail in Chapter 4.

✻ **EXERCISE 1A** ✻

Write six sentences of your own. Use the verbs in the parentheses.

Example: (sell) Mr. Rico <u>sells</u> real estate in Philadelphia.

1. (visit) _____

2. (drink) _____

3. (is) _____

4. (seem) _____

5. (appear) _____

6. (break) _____

✻ **EXERCISE 1B** ✻

In the following sentences, underline the verbs and write them on the lines at the right.

1. The train stops for only a few moments at Oakhurst.   _____

   The train stopped for only a few moments at
   Oakhurst.   _____

2. Gene hurries to get on the train already in motion.   _____

   Gene hurried to get on the train already in motion.   _____

3. He trips over a woman's suitcase in the aisle.   _____

   He tripped over a woman's suitcase in the aisle.   _____

4. Gene and the woman glare at each other.   _____

    Gene and the woman glared at each other.   _____

5. In his seat at last, he watches the dawn through
    the smeary windows of the train.   _____

    In his seat at last, he watched the dawn through
    the smeary windows of the train.   _____

The verbs in Exercise 1B form the past tense by adding **-d** or **-ed** to the base form. Most verbs follow this pattern. These are called REGULAR VERBS.

Verbs change their forms to indicate the time the action takes place. We call this sign of time TENSE. The PRESENT TENSE is used to express commands and suggestions and to indicate habitual action or continuing ability.

Examples: Command: Deliver this message immediately.
Suggestion: Discourage them from coming if you can.
Habitual action: He paints beautifully.

The PAST TENSE is used in sentences about action that happened before the present time. Say "Yesterday" at the beginning of the sentence to remind you to use the past tense.

Example: Yesterday he cut the potatoes for tonight's dinner.

Here is a chart showing the pattern of the regular verbs in the present and the past tenses.

Model Verb—Walk

Person	Present Tense Singular	Plural	Person	Past Tense Singular	Plural
1st	I walk	we walk	1st	I walked	we walked
2nd	you walk	you walk	2nd	you walked	you walked
3rd	he walks	they walk	3rd	he walked	they walked
	she walks	they walk		she walked	they walked
	it walks	they walk		it walked	they walked

Answer these questions by looking at the model verb **walk** in the chart.

1. What letter do you add to the base form of the verb for
   the third person singular, present tense?   _____

If you answered **s,** you are correct. Notice that the singular adds an **-s** to
the base form of the verb, but the plural has no **-s.**

2. What letters do you add to the base form of the verb
   to form the past tense?   _____

If you answered **-ed,** you are correct. Notice that both singular and plural
add **-ed** to form the past tense.

EXERCISE 1C

Write five sentences with <u>regular verbs</u> in the <u>present tense.</u>

1. (place) _____

2. (watch) _____

3. (hope) _____

4. (enjoy) _____

5. (decide) _____

Underline each verb in the sentences you have just written. Rewrite each
sentence and change each verb to the past tense.

1. _____

2. _____

3. _____

4. _____

5. _____

✳ EXERCISE 1D ✳

Underline the verb in each of the following sentences. Write the present tense form of each verb on the line at the right.

1. Momoko planned a ski vacation in the mountains.   _____

2. She worked extra hours in the evenings and on weekends.   _____

3. She saved half of her paycheck every week.   _____

4. Momoko opened a special bank account.   _____

5. She watched her money grow very slowly.   _____

6. She waited for the first heavy snowfall.   _____

7. She listened to the weather forecast every day.   _____

8. Finally, the weather changed.   _____

9. It snowed for three days and nights.   _____

10. Momoko withdrew her savings from the bank happily.   _____

Lesson 2 ✳ *Present and Past Tenses: Irregular Verbs*

Most verbs are regular verbs. We add **-d** or **-ed** to them to form the past tense. Verbs that do not add **-d** or **-ed** to form the past tense are called IRREGULAR VERBS. Use your dictionary to find the past tense of irregular verbs or consult the chart of irregular verbs that follows.

Here is a chart listing some of the most commonly used irregular verbs.

Present (base form) Use with I, you, we, they, and plural nouns.	**Present + -s (-es)** Use with he, she, it, and singular nouns.	**Past** Use with all pronouns and nouns.	**Past Participle** Use with auxiliary verbs (has, had, have)	**Present Participle** Use with auxiliary verbs (is, am, are, was, were).
am, are	is	was, were	been	being
beat	beats	beat	beaten	beating
begin	begins	began	begun	beginning
bite	bites	bit	bitten	biting
blow	blows	blew	blown	blowing
break	breaks	broke	broken	breaking
bring	brings	brought	brought	bringing
burst	bursts	burst	burst	bursting
buy	buys	bought	bought	buying
catch	catches	caught	caught	catching
choose	chooses	chose	chosen	choosing
come	comes	came	come	coming
dig	digs	dug	dug	digging
do	does	did	done	doing
draw	draws	drew	drawn	drawing
drink	drinks	drank	drunk	drinking
drive	drives	drove	driven	driving
eat	eats	ate	eaten	eating
fall	falls	fell	fallen	falling
fight	fights	fought	fought	fighting
find	finds	found	found	finding
fly	flies	flew	flown	flying
forget	forgets	forgot	forgotten	forgetting
freeze	freezes	froze	frozen	freezing
give	gives	gave	given	giving
go	goes	went	gone	going
grow	grows	grew	grown	growing
hang	hangs	hung	hung	hanging
have	has	had	had	having
hear	hears	heard	heard	hearing
hide	hides	hid	hidden	hiding
hold	holds	held	held	holding
know	knows	knew	known	knowing
lay	lays	laid	laid	laying
lead	leads	led	led	leading
leave	leaves	left	left	leaving
lie	lies	lay	lain	lying
lose	loses	lost	lost	losing
make	makes	made	made	making

Present (base form) Use with I, you, we, they, and plural nouns.	Present + -s (-es) Use with he, she, it, and singular nouns.	Past Use with all pronouns and nouns.	Past Participle Use with auxiliary verbs (has, had, have)	Present Participle Use with auxiliary verbs (is, am, are, was, were).
read	reads	read	read	reading
ride	rides	rode	ridden	riding
ring	rings	rang	rung	ringing
rise	rises	rose	risen	rising
run	runs	ran	run	running
say	says	said	said	saying
see	sees	saw	seen	seeing
sell	sells	sold	sold	selling
set	sets	set	set	setting
shake	shakes	shook	shaken	shaking
shine	shines	shone	shone	shining
sing	sings	sang	sung	singing
sink	sinks	sank	sunk	sinking
sit	sits	sat	sat	sitting
sleep	sleeps	slept	slept	sleeping
slide	slides	slid	slid	sliding
speak	speaks	spoke	spoken	speaking
spin	spins	spun	spun	spinning
stand	stands	stood	stood	standing
steal	steals	stole	stolen	stealing
stick	sticks	stuck	stuck	sticking
strike	strikes	struck	struck	striking
swear	swears	swore	sworn	swearing
swim	swims	swam	swum	swimming
swing	swings	swung	swung	swinging
take	takes	took	taken	taking
teach	teaches	taught	taught	teaching
tear	tears	tore	torn	tearing
think	thinks	thought	thought	thinking
throw	throws	threw	thrown	throwing
wake	wakes	waked	waked	waking
wear	wears	wore	worn	wearing
win	wins	won	won	winning
write	writes	wrote	written	writing

EXERCISE 2A

All of the verbs in the following sentences are past tense forms of irregular verbs. Underline each verb. Write the <u>present tense</u> form on the line at the right.

Example: Ricardo and his father <u>rose</u> early.   _____rise_____

1. Ricardo and his father drove to the lake cabin together.   _____

2. The next morning they awoke to a bright frost on the grass.   _____

3. The sweet smell of coffee came from the kitchen.   _____

4. After a breakfast of fruit and pancakes, they took a boat out on the lake.   _____

5. Ricardo held tightly to the fishing pole.   _____

6. He threw the line far out into the water.   _____

7. Suddenly the rod bent in his hands.   _____

8. A large trout hung on his hook.   _____

9. He brought the large trout into the boat.   _____

10. Ricardo and his father caught several fish that day.   _____

EXERCISE 2B

All of the verbs in the following sentences are present tense forms of irregular verbs. Underline each verb. Then write the past tense form of each verb on the line at the right.

Example: The convention <u>begins</u> on Thursday.   _____began_____

1. Jugglers meet once a year at an international convention.   _____

2. They come from all age groups and many occupations.   _____

3. Each one gives a demonstration of a specialty.   _____

4. Everyone makes a unique presentation.   _____

5. These artists throw just about everything from cigar boxes to bean bags up in the air.   _____

6. Some ride unicycles during their performances.   _____

7. One man even eats parts of an apple and a cucumber in his act.   _____

8. Jugglers have their names in the *Guinness Book of World Records*.   _____

9. Rastelli, an Italian juggler, set the record: ten balls or eight plates in motion at once.   _____

10. Amateur or professional, jugglers keep things on the move.   _____

G R O U P   A C T I V I T Y

Change the following story to the past tense by writing the past tense form above each underlined verb. Form a group and check your answers with members of the group. Then, as a group, write a paragraph about how you spent a weekend recently. Use the past tense. When you have completed it, underline the verbs. Exchange this paragraph with one written by another group in your class. Change the verbs in that paragraph to the present tense.

Marla and Jack <u>live</u> in an apartment on the third floor. They <u>enjoy</u> the view from their apartment. Marla usually <u>watches</u> TV in the living room while Jack <u>cleans</u> the apartment on weekends. Sometimes they <u>tour</u> the city together when out-of-town visitors <u>come</u>. Jack's stories <u>amuse</u> Marla and the visitors. They often <u>see</u> unusual sights on their tours. One afternoon as they <u>travel</u>, Marla <u>asks</u> Jack if he <u>sees</u> the artist drawing a picture of the scenery. Jack <u>shrugs</u> his shoulders and <u>remarks</u> about the beautiful model who <u>poses</u> for the cameraman nearby. Marla <u>looks</u> angry. She <u>thinks</u> she <u>understands</u> Jack well. But sometimes he <u>disappoints</u> her. She <u>plans</u> to discuss this problem with him soon. Meanwhile she <u>tries</u> to enjoy the rest of the tour of the city.

Lesson 3 ❋ *Principal Forms of Verbs*

When you change the spelling of a verb, you are changing the form of the verb. All verbs have five principal forms.

1. The PRESENT or BASE FORM is the verb without any changes in spelling. It is used with the pronouns I, <u>you</u>, <u>we</u>, and <u>they</u> and with plural nouns.

   Example: walk   see

2. The PRESENT + S FORM is spelled by adding an **-s** or **-es** to the base form. It is used with singular nouns and with the pronouns <u>he</u>, <u>she</u>, and <u>it</u>.

   Example: walks   sees

3. The PAST FORM is spelled by adding **-d** or **-ed** to a regular verb. Irregular verbs change the base form spelling in different ways. They should be memorized. The past form is used with all pronouns and nouns.

   Example: walked   saw

4. The PAST PARTICIPLE is spelled the same as the past form in regular verbs. Irregular verbs that change the spelling should be memorized. The past participle is usually used with a form of the auxiliary verb *have*.

   Example: has walked   has seen

5. The PRESENT PARTICIPLE is formed by adding **-ing** to the base form of the verb. It is used with a form of the auxiliary verb *be*.

   Example: am walking   am seeing

EXERCISE 3A

Write the principal forms of the following regular verbs. Use your dictionary.

Present	Present + -s	Past	Past Participle	Present Participle
(base form) Use with I, you, we, they, and plural nouns.	Use with he, she, it, and singular nouns.	Use with all pronouns and nouns.	Use with auxiliary verbs (has, had, have).	Use with auxiliary verbs (is, am, are, was, were).

Example:

walk	walks	walked	walked	walking
1. stop				
2. carry				
3. watch				
4. try				
5. hope				

All VERBS form the PRESENT PARTICIPLE by adding **-ing** to the PRESENT form:

Present	*Present Participle*	*Present*	*Present Participle*
walk	walking	try	trying

Some verbs, however, require a spelling change:

A. Drop a final, unpronounced **-e** before adding a suffix beginning with a vowel.

    Examples: like, liking   use, using   come, coming,
                  dine, dining

B. Double a final single consonant before a suffix beginning with a vowel:
    (1) if the consonant ends a stressed syllable or a word of one syllable, and
    (2) if the consonant is preceded by a single vowel.

    Examples: run, running   hop, hopping   begin, beginning
                  drag, dragging

Note: When the verb phrase is underlined in this book, one line will indicate the auxiliary verb and two lines, the main verb. *Example*: will be speaking

The auxiliary verb has two main uses. First, the auxiliary verb indicates shades of meaning that cannot be expressed by a main verb alone.

He might go to college.   He can go to college.
He should go to college.   Would he go to college?

Second, the auxiliary verb indicates tense—the time the action of the verb takes place.

He is going to college.   He will go to college.
He has gone to college.   He does go to college.

Note that in a question, the subject separates the auxiliary verb and the main verb.

Will he go to college?

Auxiliary verbs are commonly divided into two groups.

Group 1:   These words are used with main verbs, but they are *not* used as verbs alone except in answer to a question. They *signal* the approach of a main verb.

Group 1 Auxiliary Verbs				
can	may	shall	will	must
could	might	should	would	ought to

EXERCISE 4A

Underline the auxiliary verb or verbs once and the main verb twice.

Example: I would like to place an order.

1. Can you shop at home?

2. You might have received a mail-order catalog from time to time.

3. Many people have found these catalogs convenient.

4. Years ago farm families could send for clothes and household needs.

5. Today urban shoppers can order a variety of goods from specialty stores.

6. The wide choice of items should appeal to families.

7. They may be surprised to see everything from a twelve-unit condo for birds to a goose-down mask.

8. The order form must be filled out carefully.

9. The merchandise will arrive in good condition.

10. Perhaps you ought to shop by mail.

❋ EXERCISE 4B ❋

Write sentences of your own using the auxiliary verbs listed below. Underline the auxiliary verb once and the main verb twice.

1. will _____

2. can _____

3. should _____

4. may _____

5. would _____

Group 2:   These verbs may be used as auxiliary verbs or as main verbs. When they serve as auxiliaries, another form of a verb is used as the main verb of the verb phrase.

Group 2 Auxiliary Verbs			
be	am	have	do
being	is, are	has	does
been	was, were	had	did

Study the way these verbs are used both as auxiliary verbs and as main verbs. As you study, underline the auxiliaries with one line and the main verbs with two lines. Then label each verb.

Remember

1. A sentence must always have a main verb, but it may or may not have an auxiliary verb.
2. If the sentence has an auxiliary verb, it is always placed in front of the main verb.
3. In a question, the subject separates the auxiliary verb and the main verb.

EXERCISE 4C

In the following sentences, underline the auxiliary verb or verbs once and the main verb twice. Do not underline the contraction for *not (n't)*.

Example: He <u>didn't</u> <u>understand</u> the procedure.

1. Many injured athletes have been helped by a new instrument called an arthroscope.

2. With the arthroscope, doctors can see inside the knee.

3. The doctor can examine bones and tissues.

4. The surgery may be done within an hour.

5. Without the arthroscope, a doctor must cut open the knee.

6. Even then, a doctor can't be sure of the diagnosis.

7. Now, many doctors are using the arthroscope for diagnosis and surgery.

8. They don't think of it as miracle surgery.

9. But many injured athletes are playing in games within a week after surgery.

10. Doesn't that seem like a miracle to you?

EXERCISE 4D

Write sentences of your own using the auxiliary verbs listed below. Underline the auxiliary verb once and the main verb twice in each sentence.

Example: I <u>have</u> just <u>read</u> a fascinating book.

1. has dreamed

   _____

   _____

2. were wondering

   _____

   _____

3. doesn't think

   _____

   _____

4. are enjoying

   _____

   _____

5. have left

   _____

   _____

Summary

1. Present and past participles must be accompanied by an auxiliary verb.
2. Present and past participles cannot function alone as the verbs of a sentence.
3. *Be, have,* and *do* sometimes function as auxiliary verbs.

   I <u>have</u> <u>finished</u> my homework. I <u>didn't</u> <u>speak</u> to him. I <u>was</u> <u>eating</u>.

4. *Be, have,* and *do* often function alone in a sentence as main verbs.

   I <u>have</u> a penny. I <u>do</u> my homework. I <u>was</u> an only child.

EXERCISE 4E

Fill in the correct form of the main verb in parentheses to complete the sentence. Consult the chart of irregular verbs or your dictionary.

1. (run)   Since the retirement of his father, Nick has _____ their restaurant.

2. (become)   Located downtown in a large city, it had _____ a popular place to eat.

3. (think)   For some time, Nick had _____ about making a few changes in the business.

4. (begin)   As a start, he has now _____ faxing his menu to customers on request.

5. (take)   Have many people _____ advantage of this service?

6. (hear)   New patrons often have _____ of the restaurant's excellence.

7. (find)   Many people who are planning parties have _____ that seeing the menu is very helpful.

8. (make)   Businesses have _____ the most frequent requests for these faxed menus.

9. (see)   Nick has _____ his take-out orders during the day increase appreciably.

10. (eat)   These business customers who have _____ Nick's lunches sometimes bring in their friends to dine in the evening.

Make a habit of consulting your dictionary to find the principal forms of irregular verbs. Do not guess.

EXERCISE 4F

Consulting the chart of irregular verbs or your dictionary, write five sentences using the past participle form of five irregular verbs. Use a form of the verb **have** as an auxiliary verb. Use a different main verb in each sentence.

Example: He <u>has</u> <u>driven</u> to Detroit.

1. _____

2. _____

3. _____

4. _____

5. _____

EXERCISE 4G

Consulting the chart of irregular verbs or your dictionary, write five sentences using the present participle form of five irregular verbs. Use a form of the verb **be** as an auxiliary verb. Do not use the same main verbs that you used in Exercise 4F. Use a different verb each time.

Example: She <u>is</u> <u>writing</u> her composition.

1. _____

2. _____

3. _____

4. _____

5. _____

Adverbs

An adverb is a modifier that adds further information about verbs, adjectives, and other adverbs. The following adverbs, in addition to others, frequently appear between auxiliary verbs and main verbs. These words are not auxiliary verbs. Do not underline them as verbs.

never	always	often	sometimes
not	still	seldom	completely
just	ever	frequently	

Examples: The quarterback <u>will</u> never <u>attempt</u> a pass now.
The football game <u>has</u> just <u>ended</u>.

NOTE: The contraction for *not (n't)* may be added to many auxiliary verbs, but *n't* is not an auxiliary verb; do not underline it as one.

Examples: We <u>had</u>(n't) <u>driven</u> the car for a week.
The mechanic <u>could</u>(n't) <u>repair</u> the car in one day.

EXERCISE 4H

In the following sentences, underline the auxiliary verb or verbs once and the main verb twice. Put parentheses around any adverbs or contractions.

Example: The past president <u>could</u>(n't) <u>serve</u> on the new board.

The condo association meeting has just ended. The homeowners have voted for the new officers of the condo board. They have selected some owners who had been complaining about the past president. The owners said that the president had not returned their phone calls when the windstorm had damaged their roofs. The president had been out of town, and when she returned, she didn't want to return all of the irate homeowners' phone messages as she did not have a reply for them. What could she do? The new board members are discussing ways to finance repair of the roofs.

EXERCISE 41

Underline the auxiliary verbs once and the main verbs twice. Put parentheses around any adverbs or contractions.

Example: Mr. Williams <u>has</u> (just) <u>seen</u> a bear in his backyard.

As Southern California developers have built homes closer and closer to forests and mountains, residents of these communities must often share the territory with its former four-legged inhabitants. Possums are now surveying backyards from utility wires, coyotes are snatching pet cats and small dogs from their owners' patios, and raccoons are accepting nightly handouts from willing human neighbors. Bears in search of food have appeared as well. One bear had even found a convenient home in a large tree. He was taking his exercise in nearby swimming pools and his dinner from trash cans. What bear wouldn't enjoy the good life?

A crew was finally summoned to convince him that he wasn't welcome. Recently a 300-pound black bear was relocated from a residential area with the aid of a helicopter, three sheriff's deputies, a game warden, and tranquilizing darts. From the bear's point of view, this reception must not have seemed very neighborly.

EXERCISE 4J

Add auxiliary verbs in the blank spaces to complete the following sentences.

1. The students _____ enrolling for the fall semester now.

2. They _____ already received class schedules in the mail.

3. They _____ been given a specific time to telephone the college.

4. Some students _____ not chosen their courses yet.

5. By the time they telephone next week, they _____ _____ chosen their courses for the new semester.

GROUP ACTIVITY

Cut out a short article from a newspaper or a magazine. Underline the auxiliary verbs once and the main verbs twice. Put parentheses around any adverbs or contractions. Bring your article to class. Exchange your work with a member of your group to check each other's work.

Lesson 5 ❈ *Future Tense*

The FUTURE TENSE is used for sentences about something that will happen in the future. Say "tomorrow" before the subject: "Tomorrow I will walk."

The future tense is formed by using the auxiliary verbs <u>will</u> or <u>would</u> and the base form of the main verb. Here is a chart showing the pattern of all verbs in the future tense.

Model Verb—Walk			
Person	**Singular**	**Person**	**Plural**
1st	I will walk	1st	we will walk
2nd	you will walk	2nd	you will walk
3rd	he will walk	3rd	they will walk
	she will walk		they will walk
	it will walk		they will walk

Although it is correct to express future action by using the present progressive tense (I **am going** to graduate in June.), use only the future tense (I **will graduate** in June.) when you are writing the exercises in this lesson.

❈   **EXERCISE 5A**   ❈

Complete the following sentences by using the future tense of the verb in the parentheses.

1. (begin)   Tomorrow Linda _____ her new job.

2. (set)   Tonight she _____ her alarm clock for 6 A.M.

3. (take)   Tomorrow morning she _____ the 7:30 bus to work.

4. (be)   She hopes the bus _____ on schedule.

5. (earn)   Very soon Linda _____ her first paycheck.

EXERCISE 5B

Write five sentences telling about something that will happen to you in the future. Underline the auxiliary verb once and the main verb twice. Use a different main verb in each sentence.

1. ____

2. ____

3. ____

4. ____

5. ____

<u>Will</u> and <u>Would</u>

WILL points to the future from the present.	KNOW/WILL
WOULD points to the future from the past.	KNEW/WOULD

a. You <u>know</u> that you <u>will</u> do well in this class.

In sentence a, "you know" <u>now</u> (in the present) that "you will do well" in the <u>future</u>.

b. You <u>knew</u> that you <u>would</u> do well in this class.

In sentence b, "you knew" <u>then</u> (in the past) that "you would do well" in the <u>future</u>.

EXERCISE 5C

In the following sentences, fill in <u>will</u> or <u>would</u> to indicate the future.

1. Herb knows that he _____ win someday.

2. Herb knew that he _____ win someday.

3. Wu arrives early so he _____ get the best seats.

4. Wu arrived early so he _____ get the best seats.

5. He says that he _____ hire a band.

6. He said that he _____ hire a band.

EXERCISE 5D

Complete the following sentences with a <u>future</u> form of the verb in parentheses.

1. (come)   Where _____ fish and shrimp _____ from in the future?

2. (need)   The world _____ _____ an additional 16 million tons of fish annually.

3. (fill)   The United Nations hoped that fish farms _____ _____ this need.

4. (supply)   Japan and China _____ _____ 1.5 billion pounds of shrimp each year.

5. (raise)   The Norwegians have promised that they _____ _____ salmon in protected fish farms.

Lesson 6 ✳ *Perfect Tenses*

In the lesson on auxiliary verbs, you used the perfect tenses in some of the verbs that you identified or wrote. The name **perfect tenses** gives no clue to the uses of these tenses. Study the examples given below to learn how to use the perfect tenses.

A. The PRESENT PERFECT TENSE is formed by using the auxiliary verb **have** in the present tense plus the past participle of the main verb.

Model Verb—Run			
Person	**Singular**	**Person**	**Plural**
1st	I have run	1st	we have run
2nd	you have run	2nd	you have run
3rd	he has run	3rd	they have run
	she has run		they have run
	it has run		they have run

Use the present perfect tense to show that an action began in the past and has continued until now, or that an action has just happened. It is often used to show that an action occurred at an indefinite time in the past. Adverbs such as *just* and *already* are commonly included.

✳ EXERCISE 6A ✳

Fill in the present perfect tense of the verb given in the parentheses. Use the chart of irregular verbs or your dictionary.

Example: (study) <u>Has</u> Dr. Sandoval <u>studied</u> about Nicaragua?

1. (teach) Dr. Sandoval _____ _____ in the history department for the past five years.

2. (specialize) He _____ _____ in the history of Latin America since graduate school.

3. (enjoy) His students _____ always _____ his lectures about Guatemala.

4. (be) For the past semester he _____ _____ on a sabbatical leave.

5. (do) Dr. Sandoval _____ _____ research about his favorite subject in the library.

B. The PAST PERFECT TENSE is formed by using the auxiliary verb **had** plus the past participle of the main verb.

Model Verb—Run			
Person	**Singular**	**Person**	**Plural**
1st	I had run	1st	we had run
2nd	you had run	2nd	you had run
3rd	he had run	3rd	they had run
	she had run		they had run
	it had run		they had run

Use the past perfect tense to show that one action happened before another action in the past. Use it only when you are writing in the past tense.

EXERCISE 6B

Fill in the past perfect tense of the verb given in parentheses. Use the chart of irregular verbs or your dictionary.

Example: After we <u>had</u> <u>seen</u> the play, we went to a restaurant for dessert.

1. (read) The English class _____ already _____ the play last week.

2. (promise) The instructor _____ even _____ to meet the students at the theater.

3. (have) The play _____ _____ a long run in Boston and New York before opening here.

Progressive Tenses

Verbs have a progressive form indicating continuing actions. These forms are the same for both regular and irregular verbs. The progressive tenses use a form of the verb **be** as an auxiliary verb and the "**-ing**" form or present participle form of the main verb to show that an action is "in progress." For example, the present progressive tense indicates that some action is taking place right now.

PROGRESSIVE FORMS

PRESENT	is waiting
PAST	was waiting
FUTURE	will be waiting
PRESENT PERFECT	has been waiting
PAST PERFECT	had been waiting
FUTURE PERFECT	will have been waiting

Lesson 7 ✳ *Tense Shift Problems*

Do *not* shift tenses in the middle of a sentence, a paragraph, or an essay unless you have a reason to do so. If you begin writing in the present tense, don't shift to the past. If you begin in the past, don't shift to the present.

Incorrect: Bike riding is a good way to meet people. They were always willing to join me in a short or a long trip. When I was riding my bike, I enjoyed the company of other bike enthusiasts.

The tense shifts from present to past.

Correct: Bike riding is a good way to meet people. They are always willing to join me in a short or a long trip. When I am riding my bike, I enjoy the company of other bike enthusiasts.

All the verbs are in the present tense.

EXERCISE 7A

Some of the following sentences contain shifts in tense. Identify each error by drawing a line under the incorrect verb. Write the correct form above the word.

Example: All the activity began when I *started* start studying.

1. Last Tuesday night I went to the library because I had a test in history on Wednesday morning. It is too noisy at home to study. My brother is playing the stereo, my mother was vacuuming, and my little sister and her friend are chasing each other around the house. How am I supposed to concentrate with all that commotion?

2. Working in a legal office is a very demanding job. My job as a legal assistant consisted of processing many felony complaints and other legal documents. Since these complaints must be filed in court, they had to be accurate and completed on time. I was working under pressure all the time. I have to be dependable and courteous. Even when I was tired and depressed, I still have to be helpful and polite.

3. When my neighbor bought a used car, he received a lesson in odometer tampering. He thought he has bought a reliable, low-mileage car, but after he begins driving it, problems develop. His mechanic told him that the car needs a new transmission although the odometer showed only 30,000 miles. The mechanic becomes suspicious. Worn

brake and gas pedals suggest that the car had probably been driven over 75,000 miles. Scratches on the odometer further convince the mechanic that the mileage has been changed.

Summary of Chapter 3

Choose words from the box below to complete each sentence correctly.

1. Add **-s** to the verb in the _____ person singular form of the present tense.

2. Regular verbs add _____ or _____ to the present form to make the past tense form.

3. Look in the dictionary to find the principal _____ of irregular verbs.

4. To form the future tense, add the auxiliary verb _____ before the base form of the main verb.

5. To form the perfect tenses, use the auxiliary verb _____ before the _____ participle.

6. Some other examples of auxiliary verbs are _____ and _____.

7. The words that sometimes appear between the auxiliary verb and the main verb are called _____.

8. Some examples of adverbs are _____, _____, and _____.

-d -ed third forms past will be do have adverbs never always not

Sentence Combining

Here is another opportunity to sharpen your skills at combining sentences. Notice the way these six sentences have been combined into one sentence.

1. Kevin sorted the papers.
2. He sorted quickly.
3. The papers were on the desk.
4. Kevin put the papers into stacks.
5. Kevin made four stacks.
6. He made neat stacks.

Combined Sentence

Kevin quickly sorted the papers on the desk into four neat stacks.

A. Combine these six sentences into one sentence.

1. The hikers could not climb the trail.
2. The hikers were inexperienced.
3. The hikers had backpacks.
4. The backpacks were heavily loaded.
5. The trail was steep.
6. The trail led to Frog Lake.

B. Combine these five sentences into one sentence.

1. Another strip mall will eliminate our small park.
2. It is in our neighborhood.
3. It will increase traffic.
4. Our streets are narrow.
5. They are already crowded.

C. Combine these seven sentences into one sentence.

1. Wynton Marsalis played in an orchestra.
2. It was the New Orleans Civic Orchestra.
3. He played first trumpet.
4. He was in high school.
5. He attended Juilliard School of Music.
6. It was in New York.
7. He was eighteen.

D. Combine these seven sentences into one sentence.

1. Delores has heard the beat of music.
2. The beat is steady.
3. It is rock music.
4. Delores can hear voices.
5. The voices are loud.
6. The music and the voices come from the neighboring apartment.
7. She has heard it all night long.

E. Combine these seven sentences into one sentence.

1. A reporter interviewed a man.
2. The man is a candidate for mayor.
3. The interview was held on a television news program.
4. The interview was last Friday.
5. The reporter asked some questions.
6. The questions were probing.
7. The questions were about campaign funds.

WRITING ASSIGNMENT

A neighborhood is more than a collection of people, houses, and stores in the same vicinity. Neighborhoods can differ greatly, each having its own character. In this assignment you are asked to describe a neighborhood that you knew well in the past. Can you recall what some of the houses and nearby stores looked like? Do any of the neighbors themselves stand out in your memory? What were the sights, sounds, and smells of the place? Write down details you can remember about that neighborhood. Tell the reader where the neighborhood is.

1. _____

2. _____

3. _____

4. _____

5. _____

6. _____

7. _____

8. _____

9. _____

10. _____

11. _____

12. _____

Look over your list and decide what impressed you most about the neighborhood. You will want to focus on a single impression since you cannot describe everything in your neighborhood in a paragraph. Perhaps the people in your neighborhood were very sociable, and you believe that the Fourth-of-July block party best showed that trait. You might write an opening sentence such as this one:

"Every Fourth of July, our neighborhood joined together in a huge dawn-to-dark celebration."

Or perhaps you prefer to show how a certain person reflected the spirit of your neighborhood. You might write: "Joe Marshall, who lived on our block, was typical of the helpful, friendly spirit in our neighborhood."

Remember that you want to make your readers see and hear what you saw and heard in that neighborhood. Don't just write that the man next door was a good guy. Show him helping you change a tire. Let your reader hear his favorite greeting, "Hi, neighbor, come on in. How about a cup of coffee?" You must write in specific, precise words if you are going to give your readers a sense of the place and the people in your neighborhood.

ALTERNATE WRITING ASSIGNMENT

Describe in detail a place on your college campus that has made an impression on you or has a strong attraction for you. If you write about this topic, you will not be recalling a memory of the past, but observing a scene firsthand. Read the paragraph about the guitar store in Chapter 4, Exercise 2D, page 125 as an example of observation and description.

Choose a place where you can sit comfortably and take notes as you observe what is going on around you. Describe the people you see. What activities are taking place? What do you hear? Imagine that your reader is a friend or a relative living in another state who has not seen your campus. To recreate your experience, what notes must you take to be able to write in specific and concrete detail? After you have completed your notes, decide what is most significant about your experience. As you plan your paragraph, select only those details from your notes that will support your topic sentence (Chapter 1, pages 12–16). Focus on a single impression. For example, perhaps you enjoy the weekly campus concerts. You might say, "The Wednesday noon concerts provide a welcome break from the lectures and tests of the school week." Find a place that's special to you, look at it as if you were seeing it for the first time, and start taking notes.

Chapter 3 Practice Test: Verbs

Name _____

Date _____ Class Time _____

Instructor _____

I. Underline the verb. Write the past tense form of each verb on the line
    at the right.

1. Our class plans a reunion for the third weekend in
    June.   _____

2. Cars spin out of control on the icy streets.   _____

3. Mr. Fuller is a traffic controller at the airport.   _____

4. The shortstop throws the ball to the first baseman.   _____

5. My new job offers a number of advantages.   _____

II. Underline the main verbs twice and the auxiliary verbs once. Some
    sentences may have no auxiliary verbs, and others may have more
    than one auxiliary verb.

1. Rosa Sanchez has completed her plans already.

2. The senator is campaigning for a second term.

3. All the stores had sales after New Year's Day.

4. Flames were already shooting through the garage roof.

5. Why do so many couples marry in Las Vegas?

6. I have never heard that excuse before.

7. Did the architect finally complete the house plans?

8. Here is one answer to a difficult question.

9. You may need hotel reservations during the holidays.

10. Walter and Tanya had met for the first time at a conference in Dallas.

✍ Chapter 3 Practice Test: Verbs (cont.)

III. Fill in the blanks with auxiliary verbs to make complete sentences.

1. An election _____ _____ held next Tuesday.

2. She _____ never run for political office before.

3. Yesterday we _____ discussing the election issues in class.

4. The candidates _____ speaking at an open meeting now.

5. _____ you vote yet?

IV. Complete the following sentences with the future tense of the verb in parentheses.

Example: (walk) John <u>will</u> <u>walk</u> to work today.

1. (retire) Our office manager announced that he _____

_____ in July.

2. (receive) Ben hoped that he _____ _____ a promotion soon.

3. (honor) Many television programs next January _____

_____ Dr. Martin Luther King.

4. (hold) The astronomy club _____ _____ a star watchers' class Friday evenings during January.

5. (serve) Carmen promises that she _____ _____ as chairman of the membership drive.

V. In the following sentences, supply an auxiliary and a main verb using the verb given in parentheses. Use one of the perfect tenses.

Example: (raise) The news report <u>has</u> <u>raised</u> some questions.

1. (see) A farmer reported that he _____ _____ an alien spaceship in his pasture.

✍ Chapter 3 Practice Test: Verbs (cont.)

2. (verify)   So far, no one else _____ _____ the report.

3. (refuse)   His wife _____ already _____ to talk to the press.

4. (make)   Several people _____ _____ similar claims last year.

5. (convince)   These reports _____ not _____ most people of the existence of alien spaceships.

VI.   Write the principal forms of the following verbs.

Present	Present + s	Past	Past Participle	Present Participle
cry	_____	_____	_____	_____
break	_____	_____	_____	_____
am, are	_____	_____	_____	_____
tape	_____	_____	_____	_____
plan	_____	_____	_____	_____

VII.   a.   In the following sentences, bracket the adverbs and the contractions.
       b.   Then underline the main verbs twice and the auxiliary verbs once.

1. Tony has always been a loyal fan of the Broncos.

2. Haven't they ever gone to a rock concert?

3. I can certainly understand the citizens' opposition to the landfill proposal.

4. Troy has recently won a scholarship award.

5. Mr. Loeb will seldom watch situation comedies on television.

Chapter 3 Answer Key

Exercise 1A
Your instructor will check your sentences.

Exercise 1B
1. stops, stopped   2. hurries, hurried   3. trips, tripped   4. glare, glared
5. watches, watched

Exercise 1C
Your instructor will check your sentences.

Exercise 1D
1. plans   2. works   3. saves   4. opens   5. watches   6. waits   7. listens   8. changes
9. snows   10. withdraws

Exercise 2A
1. drive 2. awake 3. comes 4. take 5. holds 6. throws 7. bends 8. hangs 9. brings 10. catch

Exercise 2B
1. met   2. came   3. gave   4. made   5. threw   6. rode   7. ate   8. had   9. set
10. kept

Exercise 3A
1. stops, stopped, stopped, stopping   2. carries, carried, carried, carrying
3. watches, watched, watched, watching   4. tries, tried, tried, trying
5. hopes, hoped, hoped, hoping

Exercise 3B
1. letting   2. jumping   3. hitting   4. returning   5. sleeping   6. arriving   7. living
8. managing   9. blaming   10. competing

Exercise 3C
1. is, was/were, been, being   2. drives, drove, driven, driving
3. runs, ran, run, running   4. chooses, chose, chosen, choosing
5. does, did, done, doing

Exercise 4A
1. Can shop   2. might have received   3. have found   4. could send   5. can order
6. should appeal   7. may be surprised   8. must be filled out   9. will arrive
10. ought to shop

Exercise 4B
Your instructor will check your answers.

Exercise 4C
1. have been helped   2. can see   3. can examine   4. may be done   5. must cut
6. can be   7. are using   8. do think   9. are playing   10. does seem

Exercise 4D
Your instructor will check your answers.

Exercise 4E
1. run   2. become   3. thought   4. begun   5. taken   6. heard   7. found   8. made
9. seen   10. eaten

Exercise 4F and 4G
Your instructor will check your sentences.

Exercise 4H
<u>has</u> (just) <u>ended</u>; <u>have</u> <u>voted</u>; <u>have</u> <u>selected</u>; <u>had been</u> <u>complaining</u>; <u>said</u>; <u>had</u> (not) <u>returned</u>; <u>had</u> <u>damaged</u>; <u>had</u> <u>been</u>; <u>returned</u>; <u>did</u>(n't) <u>want</u>; <u>did</u> (not) <u>have</u>; <u>could</u> <u>do</u>; <u>are</u> <u>discussing</u>

Exercise 4I
<u>have</u> <u>built</u>; <u>must</u> (often) <u>share</u>; <u>are</u> (now) <u>surveying</u>; <u>are</u> <u>snatching</u>; <u>are</u> <u>accepting</u>; <u>have</u> <u>appeared</u>; <u>had</u> (even) <u>found</u>; <u>was</u> <u>taking</u>; <u>would</u>(n't) <u>enjoy</u>; <u>was</u> (finally) <u>summoned</u>; <u>was</u>(n't); <u>was</u> <u>relocated</u>; <u>must</u> (not) <u>have</u> <u>seemed</u>

Exercise 4J
1. are or were
2. have or had
3. have or had
4. have or had
5. will have

Exercise 5A
1. will begin   2. will set   3. will take   4. will be   5. will earn

Exercise 5B
Your instructor will check your answers.

Exercise 5C
1. will   2. would   3. will   4. would   5. will   6. would

Exercise 5D
1. will come   2. will need   3. would fill   4. will supply   5. would raise

Exercise 6A
1. has taught   2. has specialized   3. have enjoyed   4. has been   5. has done

Exercise 6B
1. had read   2. had promised   3. had had   4. had enjoyed   5. had chosen

Exercise 6C
1. will have bought   2. will have read   3. will have made   4. will have started
5. will have returned

Exercise 7A
Your instructor will check your answers.

Summary of Chapter 3
1. third   2. -d, -ed   3. forms   4. will   5. have, past   6. be, do   7. adverbs   8. never, always, not

4

Understanding
the Parts
of the Sentence

In Chapter 4 you will learn about the main parts of the SENTENCE.

Definitions of Terms

Every SENTENCE must have at least one subject and one verb and express a complete thought.

The SUBJECT is the person or thing the verb is asking or telling about. In a sentence with an action verb, the subject is the person or thing doing the action.

The SUBJECT OF A COMMAND is understood to be "you."

PREPOSITIONS are the words used to show position, direction, or relationship.

The OBJECT is the noun or pronoun that answers the question "what?" or "whom?" after an action verb. OBJECTS also follow prepositions.

A LINKING VERB shows a relationship between the subject and a completer. Common linking verbs are *become, feel, seem, appear,* and the forms of the verb *be.*

A COMPLETER follows a LINKING VERB to describe or rename the subject.

A COMPOUND SUBJECT is two or more subjects joined by a coordinating connective.

A COMPOUND VERB is two or more verbs joined by a coordinating connective.

A COMPOUND OBJECT is two or more OBJECTS joined by a coordinating connective.

A CONTRACTION is a word formed by combining two words with an apostrophe to substitute for the omission of letters.

A PHRASE is a group of words without a subject and a verb. Examples are noun phrases, verb phrases, and prepositional phrases.

Lesson 1 ✳ *Subjects and Verbs*

Fill in the blanks:

1. _____ <u>land</u> every few minutes at Chicago's O'Hare International Airport.

2. Have _____ <u>claimed</u> their luggage?

These word groups have verbs, but they are not complete sentences because the subject of each verb is missing. You have filled in the subjects to make them complete sentences.

The SUBJECT of a sentence is the person or the thing the VERB is asking or telling about. The subject may be a NOUN or a PRONOUN.

Example: The tourists <u>have</u> <u>returned</u> home. Subject = tourists. To find the subject ask, "Who <u>have</u> <u>returned</u> home?" The answer, "The tourists," is the subject of the sentence.

> Every sentence must have at least one subject and one verb and express a complete thought.

Subject Pronouns

Subject pronouns are used primarily as the subjects of sentences or clauses.

Example: They have claimed their luggage. To find the subject, ask "who" or "what" with the verb: "Who have claimed their luggage?" The answer, "THEY," is the subject of the sentence.

Subject pronouns also are used after all forms of the verb <u>be</u> in formal writing.

Example: It is <u>I</u>. (In conversation, most people would say, "It's me.")

Subject Pronouns		
Person	**Singular**	**Plural**
1st	I	we
2nd	you	you
3rd	he, she, it	they

EXERCISE 1A

Complete each of the following sentences by supplying a common or proper noun subject or a pronoun subject.

1. _____ bought bagels and tortillas at the market.
   <u>proper noun</u>

2. The two _____ tasted delicious, but the _____ was
   <u>common noun</u>   <u>common noun</u>
   too salty.

3. _____ traveled to Kansas by bus.
   <u>pronoun</u>

4. Her _____ left one hour ago.
   <u>common noun</u>

5. _____ requires skill and concentration.
   <u>common noun</u>

6. _____ often practices as early as 5 A.M.
   _{proper noun}

7. _____ saw a thrilling movie last week.
   _{pronoun}

8. The _____ included a number of famous actors.
   _{common noun}

9. _____ waved and smiled at the crowds lining the street.
   _{proper noun}

10. _____ came back after a month in a spaceship circling the
    _{pronoun}
    earth.

Finding Subjects and Verbs

1. First, find the verb. Underline the auxiliary verb once and the main verb twice.

   The children <u>swim</u>.   They <u>can</u> <u>play</u>.

2. Then, find the noun or pronoun subject by asking <u>who</u> or <u>what</u> with the verb. Circle the subject.

   Who <u>swim</u>? The (children) <u>swim</u>.   Who <u>can</u> <u>play</u>? (They) <u>can</u> <u>play</u>.

   The answer gives you the noun or pronoun subject circled above.

3. If the sentence asks a question, put the sentence in the form of a statement to help you find the subject and the verb.

   <u>Can</u> the children <u>play</u>? Change to: The children <u>can</u> <u>play</u>.
   Then ask: Who <u>can</u> <u>play</u>?

   The answer gives you the subject. The (children) <u>can</u> <u>play</u>.

4. Remember that every sentence must have at least <u>one</u> subject and <u>one</u> verb.

EXERCISE 1B

Underline the auxiliary verb once and the main verb twice. Circle the subject. The last sentence has more than one subject and verb.

Example: I have never traveled to Scotland. Have you ever been there?

1. Americans can experience the Scottish Highland Games without making a trip to Scotland.

2. Similar festivals are held in the United States each year.

3. We have attended the Scottish-American version of the Games in our city several times.

4. The numerous events include many tests of strength, such as contests for shot-putters, hammer throwers, and caber (pole) tossers.

5. During the caber toss, the contestants are throwing 100-pound, 18-foot poles with remarkable balance and accuracy.

6. The sheep dog trials show another kind of skill on the part of both dog and trainer.

7. In a short time, a small border collie drives the reluctant sheep through a narrow opening.

8. Bagpipers offer yet another diversion at the games.

9. They traditionally have led kilted soldiers into battle and kilted dancers through their steps.

10. Hearing the music of the bagpipers at a festival, you may think that you are in Scotland.

Commands and Requests

Each sentence must have at least one subject and one verb, but the verb can stand alone in a sentence without a stated subject in a COMMAND or REQUEST. The subject in such a sentence is "<u>YOU, UNDERSTOOD</u>." In other words, it is understood that the subject is "you."

Examples:

$\overset{V}{\underline{Look}}$! = $\overset{S}{(You)}\overset{V}{\underline{look}}$!

$\overset{V}{\underline{Hurry}}$! = $\overset{S}{(You)}\overset{V}{\underline{hurry}}$!

$\overset{V}{\underline{Pay}}$ the cashier. = $\overset{S}{(You)}\overset{V}{\underline{pay}}$ the cashier.

EXERCISE 1C

Fill in the blanks with VERBS that command or request.

1. _____ the invitations today.

2. _____ some stamps at the post office.

3. Don't _____ to seal the envelopes.

4. _____ to the party next Saturday.

5. _____ a glass of punch.

The subject of each of these five sentences is the pronoun, _____.

EXERCISE 1D

Write five commands or requests of your own similar to those in Exercise 1C.

1. _____

2. _____

3. _____

4. _____

5. ___ _____

Lesson 2 ✳ *Prepositional Phrases*

Not many sentences have subjects and verbs as easy to recognize as those in the sentences you have been working with. We usually add words to the subject and the verb to give more information about them. Sometimes we use one word, sometimes a group of words. A group of words introduced by a preposition and known as a PREPOSITIONAL PHRASE is often used to expand the subject and the verb.

> Prepositions are the short words that show position, relationship, or direction. For example, if you were trying to give the location of your pencil, you might say: The pencil is on the desk. Or, the pencil is under the desk. The prepositions are on and under. The prepositional phrases are on the desk and under the desk.

Each prepositional phrase contains at least two words: a PREPOSITION (P) and an OBJECT (O). The object (O) is always a noun or a pronoun.

             S   P O

Example: Paula enjoys a bowl of soup.

Some prepositional phrases contain adjectives that come between the preposition and the object. These words describe the object.

             S   P Adj.   Adj.   O

Example: Paula enjoys a bowl of hot minestrone soup.

of manual training for black youths; with Marcus Garvey, the black nationalist; and with the National Association for the Advancement of Colored People. In the last years of his life, Du Bois applied for membership in the Communist Party and then fled from America. He died in Ghana in 1963, a day before the Rev. Martin Luther King's March on Washington.

Lesson 5 ✳ *Compound Subjects, Verbs, and Objects*

Until now most of the sentences in this book have contained simple subjects and simple verbs. Many sentences, however, have COMPOUND SUBJECTS and COMPOUND VERBS. A compound subject is made up of two or more subjects joined by coordinating connectives, such as <u>and</u> or <u>or</u>. A compound verb is made up of two or more verbs joined by coordinating connectives, such as <u>and</u> or <u>or</u>.

Simple Subject

S   LV   C
The (melons) <u>are</u> ripe.

Compound Subject

S   S   LV   C
The (melons) and (bananas) <u>are</u> ripe.

Simple Verb

S   V
The (car) <u>skidded</u>.

Compound Verb

S   V   V
The (car) <u>skidded</u> and <u>stopped</u>.

Objects and completers can also be compound.

Compound Object

S   V   O   O   O
(She) <u>brought</u> fresh beans, squash, and tomatoes from her garden.

Compound Completer

S   LV   C   C
(He) <u>is</u> an actor and a musician.

EXERCISE 5A

Write five sentences with compound subjects. Underline and label subjects and verbs.

1. _____

2. _____

3. _____

4. _____

5. _____

Write five sentences with compound verbs. Underline and label subjects and verbs.

1. _____

2. _____

3. _____

4. _____

5. _____

EXERCISE 5B

Circle the compound subjects and underline the compound verbs in the following paragraph.

When I was in the second grade, my brother and I attended a Japanese class every day after our regular school. I resented Japanese school and complained frequently to my parents. The Japanese language and customs meant nothing to me. I wanted to play after school and envied the other children who did not have to go. Mother and Dad were sympathetic but firm. However, as I continued going to Japanese school, my interest and enjoyment grew. After a while I was able to communicate with my relatives in Japan and also act as a translator at school when a new student arrived from Japan. In time I realized that knowing two languages well and communicating with people were very important to me. Today I have decided to major in the Japanese language, and I hope to become a translator. Therefore, I am attending a community college and preparing myself for the university. I also speak Japanese daily while working part-time at a Japanese import company. Mother and Dad, meanwhile, recall my complaints about Japanese school and smile.

Pronouns in Compound Subjects and Objects

Compound subjects and objects can be a problem when they include pronouns. For example, what pronouns would you place in these blanks?

1. Bob and _____ (me, I) went to the game Friday.

2. We waited for Tom and _____ (he, him) after class.

I is correct in sentence 1 because I is the subject of the verb. Him is correct in sentence 2 because him is the object of the preposition for.

When you are in doubt about the form of a pronoun in sentences like these, leave out the noun subject or the noun object and the connective and read the sentence with the pronoun by itself.

1. Bob and I went to the game Friday. (You read, "I went to the game Friday" because you wouldn't say, "Me went to the game Friday.")

2. We waited for Tom and him after class. (You read, "We waited for him after class" because you wouldn't say, "We waited for he after class.")

Sometimes you might have to change the sentence slightly:

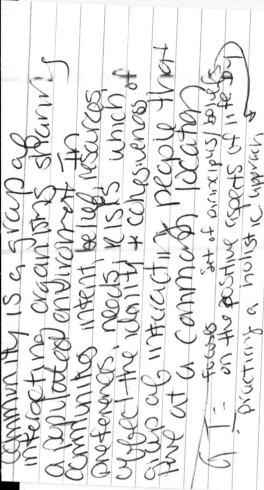

___e, I) have been friends for years.
___ob's friend for years.

EXERCISE 5C

___wing sentences aloud, leave out **one** of the sub-
___ connectives; then write the correct form of the

___isor asked Carol and <u>me</u> (I, me) to work an
___ on Saturday.
___d, The supervisor asked <u>me</u> to work an extra
___turday.)

___ing as a volunteer in the hospital. Carol first met

_____ (she, her) at the hospital last year.

___et Donna and _____ (I, me) at the hospi-
___ch.

___ drive to work together. Carol met Andy and

_____ (she, her) when they were walking to the hospital
parking lot.

4. Carol thanked Donna and _____ (he, him) for the ride home.

5. _____ (We, Us) parents should be concerned about our children's low test scores.

6. The principal and several teachers came to the PTA meeting. The

parents asked the teachers and _____ (she, her) to explain the
drop in test scores.

7. Victor and Wes tried out for the team last week. Both Victor and

_____ (he, him) made the varsity squad.

8. Brian asked Wes and ___________ (he, him) to meet him after football practice.

9. Carmen and ___________ (I, me) misunderstood the directions.

10. The instructor gave Carmen and ___________ (I, me) another day to complete our assignments.

EXERCISE 5D

Underline the correct pronoun.

Example: My brother and (I, me) want to buy a condominium together.

1. We want to find one that has a bedroom for (he, him) and one for me.

2. (He, Him) and (I, me) have been sharing one bedroom for a long time.

3. There has never been any trouble between (we, us).

4. The real estate agent asked whether my brother and (I, me) need two bathrooms.

5. My brother said that (he, him) and (I, me) need two bedrooms and two bathrooms.

6. Between you and (I, me), I think that is a good idea.

7. The agent told my brother and (I, me) to consider sharing a bathroom to save money.

8. We're going to inspect some condominiums that (she, her) and her partner have listed.

9. Now my brother and (I, me) may have to compromise in order to find a place we can afford.

10. I hope that my brother and (I, me) can find one we like.

Lesson 6 ✖ *Contractions*

A pronoun is sometimes combined with the verb that follows it to form a contraction. In writing the contraction, do not omit the apostrophe that takes the place of the omitted letters.

 I have = I've   she will = she'll   you are = you're

Omitting the i in Here is and There is

Contractions may also be formed by combining there with is and here with is.

Examples: There is John now. There's John now.
 Here is your book. Here's your book.

In both cases the apostrophe takes the place of the letter i in is. Note: There are and here are are never contracted. Furthermore, when a sentence begins with the words here is or there is, the noun that follows the verb is the subject.

EXERCISE 6A

Supply the contractions for these words.

1. she will ___she'll___   6. I am _____

2. they have _____   7. we have _____

3. he had _____   8. here is _____

4. he is _____   9. it is _____

5 I will _____   10. we are _____

EXERCISE 6B

A. Supply the missing apostrophes. Write out the pronoun and the verb on the line.

1. Hell meet us in an hour.   _____

2. Well shoot some baskets.   _____

3. Heres your basketball.   _____

4. After dinner theyre going to a play.   _____

5. Theres the entrance to the theater.   _____

6. Shell be late for the first act.   _____

7. Theyll have some dessert after the play.   _____

8. Youre wanted on the telephone.   _____

9. Whos calling please?   _____

10. Were not interested in subscribing to that magazine. _____

B. Now write the subjects and the complete verbs of the sentences. Omit the apostrophes and supply the missing letters of the verb if necessary. The first one has been completed for you.

	S	Aux. V	MV		S	Aux. V	MV
1.	he	will	meet	6.	___	___	___
2.	___	___	___	7.	___	___	___
3.	___	___	___	8.	___	___	___
4.	___	___	___	9.	___	___	___
5.	___	___	___	10.	___	___	___

It is a good idea to limit your use of contractions to informal writing. Do not use contractions in formal letters, essays, or term papers.

Summary of Chapter 4

Complete these sentences by choosing the appropriate words from the box below. Check your answers with the Answer Key.

1. In order to write complete sentences, remember to write a complete

   _____ and a noun or pronoun _____.

2. To help you find the verbs and their subjects, get in the habit of

   bracketing _____ phrases.

3. Some action verbs may be followed by a noun or pronoun which is

   called the _____ of the verb.

4. A special group of verbs _____ the subject to a completer.

5. Two or more subjects or verbs joined by a coordinating connective are

   called _____ subjects or verbs.

6. The subject of a verb that commands or requests is the pronoun

   _____.

prepositional	subject	links	verb
object	compound	"You"	

Sentence Combining

Study the way the writer combined these six sentences in one sentence before you complete the exercise that follows.

1. It was Sunday evening.
2. Ashley settled down.
3. Eric settled down.
4. They were on the couch.
5. They were in front of the television.
6. They watched their favorite program.

Combined Sentence

On Sunday evening Ashley and Eric settled down on the couch in front of the television and watched their favorite program.

Notice that the writer has used a compound subject in addition to prepositional phrases to combine six sentences into one.

On Sunday evening = prepositional phrase

Ashley and Eric = compound subject

in front of the television = prep. phrase

A. Combine these four sentences into one sentence with a compound subject.

1. The members of the cast took their bows.
2. The members of the orchestra took their bows.
3. They took their bows to the applause of the audience.
4. It was the final performance of the play.

B. Combine these four sentences into one sentence with a compound verb.

1. The gardener finished his work.
2. He loaded his tools on his truck.
3. He loaded them quickly.
4. He drove off to his next job.

C. Combine these five sentences into one sentence with a compound subject.

1. I am going on a trip.
2. My friend is going too.
3. We are going on a barge.
4. We are going in November.
5. We are going through the French countryside.

D. Combine these six sentences into one sentence with a compound verb.

1. The sports car skidded on the road.
2. The sports car spun around.
3. The road was a mountain road.
4. The road was icy.

5. The sports car nearly rear-ended a truck.
6. The truck was huge.

E. Combine these five sentences into one sentence with a compound verb.

1. The driver of the sports car was frightened.
2. He turned the wheel sharply.
3. He brought the car to a stop.
4. It was a skidding stop.
5. He brought the car to a stop just in time.

WRITING ASSIGNMENT

Look back at the Group Activity on page 135. After reading over the paragraph about W.E.B. Du Bois, you might be reminded of some friend or acquaintance of yours who is outstanding in some ways but has difficulty getting along with colleagues and friends. Or you might consider writing about some public figure who has achieved some fame but has had difficulty with colleagues or with the news media. Consult your instructor for approval of the subject if you plan to write about a public figure.

Begin by writing the name of the person you are going to write about in the middle of a piece of paper. Draw a circle around the name. Then make a cluster of circles listing the achievements or good qualities on one side of the central circle and a cluster of circles listing the problems or difficulties on the other side of the central circle. (For further discussion of "clustering," see Chapter 1, pages 5–7.)

Ask yourself which ideas interest you most, which ones will make the writing assignment more interesting for your readers. Decide how many items from your list of clustered achievements you will include and how many from your list of character problems you will include.

Before you begin to write, consider who will be reading this work. As you write, keep your reader in mind.

Then write a rough draft including a topic sentence with an evaluation of your subject's strengths and weaknesses. (See the original paragraph on Du Bois for an example of a topic sentence.)

ALTERNATE WRITING ASSIGNMENT

Look back at the paragraph in Exercise 5B on pages 137–138 by the student whose parents sent her to Japanese school despite her protests.

Write a paragraph about a past activity of yours which gave you little sense of purpose or a good reason for participating in it at the time. Today, however, the experience has proved valuable to you, and you are glad that you made the effort.

If you do not wish to write about yourself, perhaps you know someone you can interview who has had such an experience and is willing to serve as your subject.

When you are planning your paragraph, jot down questions that lead to an evaluation of the experience rather than just a narrative or description of it. You, of course, may use both narration and description in the development of the subject. To begin, ask yourself questions such as these that follow:

1. What specifically was the activity? Where and when did it take place? Is this an unusual activity? Will your reader require any special definitions?
2. Did someone else persuade you to participate in it, or was it your own idea?
3. What pressures, your own or someone else's, did you face?
4. Why did you continue despite your negative feelings and objections?
5. Why do you now regard this as a valuable experience?

Write a topic sentence summing up the change in your thinking that took place. For example:

"As I continued going to Japanese school, my interest and enjoyment grew."

Decide how many items on your list you will include in your paragraph. For each item jot down specific details and examples that you will need to support the topic sentence.

What is the best way to organize the material? Like the writer of the paragraph on pages 137–138, you may want to explain your objections first, leading into your topic sentence. She goes on to discuss the advantages that resulted as she became older. Notice that she refers back in the last sentence to conclude her paragraph by referring to her early objections. You have other options, depending upon your subject. Refer to pages 25–30 in Chapter 1 as a review of ways to organize a paragraph.

Chapter 4 Practice Test: Understanding the Parts of the Sentence

Name _____

Date _____ Class Time _____

Instructor _____

I. Write the subjects, the auxiliary verbs, and the main verbs on the lines at the right. Some sentences may have more than one auxiliary verb, and some may not have any auxiliary verb, but all the sentences have main verbs and subjects.

	Subject	Auxiliary Verb(s)	Main Verb
1. Tom's license plates have expired.	_____	_____	_____
2. Why didn't he renew them last month?	_____	_____	_____
3. Pull over to the curb!	_____	_____	_____
4. The officer listens politely to Tom's excuse.	_____	_____	_____
5. He is smiling and writing a citation.	_____	_____	_____
6. Nola has recently been to traffic school.	_____	_____	_____
7. She had been driving over the speed limit.	_____	_____	_____
8. Across the street from the police station is the library.	_____	_____	_____
9. Traffic school is usually held in the library.	_____	_____	_____
10. Nola's class met for six hours.	_____	_____	_____

Chapter 4 Practice Test: Understanding the Parts of the Sentence (cont.)

II. a. Bracket the prepositional phrases and underline the verbs.
    b. Write the word that is the object of the verb on the line at the right.
    c. If there is no object of the verb, leave the space blank.

Example: Do you eat eggs [for breakfast]?   _____eggs_____

1. May I ride with you to school on Wednesday?   _____

2. Write the verbs on the lines at the right.   _____

3. Eddie will be working for a tax consultant during
    March.   _____

4. The students in the political science class recently
    heard some startling facts about the CIA.   _____

5. Tina studies French daily from 10 A.M. until noon.   _____

III.   Write a word of your choice in each blank. The words that are
       called for are linking verbs (LV) and completers (C). Do not use any
       form of a verb more than once, including the verb "to be" (am, is,
       are, was, were).

1. (C) Did Joanna feel _____ about the interview?

2. (LV) The rent for the apartment _____ too high.

3. (C) Bert will probably be (a/an) _____ next year.

4. (LV) The children _____ hungry again soon after lunch.

5. (LV) The circus bear _____ harmless.

IV. 1. Write a sentence with a compound verb.

     _____

     _____

Chapter 4 Practice Test: Understanding the Parts of the Sentence (cont.)

2. Write a sentence with a compound subject.

_____

_____

3. Write a sentence with a compound object or a compound completer.

_____

_____

V. In the following sentences, underline the correct form of the pronoun in the parentheses.

1. Brenda, her brother, and (me, I) have decided to buy tickets for a concert.

2. (Her, She) and her brother have been saving money for the tickets.

3. Her brother will drive Brenda and (I, me) downtown to the box office.

4. I like to go to concerts with Brenda and (he, him).

5. (He, Him) and Brenda enjoy going to concerts together with me.

VI. In the following sentences, bracket the prepositional phrases.

1. Aretha has been practicing tennis with her coach for many months.

2. Despite the pain in her arm, Aretha comes to the court every morning.

3. After a half hour, she puts an ice pack on her shoulder.

4. Aretha, together with her coach, runs around the track in the afternoon.

5. She cannot play in the tournament because of the injured shoulder.

Chapter 4 Practice Test: Understanding the Parts of the Sentence (cont.)

VII. A. Supply the missing apostrophe.

1. Well help you with those heavy suitcases.

2. Theyre too heavy for you to carry alone.

3. Youre going to drive us to the airport.

4. Ive been looking forward to this vacation for a long time.

5. Youll get a post card from us soon.

VII. B. Now write the subjects and the complete verbs of the sentences in II.A. Omit the apostrophes and supply the missing letters of the verb if necessary.

Subject	Auxiliary Verb(s)	Main Verb
1. _____	_____	_____
2. _____	_____	_____
3. _____	_____	_____
4. _____	_____	_____
5. _____	_____	_____

Chapter 4 Answer Key

Exercise 1A
Your instructor will check your answers.

Exercise 1B

Subject	Auxiliary Verb	Main Verb
1. Americans	can	experience
2. festivals	are	held
3. We	have	attended
4. events		include
5. contestants	are	throwing
6. trials		show
7. collie		drives
8. Bagpipers		offer
9. They	have	led
10. you	may	think
you		are

Exercises 1C and 1D
Your instructor will check your answers.

Exercise 2A
1. [Since 1789], [between the ages], [of fourteen and eighteen], [as congressional pages], [in our nation's capital]
2. [during vacation], [in Washington, D.C.], [for a year], [at Page School], [in the Library of Congress]
3. [for members], [of Congress], [from 9 A.M.], [to 5 P.M.]
4. [of the present system], [at home], [with their parents]
5. [despite the pressures], [of a busy schedule], [of national political life]

Exercise 2B
1. [to a baseball game] [along with two friends]
2. [contrary to the weather forecast]
3. [on account of the large crowd] [at the box office]
4. [in front of us] [about the long wait] [in line]
5. [After six innings] [because of rain]

Exercise 2C
1. The (rangers) [in Glacier National Park] <u>must</u> <u>inform</u> campers [about cow parsnip].

2. The cow (parsnip,) a member [of the parsley family], <u>is</u> the favorite food [of the grizzly bears].

3. (Grizzlies) <u>graze</u> [like cattle] [on moist slopes] [of cow parsnips].

4. [At the time] [of year] when (backpackers) <u>are</u> <u>entering</u> the park [in large numbers], the (grizzlies) <u>are</u> <u>looking</u> [for cow parsnips].

5. [According to the park rangers], the grizzly (bears) <u>are</u> never far [from the campers].

Exercise 2D

(Central Guitar) is <u>located</u> [along with a number] [of other guitar stores and studios] [on one long block] [in the middle of a large city]. Last month (Jerry Montgomery,) a college sophomore, <u>started</u> a part-time job [at Central]. Rock 'n' roll (music) has always <u>been</u> one [of Jerry's enthusiasms], and his record (collection) <u>includes</u> artists [from Les Paul and Roy Orbison] [to Eddie Van Halen and the Wallflowers]. The store's (customers) <u>vary</u> widely. A beginning (player) [with only six weeks] [of instruction] <u>may be</u> <u>standing</u> [in front of the counter] [beside a star performer]. (One) <u>is</u> <u>shopping</u> [for a $95 guitar], and the (other) <u>admires</u> the finish [on a $20,000 instrument]. Autographed (pictures) [of the top rock stars] <u>decorate</u> the walls while the (sound) [of guitar music] <u>surges</u> [into the shop] [from the studios] just [down the street]. (Jerry) <u>posts</u> a notice [of a rock concert] [above a rack] [of music] and <u>turns</u> [towards his next customer]. (Jerry,) [at this particular time], <u>has</u> <u>found</u> the perfect job.

Exercise 3A
1. it   2. us   3. her   4. them   5. me

Exercise 3B

1.   [In 1947], a (team) [of scientists] [at Bell Laboratories] <u>created</u>
the first transistor.   _____transistor_____

2.   (transistor) <u>did receive</u> [in the beginning]   _____attention_____

3.   (it) <u>replaced</u> [in radios and televisions]   _____tubes_____

4.   (transistors) <u>power</u> [from radios to computers] [from jets]
[to satellites]   _____everything_____

5.   (Millions) [of transistors] <u>can fit</u> [on a computer chip]   _____no object_____

Exercise 3C
Your instructor will check your sentences.

Exercise 3D

1. <u>have been</u> <u>coming</u> (no object)

2. <u>read</u> instructions

3. <u>is</u> <u>writing</u> (no object)

4. <u>did</u> <u>pass</u> test

5. <u>will</u> (not) <u>know</u> results

6. <u>Did</u>(n't) <u>post</u> grades

7. <u>Open</u> door

8. <u>has</u> (not) <u>completed</u> assignment

9. <u>is</u> <u>going</u> (no object)

10. <u>are</u> <u>driving</u> (no object)

Exercise 4A

1. My (daughter) <u>is</u> a freshman at Jackson Community College.
      S LV   C

2. (She) <u>is</u> a physical education major.
   S LV   C

3. The traffic (light) <u>is</u> finally <u>turning</u> green.

4. The (pedestrians) <u>seemed</u> impatient.

5. Can (you) <u>be</u> the moderator of our next discussion?

6. The (discussion) <u>should be</u> interesting.

7. <u>Is</u> (Mrs. Chavez) your friend?

8. During high school (Mrs. Chavez) <u>was</u> both a friend and an adviser to me.

Exercises 4B
Your instructor will check your answers.

Exercise 4C

1. (Marla) <u>has</u> just <u>arrived</u> home [from work].   <u>no object</u>

2. Her last (appointment) [at the office] <u>was</u> late.   <u>late</u>

3. (Jack) <u>has been</u> <u>waiting</u> [for her] [for an hour].   <u>no object</u>

4. (They) both <u>feel</u> tired and hungry.   <u>tired and hungry</u>

5. The (refrigerator) <u>looks</u> almost empty.   <u>empty</u>

6. (Marla) <u>finds</u> some leftover chicken [in the meat saver].   <u>chicken</u>

7. (Jack) <u>makes</u> a tossed salad and <u>slices</u> some French bread.   <u>salad and bread</u>

8. The (bread) tastes a bit stale.   <u>stale</u>

9. (Marla) prepares some fresh fruit [for dessert].   <u>fruit</u>

10. (Jack) does not <u>seem</u> very enthusiastic [about the dessert].   <u>enthusiastic</u>

11. (Marla) <u>comes</u> [to the rescue].   <u>no object</u>

12. (She) <u>discovers</u> a pint [of chocolate ice cream] [in the freezer].   <u>pint</u>

Exercise 5A
Your instructor will check your answers.

Exercise 5B

1. (brother and I)   2. <u>resented and complained</u>   3. (language and customs)

4. <u>wanted and envied</u>   5. (Mother and Dad)   6. (interest and enjoyment)

7. (knowing and communicating)   8. <u>attending and preparing</u>   9. (Mother and Dad)

10. <u>recall and smile</u>

Exercise 5C
1. her   2. me   3. her   4. him   5. We   6. her   7. he   8. him   9. I   10. me

Exercise 5D
1. him   2. He, I   3. us   4. I   5. he, I   6. me   7. me   8. she   9. I   10. I

Exercise 6A
1. she'll   2. they've   3. he'd   4. he's   5. I'll   6. I'm   7. we've   8. here's   9. it's
10. we're

Exercise 6B
A. 1. He'll   2. We'll   3. Here's   4. they're   5. There's   6. She'll   7. They'll
8. You're   9. Who's   10. We're
B.

Subject	Auxiliary Verb	Main Verb
2. We	will	shoot
3. basketball		is
4. they	are	going
5. entrance		is
6. She	will	be
7. They	will	have
8. You	are	wanted
9. Who	is	calling
10. We	are	interested

Summary of Chapter 4
1. verb, subject   2. prepositional   3. object   4. links   5. compound   6. "You"

5

Expanding the Sentence

In Chapter 5 you will learn about several ways to expand the sentence.

Definitions of Terms

An ADJECTIVE modifies a noun or pronoun by limiting or describing it.

A PARTICIPLE is a verb form that may function as part of a verb phrase (was <u>winning</u>) or as an adjective (<u>winning</u> team).

The COMPARATIVE form of the adjective or adverb is used to compare two persons, places, ideas, things, or actions.

The SUPERLATIVE form of the adjective or adverb is used to compare three or more persons, places, ideas, things, or actions.

An ADVERB can modify verbs, adjectives, or other adverbs. It answers one of the following questions: When? How? Where? Why?

VERBALS are formed from verbs but cannot function as main verbs. They are used as nouns, adjectives, and adverbs.

A VERBAL PHRASE includes a VERBAL plus a noun and/or a prepositional phrase.

A MODIFIER describes, limits, or makes specific another word in the sentence.

A MISPLACED MODIFIER is an adjective or adverb that has been placed next to a word it does not modify.

A DANGLING MODIFIER is an adjective or adverb that does not modify any word in the sentence.

Lesson 1 ❋ *Adding Details with Adjectives*

The sentences you have written for the exercises so far are just a beginning. Readers usually ask more of the writer: more color, more variety, more information, more specific details. Adjectives and adverbs give the reader additional information by further describing and qualifying nouns and verbs.

Adjectives

An adjective makes a noun or pronoun specific or concrete by limiting and describing it.

     N   N   Adj   Adj   N   Adj   N

a. Zoos protect species. Some new zoos protect endangered species.

     N   N   Adj   N   Adj   Adj   N

b. Zoos breed animals. Farsighted zoos breed rare and exotic animals.

     N   N   Adj   N   Adj   Adj   N

c. Zoos need support. All zoos need continued public support.

Kinds of Adjectives

This lesson will discuss four kinds of adjectives:

1. possessive forms
2. noun markers
3. numbers
4. descriptive words

1. Possessive Pronouns and Possessive Nouns   The possessive forms of nouns and pronouns describe and qualify nouns: Gene's book, his book. Your reader knows exactly what book you are talking about.

❋	*EXERCISE 1A*	❋

Bracket all possessive pronouns and possessive nouns. There are two adjectives in each sentence except for sentence 8, which has one adjective, and sentence 10, which has four.

Example: The bike [riders'] protests were loud when they heard that [their] lanes of traffic would be closed.

1. New York City's chief engineer is responsible for maintaining its highways and bridges.

2. His main job is to keep the city's bridges from decaying and collapsing.

3. Today's larger trucks have ruined many of America's roads and bridges.

4. In addition, although salt is used successfully to melt snow, the salt's acidity has destroyed our highways.

5. The chief engineer's judgments about repairs affect many people's lives.

6. Yet those people whose safety he fights for complain when their lanes of traffic are closed.

7. Also, the politicians' budget cuts have limited his inspection staff.

8. The chief engineer's plan to save a bridge might involve selling rotten wire for $50 a bundle.

9. Many of New York City's citizens agree that the engineer's job is difficult.

10. Their opinion is based on their knowledge that New York's roads are their most valuable asset.

2. *Noun Markers* Noun markers indicate that a noun will follow.

Noun Markers				
a	that	all	either	more
an	these	any	every	most
the	this	both	few	much
some	those	each	many	neither

Some of these words seem to point to the noun: that truck.
Others limit the noun: few people.

3. Numbers   All numbers are adjectives. They modify and qualify the noun by telling how many.

Examples: five apples   fifty dollars   twenty-four hours

EXERCISE 1B

Underline the possessive pronouns, noun markers, and numbers in the following paragraphs. Refer especially to the chart on page 157.

Example: Not all hunters in this jungle are stalking big game.

Three people, one woman and two men, are making their way cautiously through the jungle. Far from home they are aware of the many dangers around them. What are those strangers looking for? The solution to an environmental problem? New medicines to add to our fight against disease? Neither suggestion is correct. They are hoping to find some new ingredients to use in the manufacture of perfume. Each explorer carries a computerized device to capture any fragrances jungle flowers may contain. With these, the designers in their laboratories will create those exotic fragrances both men and women seem to find so appealing. And where are these perfumes manufactured? If your answer is Paris, that sophisticated European center of fashion, you are mistaken. Few people know that the small city of Teaneck, New Jersey, holds this distinction. Perhaps it is just as well that this fact is not commonly known; it might rob that $50 cologne of its appeal.

4. *Descriptive Adjectives*   To give the reader a mental picture of something, the writer chooses adjectives that describe the qualities or characteristics of it, including color and size.

Adj.   N   Adj.
Six clowns entertained the excited children under the top of the

     Adj   Adj   Adj   N
enormous white canvas tent.

                    Adj   Adj   N   Adj   Adj   N
A clown with curly orange hair kept falling off a small red tricycle.

Special Forms of Adjectives

1. Sometimes present and past participles are used as adjectives:

    Adj   N   Adj   N   Adj   N   Adj   N
    excited fans   winning pass   opening game   defeated team

2. When a noun precedes another noun, the first noun is used as an adjective to describe or limit the second noun:

    Adj   N   Adj   N   Adj   N   Adj   N
    canvas tent   circus tent   plastic cushions   cotton candy

3. Prepositional phrases are also used as adjectives.

       N   Adj
    Toshiro sent five letters of application.

    Of application specifies the kind of letters that Toshiro sent; therefore, the phrase is an adjective.

EXERCISE 1C

In the following sentences, bracket all the participles and nouns used as adjectives.

Example: Alex spent an [exciting] time at the [opening football] game.

1. In his reserved seat, Alex watched a closely fought game on a chilly night.

2. During half time he bought a hot dog with mustard and relish and a paper cup of hot coffee.

3. Victory came for the home team during the closing minutes of the game.

4. The fans, rising from their seats, cheered the rookie quarterback as he carried the ball into scoring territory.

5. As he left the sports stadium, Alex hoped that this game marked the beginning of an Eagle winning streak.

6. The wind was cold, so he zipped up his nylon parka, pulled on his leather gloves, and wished he had worn a wool sweater under his parka.

7. But Alex's evening ended on a low note, for he could not find his car in the crowded lot.

8. A stadium guard had called the tow truck to remove Alex's car from the no-parking zone.

Position of Adjectives

1. The adjective usually appears in front of the noun:

Adj	N		Adj	N		Adj	N
spring	vacation		freshman	class		term	paper

2. But the adjective can follow the noun it modifies:

               N   Adj   Adj
The woman's answer was <u>polite</u> but <u>guarded</u>.

These adjectives are completers following the linking verb <u>was</u>.

     Adj   N   Adj   Adj
The <u>winning</u> team, <u>laughing</u> and <u>shouting</u>, ran off the field.

These present participles are adjectives modifying the noun <u>team</u>. Notice that two of them, <u>laughing</u> and <u>shouting</u>, follow the noun.

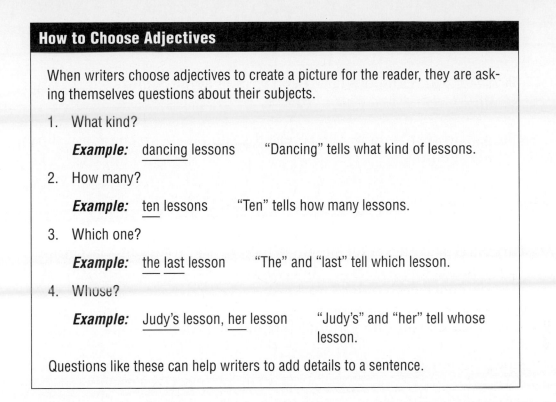

How to Choose Adjectives

When writers choose adjectives to create a picture for the reader, they are asking themselves questions about their subjects.

1. What kind?

   Example: dancing lessons   "Dancing" tells what kind of lessons.

2. How many?

   Example: ten lessons   "Ten" tells how many lessons.

3. Which one?

   Example: the last lesson   "The" and "last" tell which lesson.

4. Whose?

   Example: Judy's lesson, her lesson   "Judy's" and "her" tell whose lesson.

Questions like these can help writers to add details to a sentence.

EXERCISE 1D

Fill in each blank with an adjective. You may use numbers, possessive nouns or pronouns, participles, descriptive words, or noun markers.

1. Frida Kahlo was a _____ artist.

2. _____ paintings are in the collections of many large museums.

3. She had a _____ accident when she was a young girl.

4. To show her _____ feelings, she painted herself weeping.

5. Many of her paintings depict her _____ pain.

6. A few of her paintings show her with a monkey on _____ shoulder.

7. She was married to _____ painter, Diego Rivera.

8. A number of her paintings reveal her _____ relationship with Rivera.

9. _____ books have been written about Kahlo's _____ life.

10. As a woman painter, she received _____ recognition during her lifetime.

GROUP ACTIVITY

Part A: First, bracket all the adjectives in the following paragraph as shown in the first sentence. Then, together with members of your group in class, check each other's work.

It is [a] [beautiful], [sunny] day in [a] [popular] [theme] park in [the] United States. Mr. and Mrs. Tomita, on their first trip to this country, listen attentively to a tour guide's claim that thirty-five thousand adults and children visit the park every day. Most visitors to this magical place are attracted by an amazing variety of shows, rides, exhibits, and restaurants. Both Mr. and Mrs. Tomita, however, are impressed by the clean surroundings. They are staying at the vacationland's hotel where the rooms have immaculately clean, blue plastic furniture, green and beige walls, and beds covered with purple-green spreads. The hotel's parking lot, with its carefully planted vegetation, is also sparkling and clean. The smallest scrap of litter is sucked underground and rushed via pipes to a fabulous trash compactor. Even the friendly birds do their part by picking some bread crumbs off the restaurant's patio at the hotel. Mr. and Mrs. Tomita know that they will enjoy themselves in this spotless American tourist attraction.

Part B: Working as a group, write five sentences about an amusement park that you have visited. In these five sentences, use at least one possessive pronoun, one possessive noun, one noun marker, one color, and one number as adjectives. You, of course, may use more of these words if you wish. Exchange your sentences with those of another group in the class. Check each other's work by bracketing the adjectives in each sentence.

1. _____

_____

_____

2. _____

_____

_____

3. _____

_____

_____

4. _____

_____

_____

5. _____

_____

_____

EXERCISE 1E

On a separate piece of paper, write five brief sentences of your own. Expand each sentence by adding adjectives and prepositional phrases to the nouns.

Punctuating Adjectives Before a Noun

Use commas to separate two or more adjectives that modify the same noun if a coordinating connective such as **and** or **but** can be inserted between the adjectives. For a more detailed explanation, see Chapter 9, Lesson 2.

Examples: a. The enthusiastic candidate spoke in a loud <u>and</u> excited voice.
b. The enthusiastic candidate spoke in a loud, excited voice. (A comma separates the adjectives.)

EXERCISE 1F

Insert commas as needed in the following sentences.

1. The scenic rugged lands of northeastern Arizona attract tourists from everywhere.

2. Glowing sunsets illuminate the purple red and blue-gray sediments in the curving mounds of the Painted Desert's surreal landscape.

3. Steep red sandstone cliffs surrounding Lake Powell provide a stark contrast to its clear intense emerald-green water.

4. The mineralized rainbow-colored giant stone trees now lie exposed upon the floor of the Petrified Forest through the action of wind and water.

5. Some of the most remarkable breathtaking and memorable views of secluded sandstone canyons, rivaling those of the Grand Canyon, perhaps not in immensity, but surely in beauty, await the visitor to Canyon de Chelly (de shay).

Lesson 2 ✾ *Comparison of Adjectives*

Most adjectives change their form for use in comparisons. For example, **soft, softer, softest** show differences in degree.

Comparative Degree

A. Walt is <u>strong</u>.
B. Dan is <u>stronger</u> than Walt.

Sentence B compares the strength of Walt and Dan. Stronger is the COMPARATIVE form of the adjective strong.

Superlative Degree

   A. Pete is the strongest of all.
   B. He is the strongest wrestler on the team.

Strongest is the SUPERLATIVE form of the adjective strong. Superlative forms are often followed by prepositional phrases as shown in the examples above.

Forming Comparatives and Superlatives

1. Add **-er** to adjectives of one syllable   Add **-est** to adjectives of *one* syllable.

Positive	Comparative	Superlative
rich	richer	richest
sweet	sweeter	sweetest
tall	taller	tallest

(Exceptions)

good	better	best
bad	worse	worst

2. Place the words *more* or *most* before adjectives of two or more syllables.

brilliant	more brilliant	most brilliant
dangerous	more dangerous	most dangerous
exciting	more exciting	most exciting

Exception: There is an exception to the rule that two-syllable adjectives add *more* to the comparative form. To form the comparative of two-syllable adjectives ending in **-y,** change the **-y** to **-i** and add **-er.** To form the superlative, add **-est.**

happy	happier	happiest
lovely	lovelier	loveliest
lazy	lazier	laziest

Use the comparative form to compare two persons, places, ideas, or things.

Use the superlative form to compare more than two persons, places, ideas, or things.

Example: Marion is taller than Andy.
         Marion is the tallest player on our team.

Less and Least   <u>Less</u> and <u>least</u> may be substituted for <u>more</u> and <u>most</u> to show a lesser degree in a comparison.

Comparative   (followed by *than*)   **Superlative**   (followed by *of* or other prepositions)

less dangerous   least dangerous
less comfortable   least comfortable

EXERCISE 2A

Fill in the blanks with words that show a <u>lesser</u> degree of comparison.

Example: The driver's account of the accident was <u>less</u> factual than the traffic officer's.

1. The speaker was _____ interesting than I had expected.

2. Highway 10 is the _____ dangerous way of all through the mountains.

3. That house is _____ expensive than the one we looked at this morning.

4. I am the _____ creative member of our family.

5. The baby seems _____ sleepy than she was an hour ago.

EXERCISE 2B

Change the adjective in parentheses into the comparative or superlative degree. The first sentence is completed as an example.

1. Buying a computer for home or business may be the

   <u>most important</u> purchase you will make in the next ten years.
   (important, superlative)

2. The computer you choose for the home is almost _____ to use
   (easy, comparative)

   than the telephone.

3. It enables you to have a _____ method of controlling the
   (good, comparative)

   family budget.

4. You should be sure to buy a computer that can be upgraded to a

   _____, _____ model sometime in the future.
   (big, comparative)   (powerful, comparative)

5. The data-processing computer has become the _____
   (recent, superlative)

   addition to the business world.

6. Some computerized information systems offer businesses

   _____ productivity.
   (great, comparative)

7. They even promise _____ use of energy.
   (efficient, comparative)

8. The use of computers encourages _____ business
   (simple, comparative)

   procedures.

9. The _____ computer systems are powerful enough to process
   (large, superlative)

   company payrolls.

10. The computer you buy for home or business should be the

    _____ quality at the _____ price.
    (good, superlative)   (low, superlative)

EXERCISE 3B

Completing this exercise will give you a further review of adjectives and adverbs. Combine the sentences in each part according to the directions. A, B, and C focus on adjectives and D and E on adverbs.

A. Combine these five sentences into one sentence. Use a prepositional phrase to describe the sale. Use a participle to describe the books and the customers.

1. The bookstore was having a sale.
2. They were selling reduced books.
3. The books were slightly soiled.
4. But the customers didn't mind the smudge marks.
5. The customers were delighted.

_____

_____

_____

_____

B. Combine these seven sentences into one sentence in which the subject is compound. Use <u>approaching</u> and <u>salesman's</u> as adjectives.

1. Books filled the briefcase.
2. Magazines filled the briefcase.
3. The briefcase belonged to the salesman.
4. The salesman was approaching.
5. The briefcase was large.
6. It was brown.
7. It was leather.

_____

_____

_____

_____

C. Combine these seven sentences into one sentence that shows a contrast. Use modifiers to describe the nouns <u>bicycle</u> and <u>roads</u>.

1. Carola has a bicycle.
2. The bicycle is lightweight.
3. But it is strong enough.
4. She can ride it on city streets.
5. The streets are paved.
6. She can ride it on country roads.
7. The roads are unpaved.

_____

_____

_____

_____

D. Combine these six sentences into one sentence.

1. It was Monday.
2. The foreign minister arrived.
3. He was a new one.
4. He arrived early.
5. It was in the morning.
6. He arrived in Helsinki.

_____

_____

_____

_____

E. Combine these six sentences into one sentence.

1. Mrs. Konitz joined her friends.
2. She usually met them every Sunday afternoon.
3. They sat on the same bench.
4. The bench was just inside the gate.
5. It was the gate to the park.
6. The gate was at the south end of the park.

_____

_____

_____

_____

_____

EXERCISE 3C

On a separate piece of paper, write five brief sentences of your own. Expand each sentence by adding adverbs and prepositional phrases to the verbs, adverbs, and/or adjectives.

Comparison of Adverbs

Adverbs, like adjectives, have degrees of comparison: the positive, the comparative, the superlative.

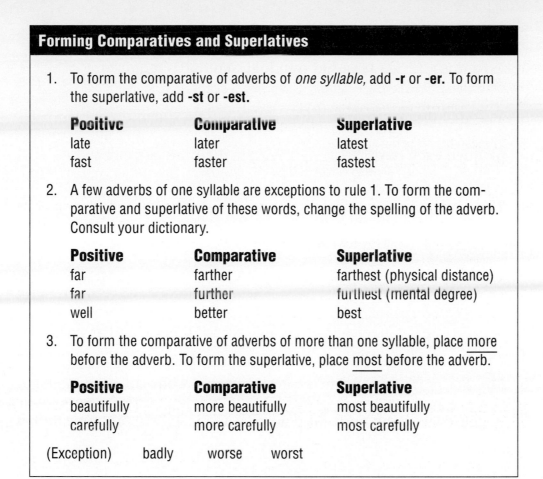

Forming Comparatives and Superlatives

1. To form the comparative of adverbs of *one syllable,* add **-r** or **-er.** To form the superlative, add **-st** or **-est.**

Positive	Comparative	Superlative
late	later	latest
fast	faster	fastest

2. A few adverbs of one syllable are exceptions to rule 1. To form the comparative and superlative of these words, change the spelling of the adverb. Consult your dictionary.

Positive	Comparative	Superlative
far	farther	farthest (physical distance)
far	further	furthest (mental degree)
well	better	best

3. To form the comparative of adverbs of more than one syllable, place <u>more</u> before the adverb. To form the superlative, place <u>most</u> before the adverb.

Positive	Comparative	Superlative
beautifully	more beautifully	most beautifully
carefully	more carefully	most carefully

(Exception)   badly   worse   worst

Use the comparative form when comparing two actions. Use the superlative form when comparing three or more actions.

Example: I had thought that Jan skated <u>more gracefully</u> than Marie, but then I saw Adele skate. Adele skated <u>most gracefully</u> of all.

EXERCISE 3D

Change each adverb in parentheses into the comparative or superlative degree. The first is completed as an example.

1. Marty Porter, a night school student and the mother of three children

   under the age of ten, had decided <u>most reluctantly</u> to give up her
   (reluctantly, superlative)

   full-time job.

2. She found herself performing these three demanding roles

_____ than her own high standards required.
(efficiently, comparative)

3. The inability to organize her activities was not the problem; she

planned each day _____ than the last.
(systematically, comparative)

4. The company she worked for, however, did not want to lose one of its

_____ employees.
(valuable, superlative)

5. Her supervisor arranged a flexible schedule that allowed her to fulfill

_____ her obligations at home, at school, and at work.
(easily, comparative)

6. Mrs. Porter is one of an increasing number of white-collar workers with

staggered working hours who now fare _____ at home and at
(well, comparative)
work.

7. The companies adopting flexible scheduling for employees

_____ than not benefit as well.
(often, comparative)

8. Absenteeism drops _____, and employees
(significantly, superlative)

_____ request time off for medical and dental appoint-
(frequently, comparative)

ments. In addition, many companies find that flexible scheduling

improves production and raises worker morale.

G R O U P   A C T I V I T Y

Read the following paragraph. Then, writing in complete sentences, answer the questions at the end of the paragraph. Use adverbs in your sentences and underline each one. In class get together with one or two classmates and compare your sentences.

A baseball can carry farther in some stadiums than in others. Most hitters already know that fact. There is also evidence that, on some days and in some stadiums, a ball will go even farther. The ideal day would be very hot and very humid. The stadium in Denver, because of its altitude of more than 5,000 feet, is the ideal place. Many players hit best of all in Denver's stadium, and they hit worst of all in the stadium in San Diego. The stadium in that city is at sea level, and there is almost no humidity. A baseball travels fastest and farthest on hot, humid days and at high altitudes. So if you are seriously interested in becoming a "home-run king," you should travel to Denver on an exceptionally hot day in August, and you should be able to hit the ball harder and faster.

1. What is the ideal weather for hitting a baseball?
2. What is the ideal stadium for hitting a baseball?
3. What stadium poses the greatest challenge to a hitter?

_____

_____

_____

_____

_____

Lesson 4 ✳ *Adding Details with Verbal Phrases*

Verbal phrases can be indispensable additions to a basic sentence because they greatly increase the possibilities for expanding it.

Example: Carla waited.

Breathless and exhausted, Carla waited to hear the choreographer's opinion of her audition.
Anxious to hear the choreographer's opinion of her dancing, Carla waited, forgetting her exhaustion.

Verbals are formed from verbs but cannot function as main verbs. They introduce verbal phrases and usually include a noun and/or a prepositional phrase. They are used as nouns, adjectives, and adverbs in sentences.

Verbal Phrase

1. to choose a pet   The verbal is to choose, formed from to plus the present form of the verb.

2. chosen for its intelligence   The verbal is chosen, the past participle.

3   choosing a Seeing Eye dog   The verbal is choosing, the present participle.

Pay special attention to the first type of verbal phrase (to choose a pet) because it looks like a prepositional phrase. Read the information below carefully.

Note:

The word *to* is used to introduce both verbal phrases and prepositional phrases.

TO + A VERB = A VERBAL PHRASE (INFINITIVE PHRASE)

Example: to send

TO + A NOUN AND ITS MODIFIERS = A PREPOSITIONAL PHRASE

Example: to the moon

> ## EXERCISE 4A

Complete the following sentences by writing verbal phrases on the lines. Form the verbal from the verb in parentheses.

Example: (hike)   Laurel likes <u>to hike in the mountains</u> every summer.

1. (begin)   Curtis has decided _____.

2. (reduce)   Mr. Gleason has increased the company's profits by _____.

3. (drive)   _____, Robin listened to her CD player.

4. (encourage)   The author, _____, began work on a second book.

5. (understand)   Mrs. Rodman tried _____.

> ## EXERCISE 4B

In the following paragraphs, bracket the verbal phrases and prepositional phrases. Then, answer the questions following the paragraph, using complete sentences that include verbal phrases wherever possible.

The water in the Amazon is muddy. It is hard to see just a few feet down, and twenty feet down, it is impossible to see anything. But electric fish are able to navigate at that depth without vision. They use electric organs to generate electric fields around their bodies to sense other living things. Catfish, using feelers, probe the muddy waters. They also have taste buds all over their bodies, allowing other senses to dominate over sight. Researchers have found many eyeless fish swimming at the bottom of the

Amazon. They survive by eating the tails of other fish. The fish can then grow new tails.

Another unusual group of fish found in the Amazon survive by eating dead wood found along the banks of the river. Hoping to discover more rare species, researchers are dragging nets along the bottom of the muddy river to bring them to the surface for study. The nets have brought in a tiny transparent catfish that is only one-third of an inch long. It is also blind, but it has thickened bones and armored plates on its side to protect it from larger fish. So far the waters of the Amazon are estimated to harbor at least 200 million fish species. That number is nearly twice the number in all of North America.

1. What special adaptation do electric fish have to the muddy waters of the Amazon River?

   _____

2. How do the catfish "see" in the dark? Describe two different methods.

   _____

   _____

3. How do these eyeless fish survive? Describe at least two different survival tactics.

   _____

   _____

4. Why does the tiny transparent catfish have protective armor?

   _____

Punctuation

At the beginning of a sentence, use a comma after an introductory verbal phrase.

Examples: Standing at the end of the line, I had little hope of getting a ticket.
Discouraged by the long line, I gave up and went home.

EXERCISE 4C

Insert commas after the introductory verbal phrases.

1. Hoping to make a profit Carolyn invested in the stock market.
2. Trying to get to the airport on time Josephine got a ticket for speeding.
3. Snowed in for a week in the mountains we couldn't get back in time to take our final exams.
4. Having spent the day shopping unsuccessfully for shoes Tina decided to wear her old ones to the party.
5. Finding a wallet on his way to school Jerry had visions of a generous reward.

For a more detailed discussion of this use of the comma, see Chapter 9.

Lesson 5 *Misplaced Modifiers and Dangling Modifiers*

When you use modifiers in your sentences, be sure that the word order of each sentence is clear and logical. Placing a modifier in an incorrect position can change or confuse the meaning of the sentence. Modifiers should be placed close to the words that they describe or qualify. Learn to identify and correct MISPLACED MODIFIERS and DANGLING MODIFIERS.

Misplaced Modifiers

Misplaced modifiers are exactly what the term suggests: these modifiers arc called misplaced because they have been incorrectly placed next to words that they are not intended to modify.

Examples:

a. I <u>nearly</u> ate all the brownies. (misplaced modifier)

   This sentence suggests that you didn't eat anything at all. You should place <u>nearly</u> in front of *all the brownies.*

   I ate <u>nearly</u> all the brownies. (correctly placed modifier)

b. I heard that our nation needs additional preschool teachers <u>on the television news.</u> (misplaced modifier)

   The preschool teachers are not needed on the television news, are they? You should place <u>on the television news</u> after the verb *heard.*

   I heard <u>on the television news</u> that our nation needs additional preschool teachers. (correctly placed modifier)

c. Coretta bought a German shepherd dog <u>alarmed by the robberies in the neighborhood.</u> (misplaced modifier)

   If the dog is alarmed by the robberies, it is not going to make a good watchdog. You should place the verbal phrase modifier in front of *Coretta.*

   <u>Alarmed by the robberies in the neighborhood,</u> Coretta bought a German shepherd dog. (correctly placed modifier)

EXERCISE 5A

Revise the following sentences by placing the words or phrases in parentheses next to the words that they modify.

Example: Eileen ran after the bus. (carrying a heavy briefcase)
<u>Carrying a heavy briefcase, Eileen ran after the bus.</u>

1. Nick saved $100 by making his own repairs on his car.
   (almost)

_____

2. The candidate promised that he would reduce unemployment.
   (at the political rally)

   _____

3. Alfredo ordered a pizza to go.
   (with mushrooms and pepperoni)

   _____

4. The painters told us that they would begin painting the house.
   (on Wednesday)

   _____

5. Rex saw a woman in the front row jump up and run out the side exit.
   (suddenly)

   _____

EXERCISE 5B

Rewrite the following sentences, placing each misplaced modifier as close as possible to the word it modifies. The first sentence is completed as an example.

1. Riding around in a black and white patrol car marked K-9 Patrol, everyone noticed the new police unit in town, Barney and Fred.

   Everyone noticed the new police unit in town, Barney and Fred, rid-

   ing around in a black and white patrol car marked K-9 Patrol.

2. Unfortunately, Barney drove the car, and Fred, sitting in the back seat, was a bit too eager for action.

   _____

   _____

3. Barney would hear Fred's growls, stopping the car at a traffic light or an intersection.

   _____

   _____

4. Putting his head out of the window, Fred snarled and barked at pedestrians frequently who passed close to the car.

   _____

   _____

5. Disgruntled citizens said that Fred was supposed to protect them, not attack them in their complaints to the police department.

   _____

   _____

6. The police chief sent Barney and Fred back to training classes, hoping to restore peace and order.

   _____

   _____

7. Fred was no longer an embarrassment to Barney, trained to control his enthusiasm.

   _____

   _____

8. Now when Barney stops the patrol car, Fred sits facing the front of the car in the back seat calmly.

   _____

   _____

9. His eyes move—from left to right and from right to left only.

_____

_____

10. He doesn't bark at the cats even that he sees on the prowl.

_____

_____

Dangling Modifiers

A dangling modifier is an adjective or adverb that does not modify any word in the sentence.

> **_Example:_** Showing an interest in computers, personnel offices are flooded with applications.

Were the personnel offices showing an interest in computers? Of course not. The verbal phrase modifier, Showing an interest in computers, is left dangling. There is no word in the sentence for it to modify. To correct this problem, write the sentence as follows:

> Showing an interest in computers, students are flooding personnel offices with applications.

A word such as students must be added to the sentence to eliminate the dangling modifier.

Another method of eliminating dangling modifiers changes the dangling word or phrase into a subordinate clause. You could correct the example given above as follows:

Since students are showing an interest in computers, personnel offices are flooded with applications.

> **Remember**
>
> You cannot get rid of a dangling modifier by moving it around in a sentence. Since there is no word in the sentence for it to modify, you must rewrite the sentence and add the word that the phrase modifies.

EXERCISE 5C

Complete these sentences by adding a main clause with an appropriate subject. Do not leave any modifiers dangling. Notice that these sentences form a paragraph.

Example: <u>Walking to the front of the courtroom,</u> the defense attorney objected to the judge's ruling.

1. Summoning another witness, _____

_____

2. Turning to face his client, _____

_____

3. Frowning and looking annoyed, _____

_____

4. To make his point clear, _____

_____

5. Calling for a conference, _____

_____

EXERCISE 5D

Rewrite this paragraph on the lines on page 187. Correct the dangling modifiers in each sentence.

Expecting a robot like R2D2, the robot that was demonstrated to Willy was disappointing. Propelling itself on large wheels, Willy had hoped for useful arms and legs. Having limited mobility, stairs could not be climbed. Responding to voice command, a distance of less than seventy feet was necessary between the robot and its owner. Frustrated by the poor quality, his decision to buy a robot would have to be delayed.

_____

_____

_____

_____

_____

_____

_____

Summary of Chapter 5

In Chapter 5 you learned that modifiers are added to basic sentences to add more information and to keep the reader's interest.

Choose words from the box on page 188 to complete the following sentences.

1. To test a word to see if it is an adjective, ask _____, _____, or _____.

2. The form of some adjectives and adverbs can be changed to show the _____ degree and the _____ degree.

3. Adverbs add further information about _____, _____, and other _____.

4. To test a word to see if it is an adverb, ask _____, _____, _____, or _____.

5. Modifiers that are placed near words they are not intended to mod-

ify are called _____ _____.

how?	what kind?	verbs
when?	how many?	adjectives
where?	which one?	adverbs
why?	misplaced modifiers	comparative
		superlative

Sentence Combining

Now that you have completed the exercises in this chapter, you understand how useful modifiers can be for adding details to your sentences.
As you combine the following sentences, see if you can add a detail or two
of your own to each sentence.

Example

1. There was a council meeting.
2. It was held on Wednesday.
3. Mr. Washington was there.
4. He represented the residents.
5. He represented the community.
6. He pointed out the failure of the city government.
7. The government had not found one solution.
8. There are many inner-city problems.

Combined Sentence

At the council meeting on Wednesday, Mr. Washington, representing
the residents of his community, pointed out the failure of the city
government to find one solution to the many inner-city problems.

You might add the adjectives, *an angry,* to describe Mr. Washington. Or
perhaps you would rather add the adverb, *angrily,* to the verb *pointed out*
to show the manner in which Mr. Washington spoke.

Your sentence would read: At the council meeting on Wednesday, Mr. Washington, representing the residents of his community, angrily pointed out the failure of the city government to find one solution to the many inner-city problems.

A. Combine these five sentences into one sentence.

1. It was late summer.
2. Thunderstorms flooded the region.
3. More than seventeen inches of rain fell in places.
4. The thunderstorms sent people to higher ground.
5. There were hundreds of people.

B. Combine these seven sentences into one sentence.

1. The opponents were determined.
2. They wrote letters.
3. There were over 500 letters.
4. They circulated a petition.
5. The opponents stirred up public opinion.
6. The public was against the location of the plant.
7. The plant makes chemicals.

C. Combine these six sentences into one sentence, using a verbal phrase for sentence 4.

1. Julia told us about her trip.
2. It was a recent one.
3. She had gone to China.
4. Julia emphasized her boat ride.
5. It was exciting.
6. It was up the Yangtze River.

D. Combine these six sentences into two sentences. Sentence 2 can become a prepositional phrase. Change sentences 4 and 6 into verbal phrases.

1. Sage Ranch was a popular movie location.
2. Its big red boulders served two purposes.
3. They sheltered the good guys
4. They were camping out.
5. They concealed the bad guys.
6. They were hiding out.

E. Combine these six sentences into one sentence, using a verbal phrase for sentence 2.

1. The city was destroyed.
2. It was located on the Bay of Naples.
3. The city was an ancient one.
4. It was named Pompeii.
5. An earthquake destroyed it.
6. The earthquake occurred in A.D. 79.

WRITING ASSIGNMENT

Read the following paragraph:

Gambling is a big profit for Indians. In California there are approximately 15,000 illegal slot machines, card games, and bingo parlors. The thirty-five tribes that operate these games make about $2 billion in annual gross revenues. That is only an estimate as nobody knows exactly how much they make. It has become the biggest source of income for Native Americans all over the country. They believe that it is the only way they can overcome the poor quality of their lands and their out-of-the-way locations. Tribal members have used the profits to better their lives. They have built homes and water treatment plants, and they operate day-care centers and medical centers. Their grandparents used to walk miles to a creek to bring back a bucket of water. But today they have decent plumbing and enough money to pay for their groceries. In Florida the Seminole Indians living on a reservation near Tampa have defied the law of their state. They have been selling cigarettes without charging sales tax for many years. And now they are operating large bingo parlors built on the Tampa reservation. The bingo parlors have flourished and attracted many tourists by offering super jackpots. When the members of Congress passed the Indian Gaming Act in 1988, they gave the Indians the right to operate casinos on their reservations. Indian slot machines are actually illegal in many states, but the states cannot do anything about them. Only the federal government can do something, and the federal law enforcement agencies are reluctant to act.

Topic: What is your opinion about Indian gambling casinos operating in your state? Try to persuade your reader to agree with your views.

Step 1. Start by jotting down all the ideas that come to mind about the benefits and the problems associated with gambling. Do not try to write in sentences. Make lists of your thoughts as they occur to you. You will edit them later.

Step 2. Once you have a long list, you will need to look it over to decide what items you want to write about.

Step 3. Select two or three major reasons to support your opinion. Then, write out your opinion to serve as your topic sentence.

Step 4. Provide sufficient support for each reason you give. You might refer to the many years of genocide of the Native Americans and the policy of neglect followed by the American government. Or you might refer to the influence of mobsters in gaming casinos in the past. Whichever side you decide to write on, you should stay with just one side for the duration of your paragraph. It is too difficult to write about both sides in one paragraph. You would have to write a longer essay to consider both sides.

As You Write: Try to include verbal phrases in your sentences. Pay special attention to your choice of adjectives and adverbs as discussed in this chapter.

ALTERNATE WRITING ASSIGNMENT

As we know, people from all over the world have immigrated to the United States. Although they now are Americans, many do not wish to lose their cultural heritage and seek to keep old customs and beliefs alive in various ways. Write a paragraph about one group's efforts in this regard. Reread about the Scottish Highland Games in Chapter 2, page 62 and consider what makes these games uniquely Scottish. In this chapter on page 169, read again about the Kwanzaa ceremony, a recent attempt to bring a people together in the pursuit of moral excellence. If you have participated in a Kwanzaa rite, you may want to expand upon the brief paragraph in this chapter and give a detailed personal account.

Assume that your reader is not a member of the group you have chosen as your subject. Describe the ceremony, celebration, or whatever form the activity assumes. When did this observance begin, years ago or fairly recently? What are its distinguishing characteristics? Are any costumes, foods, props, or symbols used that reflect aspects of the culture? Is the group seeking to preserve specific values and beliefs? Would the ceremony be meaningful to someone outside the group? In what ways is it memorable? As you plan your paragraph, follow the steps above when appropriate.

Suggested Subjects

Cinco de Mayo   Japanese Oban Festival   St. Patrick's Day Parade
Korean or Chinese celebrations of the New Year   Kwanzaa

✎ Chapter 5 Practice Test: Expanding the Sentence

Name _____

Date _____ Class Time _____

Instructor _____

I. Bracket all adjectives in the following sentences.

1. The judges presented three winners with gold medals.

2. Scrambled eggs won't stick to that Teflon skillet.

3. Jayne distrusts her ex-husband's good intentions.

4. The warranty covers replacement of any damaged parts.

5. His signature was smudged and illegible.

II. In the following sentences, the adjectives have been left out. You supply the missing adjectives according to the directions in parentheses. Do not use the same adjective twice.

1. _____, Monty listened to a song _____.
   (verbal phrase)   (prepositional phrase)

2. _____ financial advice seemed _____.
   (possessive proper noun)   (adjective)

3. During _____ _____ years as a car dealer, Max was
          (possessive pronoun)   (number)

   admired for his integrity.

4. _____ _____ decision surprised everyone.
   (noun marker) (possessive common noun)

5. _____, Corliss had started _____.
   (prepositional phrase)   (verbal phrase)

✍ Chapter 5 Practice Test: Expanding the Sentence (cont.)

III. In the following sentences, bracket the adverbs. Each sentence has one adverb.

1. The hotel elevator suddenly lost power.

2. Laurel frequently skips her lunch.

3. We mustn't forget to make our reservations.

4. Ed politely refused her unreasonable request.

5. The music class has just started.

IV. Change the adjective in parentheses into the comparative or superlative degree.

1. Brenda is the _____ of all her sisters during the evening
    (energetic, superlative)
    hours.

2. My brother is a _____ cook than I am.
    (good, comparative)

3. Mr. Greer is the _____ supervisor anyone ever had.
    (bad, superlative)

4. Who is the _____ salesperson in the office?
    (competitive, superlative)

5. Before long, Casey had become _____ at repairing a fender
    (expert, comparative)
    than his instructor.

V. Change the adverb in parentheses into the comparative or superlative degree.

1. Of all the members on the panel, the district judge spoke the

    _____ about the issues.
    (intelligently, superlative)

2. Fred worked the _____ of anyone on the project.
    (hard, superlative)

3. Arthur studies _____ alone than he does with his friends.
    (well, comparative)

Chapter 5 Practice Test: Expanding the Sentence (cont.)

4. Farley has invested his inheritance _____ than his brother
   (prudently, comparative)

   has.

5. The more the other children laughed at my son's misbehavior, the

   _____ he acted.
   (badly, comparative)

VI. Correct the misplaced modifier in each sentence by placing it next
     to the word it should modify.

1. Some of the parents shouted at the members of the school board,
   angered by the new busing plan.

   _____

2. Leaking air slowly, I knew that the bicycle tire would soon be flat.

   _____

3. The defendant watched the jury return with its verdict without much
   hope.

   _____

VII. Correct the dangling modifier by rewriting the sentence and adding
      the word or words that it should modify.

1. Looking at the opposite shore, the telescope brought the waterfront
   buildings into focus.

   _____

2. Only two years old, my uncle took me to my first major-league baseball
   game.

   _____

3. The orange squirted juice all over Tricia's new silk blouse while eating
   lunch.

   _____

Chapter 5 Answer Key

Exercise 1A
1. New York City's, its   2. His, city's   3. Today's, America's   4. salt's, our
5. engineer's, people's   6. whose, their   7. politicians', his   8. engineer's
9. New York City's, engineer's   10. Their, their, New York's, their

Exercise 1B
Three people, one woman and two men, are making their way cautiously through the jungle. Far from home, they are aware of the many dangers around them. What are those strangers looking for? The solution to an environmental problem? New medicines to add to our fight against disease? Neither suggestion is correct. They are hoping to find some new ingredients to use in the manufacture of perfume. Each explorer carries a computerized device to capture any fragrances jungle flowers may contain. With these, the designers in their laboratories will create those exotic fragrances both men and women seem to find so appealing. And where are these perfumes manufactured? If your answer is Paris, that sophisticated European center of fashion, you are mistaken. Few people know that the small city of Teaneck, New Jersey, holds this distinction. Perhaps, it is just as well that this fact is not commonly known; it might rob that $50 cologne of its appeal.

Exercise 1C
1. reserved, fought   2. paper   3. home, closing   4. rising, scoring
5. sports, Eagle, winning   6. nylon, leather, wool   7. crowded
8. stadium, tow, no-parking

Exercise ID
Answers will vary. Your instructor will check your answers.

Exercise 1E
Your instructor will check your sentences.

Exercise 1F
1. scenic, rugged   2. purple, red, and blue-gray   3. Steep, red; clear, intense
4. mineralized, rainbow-colored   5. remarkable, breathtaking, and memorable

Exercise 2A
1. less interesting   2. least dangerous   3. less expensive   4. least creative
5. less sleepy

Exercise 2B
1. most important   2. easier   3. better   4. bigger, more powerful   5. most recent
6. greater   7. more efficient   8. simpler *or* more simple   9. largest   10. best, lowest

Exercise 2C
Your instructor will check your sentences.

Exercise 2D
1. most enthusiastic   2. more active   3. youngest   4. highest   5. more unusual
6. most important

Exercise 3A

Your instructor will check your answers.

Exercise 3B

A. The bookstore was having a sale of slightly soiled, reduced books, but the delighted customers didn't mind the smudge marks.
B. Books and magazines filled the approaching salesman's large, brown leather briefcase.
C. Carola's bicycle is lightweight, but it is strong enough to ride on paved city streets and unpaved country roads.
D. On Monday the new foreign minister arrived early in the morning in Helsinki.
E. On Sunday afternoons, Mrs. Konitz usually joined her friends on the same bench just inside the gate at the south end of the park.

Exercise 3C

Your instructor will check your sentences.

Exercise 3D

2. less efficiently   3. more systematically   4. most valuable   5. more easily
6. better   7. more often   8. most significantly; less frequently

Exercise 4A

Your instructor will check your answers.

Exercise 4B

Your instructor will check your answers.

Exercise 4C

1. Hoping to make a profit, Carolyn . . .   2. Trying to get to the airport on time, Josephine . . .   3. Snowed in for a week in the mountains, we . . .
4. Having spent the day shopping unsuccessfully for shoes, Tina . . .
5. Finding a wallet on his way to school, Jerry . . .

Exercise 5A

1. Nick saved almost $100 by making his own repairs on his car.
2. The candidate promised at the political rally that he would reduce unemployment.
3. Alfredo ordered a pizza with mushrooms and pepperoni to go.
4. The painters told us on Wednesday that they would begin painting the house.
     or The painters told us that they would begin painting the house on Wednesday.
5. Rex suddenly saw a woman in the front row jump up and run out . . . exit.
     or Rex . . . jump up suddenly . . . exit.

Exercise 5B

 1. Everyone noticed the new police unit in town, Barney and Fred, riding around in a black and white patrol car marked K-9 Patrol.
 2. Barney drove the car, and Fred, sitting in the back seat, was, unfortunately, a bit too eager for action.
 3. Stopping the car at a traffic light or an intersection, Barney would hear Fred's growls.
 4. Putting his head out of the window, Fred frequently snarled and barked at pedestrians who passed close to the car.

5. In their complaints to the police department, disgruntled citizens said that Fred was supposed to protect them, not attack them.

6. The police chief, hoping to restore peace and order, sent Barney and Fred back to training classes.

7. Trained to control his enthusiasm, Fred was no longer an embarrassment to Barney.

8. Now when Barney stops the patrol car, Fred sits calmly in the back seat, facing the front of the car.

9. Only his eyes move—from left to right and from right to left.

10. He doesn't even bark at the cats that he sees on the prowl.

Exercises 5C and 5D
Your instructor will check your answers.

Summary of Chapter 5
1. what kind, how many, which one   2. comparative, superlative
3. verbs, adjectives, adverbs   4. how, when, where, why   5. misplaced modifiers

 # Main Clauses

In Chapter 6 you will learn about the MAIN CLAUSE.

Definitions of Terms

A MAIN CLAUSE (also called an INDEPENDENT CLAUSE) is a group of related words with a subject and a verb that can stand alone as a sentence if the first word is capitalized and the clause ends with a mark of punctuation such as a period or a question mark.

A SIMPLE SENTENCE contains one main clause.

A COMPOUND SENTENCE contains two or more main clauses joined by a connective and appropriate punctuation.

COORDINATING CONNECTIVES (and, or, but, for, nor, so, yet) are words used with a comma to join words, phrases, and main clauses. They are also called COORDINATING CONJUNCTIONS.

A SEMICOLON (;) is a mark of punctuation that may be used to connect main clauses.

ADVERBIAL CONNECTIVES (however, nevertheless, then) are words used with a semicolon and a comma to join main clauses. They are also called ADVERBIAL CONJUNCTIONS or CONJUNCTIVE ADVERBS.

PARALLEL STRUCTURE is the placing of similar items in similar grammatical form.

A COMMA SPLICE is a grammatical error that occurs when main clauses are joined with only a comma and no connective.

A RUN-ON SENTENCE is a grammatical error made when main clauses are joined with no punctuation or connective between them.

Lesson 1 ✳ *Identifying Main Clauses*

When you studied prepositional phrases and verbal phrases, you learned that a phrase is a group of related words without a subject and a verb. A group of related words with a subject and a verb is called a CLAUSE. There are two kinds of clauses, MAIN and SUBORDINATE, but this chapter will deal only with the main clause (also called an independent clause).

To identify a main clause, look first for the verb and then for the subject. The main clause can stand alone as a sentence if the first word is capitalized and the clause ends with a mark of punctuation such as a period or a question mark. The main clause may also contain words or phrases in addition to the verb and the subject.

✳   **EXERCISE 1A**   ✳

In the following sentences, identify the underlined group of words as a phrase (P) or a main clause (MC). Write your answer on the line at the right.

1. Conservationists are trying to reintroduce wild wolves into the woods.   _____

2. They have already returned some wolves to the Rockies.   _____

3. Wild gray wolves are moving from Quebec into the United States.   _____

4. They are returning to parts of Maine.   _____

5. A wolf sometimes travels as far as 500 miles in search of a mate.   _____

✳	**EXERCISE 1B**	✳

In this exercise you supply prepositional phrases, verbal phrases, and a main clause of your choice. Follow the instructions in the parentheses.

Example: These residents hope _____ to their city by _____.
                                              (verbal phrases)

Answer: These residents hope <u>to attract tourists</u> to their city by <u>making some major improvements.</u>

1. Many of the commercial buildings need _____.
                                                            (verbal phrase)

2. They plan to add a fountain in the town square and plant flowering

   shrubs and trees _____.
                                          (prepositional phrase)

3. The planning committee also wants _____ and _____.
                                                          (verbal phrases)

4. An expanded trolley system will shuttle visitors _____.
                                                                    (prepositional phrase or phrases)

5. _____, the proposal will come before the city
      (verbal phrase or prepositional phrase)
   council for debate.

6. _____ if they are to attract tourists to the city as they hope.
        (main clause)

Lesson 2 ✳ *Connecting Main Clauses*

The Simple Sentence

In Chapters 2 through 5, you have been working primarily with the SIMPLE SENTENCE. The simple sentence contains *one* main clause. Which of the following two sentences is a simple sentence?

1. Mr. Hughes has dreamed of graduating.
2. For a long time since building his first race car nineteen years ago, Mr. Hughes has dreamed of graduating to the NASCAR Grand National Circuit.

Both sentences are simple sentences. Although the second sentence contains several phrases, it has only *one* main clause: one subject and one verb. Both sentences, as you can see, have the same subject and verb:

$$\overset{\text{S}}{(\text{Mr. Hughes})} \overset{\text{AV}}{\text{has}} \overset{\text{V}}{\underline{\text{dreamed}}}$$

The Compound Sentence

Which of the following two sentences contains *more than one* main clause and, therefore, is *not* a simple sentence?

1. Thousands of drivers like Mr. Hughes test themselves on America's hundreds of small dirt tracks, hoping to win $1,000, $100, or even just a trophy.

2. The race-car drivers hope to make it to the big-league tracks, and they love the thrill of driving at very high speeds.

The first sentence has only one subject and one verb:

$$\overset{\text{S}}{(\text{Thousands})} \overset{\text{V}}{\underline{\text{test}}}$$

It is a simple sentence with *one* main clause.

The second sentence, containing *two* main clauses, is a COMPOUND SENTENCE. It has two subjects and two verbs:

$$\overset{\text{S}}{(\text{drivers})} \overset{\text{V}}{\underline{\text{hope}}} \ldots, \text{and} \overset{\text{S}}{(\text{they})} \overset{\text{V}}{\underline{\text{love}}}$$

> A simple sentence contains *one* main clause.
>
> A compound sentence contains *two* or more main clauses.

EXERCISE 2A

Identify each of the following sentences as simple or compound. If the sentence has only one main clause, write S (Simple) on the line at the right. If the sentence has two or more main clauses, write C (Compound) on the line at the right.

Example: (David) <u>wanted</u> a new bicycle, but (he) <u>didn't</u>
<u>have</u> enough money for one.   C

1. Some people think of Iowa as flat, but some bicyclists know better now.   _____

2. Every year about seven thousand bicyclists ride slowly and painfully across the state of Iowa.   _____

3. The ride begins at the Missouri River along the state's western border, and it ends at its eastern edge along the Mississippi.   _____

4. Many riders complain about injured knees as well as sunburns.   _____

5. The bicyclists are surprised by the hills of Iowa, for the land had looked flat to them.   _____

Joining Main Clauses

There are three ways to join the main clauses of compound sentences. You may use (1) a coordinating connective, (2) a semicolon, or (3) an adverbial connective. COORDINATING CONNECTIVES (sometimes called coordinating conjunctions) are words used to join words, phrases, or clauses together.

Examples: typhoons **and** hurricanes

in the Pacific Ocean **and** along the Atlantic coastline

In the Atlantic Ocean, a tropical cyclone is called a hurricane, **but** in the western Pacific Ocean, it is known as a typhoon.

Remember These Seven Coordinating Connectives

and	for	or	yet
but	nor	so	

Put a comma before the coordinating connective when it joins two main clauses into a compound sentence.

Example: Formerly, hurricanes were named exclusively for women, but today women share this dubious honor with men.

EXERCISE 2B

Change these simple sentences into compound sentences by joining the main clauses with a comma and the coordinating connectives in the parentheses.

1. (for)   Formed in the sea, hundreds of miles from land, hurricanes become most destructive along the Atlantic seaboard. They increase their speed on their northward journey.

2. (yet)   No more than ten hurricanes of great strength develop in a year. Of these only about six become a threat to our eastern coastline.

3. (so)   Hurricanes require a high sea-surface temperature of at least 82 degrees to spawn. They usually occur in the late summer or early fall.

4. (but)   Many storms follow a fairly straight path. Others make sharp turns, loops, and reversals before pursuing a more predictable course.

5. (and)   By Columbus's fourth voyage to this part of the world, he was familiar with the native population's hurricane lore. Thus, he drew upon this knowledge to save his ships from a coming storm.

6. (for)   Many Seminole Indians in Florida still accurately predict storms by noting the height of saw grass, the flight pattern of birds, and the alligators' move to deep water. These Seminoles have more faith in their own observations than in those of the official weather forecasters.

G R O U P   A C T I V I T Y

Read the following paragraph and respond to the questions that follow it using complete sentences. Together with two or three classmates, check your sentences. Then, select the best sentences from your group and exchange your work with that of another group in your class to pick the best answers from the class.

1. In 1989 European scientists sent up a satellite to measure the position of 120,000 stars. 2. The satellite failed to reach its correct orbit after its launching, but it was reprogrammed from the ground. 3. It has been operating perfectly since 1993, and the scientists have been surprised by its findings. 4. In fact, they have had to change their thinking about the size of the universe. 5. The universe may be much bigger than the previous estimates.

Answer the following questions:

1. Which sentences are simple sentences?_____

2. Which sentences are compound sentences?_____

3. What coordinating connectives are used?_____

4. How many verbal and prepositional phrases can you find?

    _____

5. How did the European scientists plan to measure the size of the universe?

    _____

6. What was the original problem with the satellite, and how was it corrected?

    _____

7. How long has the satellite been operating successfully?

    _____

8. What have been the results of the satellite's findings?

    _____

A SEMICOLON (;) may be used to connect main clauses.

Example: Many tourists are afraid to travel around the city of New York by themselves; a volunteer Big Apple Greeter makes such travel a little less frightening.

EXERCISE 2C

On the lines at the right, identify each sentence as simple (S) or compound (C). Correct the compound sentences by joining the main clauses with semicolons.

1. The young couple on their honeymoon in New York expected to find muggers and thieves on the streets, instead they found a woman by the name of Lucy Littlefield. __________
2. Ms. Littlefield welcomed the couple to New York with free subway tokens and city maps. __________
3. She also gave them several hours of her time guiding them around New York she is a member of a group called the Big Apple Greeters. __________
4. The Big Apple Greeters help visitors discover the joys of this large metropolis no other American city offers such a service. __________
5. To the honeymooners, it seemed as though they had a mom along on their trip. __________

The ADVERBIAL CONNECTIVES (sometimes called adverbial conjunctions) listed below also may be used to join main clauses.

Addition:	also	further	in addition	moreover
Contrast:	however	instead	nevertheless	otherwise
Time:	meanwhile	then		
Result:	as a result	consequently	thus	therefore
In Reality:	in fact	indeed		

Use a semicolon before the connectives and insert a comma after them.

Example: In the 1926 hurricane, the Seminoles avoided harm by moving out of the path of the storm**; however,** loss of life and property was high among the rest of the state's population.

You may need to consult your dictionary to be sure you are using these words correctly.

EXERCISE 2D

Write five compound sentences using the words in the box below as adverbial connectives. Study the rule and the example above to help you punctuate the connectives.

however	meanwhile	furthermore	instead	nevertheless

1. _____

2. _____

3. _____

4. _____

5. _____

EXERCISE 2E

Choose an appropriate adverbial connective from the words in the following box to connect the main clauses in the following sentences. Use each connective only once. Punctuate the sentences correctly.

consequently	in addition	in fact	instead	then

1. Samuel Clemens's formal education ended at the age of twelve. This noted author represents the model of a self-made man to many people.

2. At seventeen, leaving the small town of Hannibal, Missouri, he worked for a time as a river pilot. He traveled to the West to try his hand at gold mining.

3. Clemens did not make a fortune as a miner. He found his vocation as a journalist and, more importantly, the identity of Mark Twain.

4. Leaving the West, he became a popular writer, a lecturer, and an Eastern gentleman. He won an audience among Europeans as well.

5. As an internationally known writer, Twain did not entirely leave his Midwest origins behind. Hannibal and the Mississippi River provided the material for his most widely read books.

Review: Three Ways to Connect Main Clauses

1. Use a coordinating connective and a comma (, but).
2. Use a semicolon (;).
3. Use an adverbial connective and punctuation marks (; however,).

Punctuation

In simple sentences some of the words listed above serve as adverbs and are enclosed by commas. These adverbs do not join main clauses in a sentence as the adverbial connectives do.

Examples: Eric sometimes guesses correctly the meanings of words.

He should, nevertheless, consult a dictionary.

EXERCISE 2F

Punctuate the sentences in the following paragraph correctly.

A dictionary, indeed, can tell you the meaning of a word. Besides that a dictionary shows you how to spell a word. A dictionary in addition shows you how to divide a word into syllables. It can tell you furthermore the origin and development of a word. A dictionary in fact is a good source of biographical information. Moreover if you want to know about the location of any college in the United States, just look in your dictionary. You should in fact keep a dictionary in several rooms of your house. Thus you will have a handy reference tool always at hand. You must however develop the habit of consulting it frequently.

EXERCISE 2G

Connect the two main clauses in each of the following groups of sentences by using the method suggested in parentheses. Correct the punctuation and change the capital letters to lower case.

1. Alan wanted to play in the Rose Bowl. His team's record was 0—10 for the season. (coordinating connective)

2. Alan's team will try harder next year. Perhaps they will have a better record. (coordinating connective)

3. Playing in the Rose Bowl is every football player's dream. Few achieve that goal. (adverbial connective)

4. On New Year's Day Alan will watch the game on TV. His teammates will be there too. (semicolon)

Lesson 3 ✳ *Parallel Structure*

Coordinating connectives join words, phrases, or clauses that are of equal importance. The word to notice in this definition is equal. Parallel structure, the placing of similar items in similar grammatical form, gives the writer another strategy for expanding a sentence in a balanced way.

Example a:

Ann Nguyen is now a student in a small community college.

Ann Nguyen, former gardener, secretary, and short-order cook, is now a student in a small community college.

Parallel nouns (gardener, secretary, and short-order cook) give the reader more information about Ms. Nguyen.

Example b:

She participates in student activities.

She enjoys working in the college library, serving on student council, and writing for the school newspaper.

Parallel verbal phrases (working . . . , serving . . . , writing . . .) add details about the nature of Ms. Nguyen's participation in student activities.

Faulty Parallelism

When you use parallel structure, always put the parts of the sentence that you are joining in the same grammatical form. For example, placing a noun before or, and, or but requires that another noun follow the connective (a swimmer, a golfer, or a jogger). Failure to do so results in FAULTY PARALLELISM (a swimmer, a golfer, or jogging).

Incorrect: Ann liked swimming, dancing, and to play basketball.

Correct: Ann liked swimming, dancing, and playing basketball.

or

Ann liked to swim, to dance, and to play basketball.

EXERCISE 3A

Complete the sentences by filling in the blanks according to the instructions in parentheses.

Example: As a student, I look forward to eating out, meeting with friends, or going to a movie on Saturday night.
(three verbal phrases)

1. After a week of _____, _____, and _____, I am
(Use three verbal phrases)
   ready to relax on Saturday evening.

2. Last Saturday, I went with a friend to a new restaurant called

   _____; we had heard that the food there w
   (name of restaurant)

   _____, _____, and _____.
   (Use three adjectives.)

3. The restaurant was crowded; we especially noticed _____,

   _____, and _____.
   (Use three nouns. You also may include modifiers.)

4. After giving us the menus, the waiter returned with _____

   _____, _____ _____, and _____ _____.
   (Use three nouns, each modified by a prepositional phrase.)

5. For dinner my friend _____ _____, and I
   (verb + object)

   _____ _____.
   (verb + object)

6. Ready for a change of pace, we discussed _____, _____,
   (Use verbal phrases)

   and _____.

   We finally decided to _____.   (your choice)

GROUP ACTIVITY

Read the following paragraph and underline all examples of parallel structure. Answer the questions at the end of the paragraph using complete sentences. Try to include parallel structures in your answers. Bring your work to class, get together with two classmates, and check your answers for parallel structure. As a group write five sentences describing a recent shopping experience that involved poor service.

How many times has this happened to you? You walk into a store knowing exactly what you want to buy. You have studied the store's advertisements, and you have decided exactly what color and size you need. You even have your credit card ready to facilitate the purchase. But you cannot find anyone to help you. You wander around the store for a while in search of a salesperson. Finally, disappointed, you give up, return your credit card to your wallet, and head for the exit. Or else you are lucky enough to find a salesperson only to find that the person has no idea what item you want to buy nor where to find it in the store. It is probably his first day at work. Retailers deny that they have reduced their sales staff, but they do admit that they have reduced their sales costs. That translates to fewer salespeople on the floor and fewer well-trained people to serve you. Of course there are exceptions, but customers these days cannot count on careful attention in the lingerie department, knowledgeable service in the fine china department, or cheerful service at the lunch counter.

1. How did the writer of this paragraph prepare for a shopping trip?

2. What was the experience of the writer of the paragraph when she went shopping?

3. How do retailers defend the cutbacks in service?

4. How does the retailers' policy affect the customer?

EXERCISE 3B

Write five sentences, using the group of parallel words or phrases given for each sentence.

Example: Jim was on a flight to New York.

(dozing, working a puzzle, reading a book, listening to music)

Your sentence: During the flight to New York City, Jim passed the time by dozing, listening to music, reading a book, and working a puzzle.

1. He was met by a volunteer from the Big Apple Greeters.
   (friendly, energetic, attractive)

   Your sentence: _____

   _____

   _____

2. His plans included riding on the subway.
   (climb to the top of the Statue of Liberty, eat at the Hard Rock Café, see Rockefeller Center)

   Your sentence: _____

   _____

   _____

3. Jim was amazed by the sights of New York.
   (crowds in Times Square, weirdos around SoHo, traffic on every avenue)

   Your sentence: _____

   _____

   _____

   _____

4. He walked around with his new camera.
   (equipped with a zoom lens, finished in black and chrome, fitted with a small automatic flash)

   Your sentence: _____

   _____

   _____

Punctuation

Use commas to separate three or more items in a series. The items may be single words, phrases, or clauses.

Example: Winslow Homer, an American artist of New England origins, was a master of three mediums: wood engraving, oil, and watercolor.

EXERCISE 3C

Insert commas where necessary.

Winslow Homer's love of the natural world is apparent in his choice of subjects: the sea woods and mountains. His regard for the people who lived close to this natural world also may be seen in his depiction of the simple pleasures of American life: young couples at a picnic an ice skating party on a pond and a berry-picking expedition in the woods. Children figure in many of his rural and seaside paintings. They sit on rail fences share watermelons raid sand-swallow nests and build a fire for a clambake on the beach. Making their living from the sea, their parents unload boats mend gear and haul in nets of fish. He is, perhaps, best known for his sea paintings which frequently portray a storm at sea—the power the danger the violence and the beauty of the spectacle.

(See Chapter 9 for a more detailed explanation of this use of the comma.)

Lesson 4 ❊ *Correcting Comma Splices and Run-on Sentences*

Main clauses may be joined with connecting words and appropriate punctuation marks. But sometimes students join main clauses without any connecting words or punctuation marks.

1. The (team) <u>won</u> the tournament, (they) <u>received</u> a trophy.

2. The (team) <u>won</u> the tournament (they) <u>received</u> a trophy.

The error in sentence 1 is called a COMMA SPLICE (CS). Sentence 2 is called a RUN-ON SENTENCE (RO).

Correct comma splices and run-on sentences in any *one* of the following ways:

1. Use a comma and a coordinating connective.

   The team won the tournament, <u>and</u> they received a trophy.

2. Use a semicolon.

   The team won the tournament; they received a trophy.

3. Use an adverbial connective with a semicolon and comma.

   The team won the tournament; therefore, they received a trophy.

4. Use a period and a capital letter.

   The team won the tournament. They received a trophy.

EXERCISE 4A

Circle the subjects and underline the verbs. Decide if there are two main clauses. On the line at the right, write CS for comma splice or RO for run-on sentence. Then punctuate the sentences correctly.

1. The long line of weather watchers, turning for assistance from birds, may have begun with Noah, he sent out a raven and a dove from the ark, hoping for an end to the long rain. _____

2. According to some, the distinctive calls of woodpeckers and robins signal rain the unusual silence of other birds supposedly makes the same prediction. _____

3. Hawks, perched high on power poles, are another indicator of coming rain they wait to catch small creatures heading from low creek beds to the safety of higher ground. _____

4. On some days, sea gulls remain on the shore, seeming to avoid the ocean, fishermen once took the gulls' behavior as a sign of a coming storm and also stayed in port. _____

5. Birds themselves are weather watchers during the time for migration needing good weather to navigate, they postpone their departure during uncertain weather conditions. _____

EXERCISE 4B

Correct these comma splices and run-on sentences by using coordinating connectives, semicolons, or adverbial connectives with correct punctuation.

1. More corporations are beginning to open day-care centers for their employees' children, the centers are open from nine to five.

2. With their children in these centers, working parents worry less about them these parents take fewer days off.

3. Two-paycheck families appreciate the cost benefits, the price of a full-time baby-sitter would use up an entire salary.

4. Single-parent families especially appreciate the convenience of quality child-care programs child-care programs help to recruit high–quality employees.

5. Government support helps the corporations build special facilities, preschool playgrounds and indoor classrooms are often too expensive for smaller corporations to construct.

EXERCISE 4C

Correct these comma splices and run-on sentences by using coordinating connectives, semicolons, or adverbial connectives with correct punctuation.

1. Americans of all ages are chocolate addicts each year the per capita consumption of this sweet is about nine pounds.

2. Of course American chocolate lovers still have to catch up with the Swiss, number-one consumers of chocolate in the world, however, Americans are well on their way.

3. Chocolate fanciers who want to be current on the latest news about their weakness subscribe to a bimonthly publication it is appropriately printed on brown, chocolate-scented paper.

4. Shops specializing in expensive chocolate are thriving, some "chocoholics" will pay up to $30.00 a pound to satisfy their craving.

5. No one should ever offer a carob bar or a dish of jelly beans to a chocolate-loving friend nothing but deep brown, rich chocolate appeals to a true "chocophile."

Summary of Chapter 6

Select words from the box below to complete the following sentences correctly.

1. A clause is a group of related words with a _____ and a verb.

2. A _____ clause can stand alone as a simple sentence.

3. Two or more main clauses may be joined to form a _____ sentence.

4. A _____ may be used to connect two main clauses.

5. _____ structure is the placing of similar items in similar grammatical form.

compound	semicolon	parallel
main	subject	

Sentence Combining

When you combine sentences in the exercises in this chapter, try to use compound sentences and parallel structure in addition to prepositional phrases and single-word modifiers.

Combine these six sentences into one compound sentence. Use a verbal phrase and a prepositional phrase in parallel structure for sentence 2.

1. College students are showing an interest in computers.
2. They are showing an interest in other math-related fields.
3. Personnel offices are flooded.
4. They are flooded with applications.
5. The applications are for work.
6. There are only a few jobs available.

Combined Sentence

Showing an interest in computers and other math-related fields, college students are flooding personnel offices with applications for work, but only a few jobs are available.

A. Combine these six sentences into one compound sentence. Sentences 4, 5, and 6 should be in parallel structure.

1. Shana was looking for a job.
2. She was looking for a job in the computer field.
3. The computer field is rapidly growing.
4. She sent her resume to software developers.
5. She sent it to manufacturing companies.
6. And she sent it to health maintenance organizations.

B. Combine these five sentences into one compound sentence. Use a coordinating connective that shows a contrast between the main clauses.

1. Astronomers have known about five planets.
2. These planets are in our solar system.
3. Astronomers have known about these planets for centuries.
4. An astronomer did not discover Pluto until 1930.
5. The astronomer was at Lowell Observatory in Arizona.

C. Combine these six sentences into one compound sentence. The first sentence should be used as a verbal phrase. Sentences 4, 5, and 6 can be put in parallel structure.

1. Keiko walks onto one of Tokyo's new commuter trains.
2. She notices a television screen above the door.
3. The screen is in English as well as Japanese.
4. The screen shows the current stop.
5. It shows the next stop.
6. It also gives some news and some commercials.

D. Combine these six sentences into one sentence. Use verbal phrases in parallel structure for sentences 4, 5, and 6. Use a verbal phrase for sentences 1 and 2.

1. The governor called a press conference.
2. He called it on Friday.
3. He announced his education plan.
4. He wants to provide more computers.
5. He wants to reduce class size.
6. He wants to expand the intern program for teachers.

WRITING ASSIGNMENT

Read the following paragraphs about an important invention. As you read, locate the topic sentence and underline it.

In general most people take the small conveniences of daily life for granted. They are not usually aware of the inventions that make these conveniences possible; no banner headline on the front page of a newspaper announces an invention's arrival and the possibilities ahead. In time these products reach the marketplace, and introduced through advertisements and by word of mouth, the general public buys them and soon finds them to be virtual necessities. Many of these inventions develop as a part of an evolutionary process and do not owe their existence to a single inventor. The 1.5 volt alkaline manganese battery (sizes AA and AAA), one of the most useful and widespread devices, fits this description. Batteries, of course, are not a new idea. In the 19th century, men such as Volta, Davy, Faraday, and Leclanche laid the groundwork for 20th century inventors. In the 1950s, Samuel Ruben made several important contributions that led to the small, lightweight alkaline battery. The photographic demand for a battery to power built-in flash units contributed to the development of a consumer market. By the 1970s, manufacturers were able to supply the public's demand for the products powered by these 1.5 volt batteries.

By now these batteries seem almost indispensable. They provide freedom from plugging in to an electrical outlet. Walkers and joggers put on their headsets and exercise while listening to their favorite programs. Kitchen clocks and travel alarms don't require winding; replacing batteries occasionally is a minor inconvenience. Travelers who like to take their appliances on the road pack battery-powered shavers and toothbrushes in their luggage. Calculators and small flashlights are compact enough and light enough to slip into a pocket or a purse. Even children haven't been left out of this minor revolution; many of their toys and games now rely on this source of power. These are but a few of a wide variety of products that small batteries have made possible during the past 50 years. These items serve a useful purpose, making daily life, in a minor way, easier and pleasanter.

In a paragraph or two, describe a 20th century invention that has affected or changed daily life. Explain the changes that have resulted. Do you believe the invention has increased or decreased the quality of life? The invention does not have to be as important as the automobile or the airplane; in fact, you may find it easier to develop your ideas about a less important one in a brief writing. Here are some ideas you might consider to get started.

1. Describe the invention and/or the products associated with it. Is it familiar to most people, or is it used by a specific group of people? For example, a pacemaker might require a more detailed description than the AA alkaline battery.

2. Approximately when did the invention appear? What are the changes, if any, that have resulted? Describe and explain them. Are they significant? Why or why not? Did this invention fill a specific need? Or did the product create a market that had not formerly existed?

3. If it is appropriate, consider the advantages and/or disadvantages of this invention and its applications.

Once you have made a list of answers to any of the questions above that apply to your topic, decide what your position will be. State your attitude toward the invention in a topic sentence as the writer of the second paragraph above did: "By now these batteries seem almost indispensable." Then support your topic sentence with three or four examples and/or specific details. Decide on the order in which you will present your material before you begin writing your rough draft.

ALTERNATE WRITING ASSIGNMENT

Look back at the Group Activity assignment in Lesson 3 on page 214 in this chapter. Read over the paragraph about the problems that shoppers sometimes experience with poor service. Think about any recent encounters you have had that resemble the experience described in that paragraph. Before you begin to write about your experiences, jot down the store you were in, the description of the item you wanted to buy, and what happened in your encounter with the salespeople. Include in your notes your analysis of the reasons why there has been a breakdown in service offered by most retailers. Is there something that can be done to improve the service? Can you do anything about it? Finally, describe in specific terms the improvements you recommend to solve the problem by giving some concrete suggestions.

Chapter 6 Practice Test: Main Clauses

Name _____

Date _____ Class Time _____

Instructor _____

I. On the lines at the right, write MC for main clause or P for phrase.

1. Solving the puzzle was not so easy   _____

2. Trained in the art of self-defense   _____

3. From the scientist's point of view   _____

4. Remember this   _____

5. The commuters waited impatiently for their train
    to arrive.   _____

II. Identify each sentence as simple or compound.

1. Martin wanted to eat at Bruno's restaurant, but
    Valerie was tired of eating pasta.   _____

2. Did they go to Bruno's or to her favorite Japanese
    restaurant?   _____

3. Outraged parents planned to attend the Board of
    Education meeting and to protest against the
    schedule for the school year.   _____

4. The Board of Education may vote to operate schools
    on a year-round schedule despite strong opposition
    to the plan.   _____

5. Federal surpluses of food have been reduced; as a
    result, severe cuts will be made in many school-lunch
    programs.   _____

Chapter 6 Practice Test: Main Clauses (cont.)

III. The following sentences contain words that can be used as adverbs or adverbial connectives.
   a. Begin by labeling the subjects and verbs.
   b. Next write (S) for simple sentence or (C) for compound sentence on the lines at the right.
   c. Punctuate the sentences correctly.

1. Lewis subscribes to several magazines however he rarely reads them.   _____

2. His wife meanwhile finds time to read them all.   _____

3. Molly must take the placement test in addition she must submit an essay.   _____

4. The deadline for admission applications had already passed consequently the university refused to accept Molly's essay.   _____

5. She must reapply therefore in a few months.   _____

IV. Follow the instructions and punctuate each sentence correctly.

1. Write a simple sentence, using "consequently" as an adverb.

   _____

   _____

   _____

2. Write a compound sentence, using "meanwhile" as an adverbial connective.

   _____

   _____

   _____

   _____

✍ Chapter 6 Practice Test: Main Clauses (cont.)

3. Write a sentence that includes the following words in a parallel structure: a. comprehensive, b. informative, and c. thought-provoking.

_____

_____

V. The following sentences contain errors.
   a. Identify the error by writing CS (comma splice) or RO (run-on) on the lines at the right.
   b. Then, correct the sentences using the method suggested in parentheses.

1. We could attend the anthropology lecture tonight, we could study in the library. (coordinating connective)   _____

2. Charlene prefers classical music Howard likes rock, jazz, and reggae. (semicolon)   _____

3. They buy many classical CDs, they also go to rock concerts. (adverbial connective)   _____

4. That book has been on the best-seller list for six weeks I haven't read it yet. (coordinating connective)   _____

5. The rent for the apartment was high, Calvin was looking for a roommate to share expenses. (adverbial connective)   _____

Chapter 6 Answer Key

Exercise 1A
1. phrase   2. main clause   3. phrase   4. main clause   5. phrase

Exercise 1B
Your instructor will check your answers.

Exercise 2A

	Subject	Auxiliary Verb	Verb	Type of Sentence
1.	people	—	think	
	bicyclists	—	know	compound
2.	bicyclists	—	ride	simple
3.	ride	—	begins	
	it	—	ends	compound
4.	riders	—	complain	simple
5.	bicyclists	are	surprised	
	land	had	looked	compound

Exercise 2B
1. seaboard, for they. . . .   2. year, yet of these, . . .   3. spawn, so they . . .
4. path, but others . . .   5. lore, and thus, he . . .   6. water, for these Seminoles . . .

Exercise 2C
1. Compound: streets; instead, . . .   2. Simple   3. Compound: New York; she is . . .
4. Compound: metropolis; no other . . .   5. Simple

Exercise 2D
Your instructor will check your answers.

Exercise 2E
1. twelve; consequently, this   2. pilot; then, he   3. miner; instead, he
4. gentleman; in addition,   5. behind; in fact, Hannibal

Exercise 2F
1. A dictionary, indeed,   2. Besides that, a   3. dictionary, in addition, shows
4. you, furthermore, the   5. dictionary, in fact, is   6. Moreover, if you
7. You should, in fact, keep   8. Thus, you will have   9. You must, however, develop

Exercise 2G
1. Alan always wanted to play in the Rose Bowl, but his team's . . .
2. Alan's team will try harder next year, so perhaps . . .
3. Playing in the Rose Bowl is every football player's dream; however, few . . .
4. On New Year's Day Alan will watch the game on TV; his teammates will be there too.

Exercise 3A
Your instructor will check your answers.

Exercise 3B
Your instructor will check your sentences.

Exercise 3C
1. subjects: the sea, woods, and mountains.   2. life: young couples at a picnic, an ice
skating party on a pond, and a berry-picking expedition in the woods.   3. They sit on
rail fences, share watermelons, raid sand-swallow nests, and build a fire for a clambake
on the beach.   4. their parents unload boats, mend gear, and haul in nets of fish.
5. the power, the danger, the violence, and the beauty of the spectacle.

Exercise 4A

Some suggestions for corrections:

1. The long (line) of weather watchers, turning for assistance from birds, may have begun with Noah, **for** (he) sent out a raven and a dove from the ark, hoping for an end to the long rain.   <u>CS</u>

2. According to some, the distinctive (calls) of woodpeckers and robins signal rain; **however**, the unusual (silence) of other birds supposedly makes the same prediction.   <u>RO</u>

3. (Hawks,) perched high on power poles, are another indicator of coming rain; (they) wait to catch small creatures heading from low creek beds to the safety of higher ground.   <u>RO</u>

4. On some days, (sea gulls) remain on the shore, seeming to avoid the ocean; **in fact,** (fishermen) once took the gulls' behavior as a sign of a coming storm and also stayed in port.   <u>CS</u>

5. (Birds) themselves are weather watchers during the time for migration; needing good weather to navigate, (they) postpone their departure during uncertain weather conditions.   <u>RO</u>

Your instructor will check your corrections.

Exercise 4B

Some suggestions for corrections:
1. More corporations are beginning to open day-care centers for their employees' children, **and** the centers are open from nine to five.
2. With their children in these centers, working parents worry less about them; **therefore,** these parents take fewer days off.
3. Two-paycheck families appreciate the cost benefits; **in fact,** the price of a full-time baby-sitter would use up an entire salary.
4. Single-parent families especially appreciate the convenience of quality child-care programs, **for** child-care programs help to recruit high-quality employees.
5. Government support helps the corporations build special facilities; preschool playgrounds and indoor classrooms are often too expensive for smaller corporations to construct.

Your instructor will check your corrections.

Exercise 4C

Some suggestions for corrections:
1. addicts; each year
2. world; however,
3. publication, and it
4. thriving; in fact,
5. friend, for

Your instructor will check your answers.

Summary of Chapter 6
1. subject   2. main   3. compound   4. semicolon   5. parallel

 Subordinate Clauses

In Chapter 7 you will learn about SUBORDINATE CLAUSES.

Definitions of Terms

A SUBORDINATE CLAUSE (dependent clause) is a group of related words with a subject and a verb that is introduced by a subordinator. It makes an incomplete statement, so it must be attached to a MAIN CLAUSE to be a complete sentence.

A SUBORDINATOR is a word that is used to introduce a SUBORDINATE CLAUSE. Examples: <u>because</u>, <u>that</u>, <u>although</u>.

A COMPLEX SENTENCE has a main clause and one or more SUBORDINATE CLAUSES.

A COMMA SPLICE is a grammatical error made when main clauses are joined with only a comma and no connective between them.

A RUN-ON SENTENCE is a grammatical error made when main clauses are joined with no punctuation or connective between them.

A SENTENCE FRAGMENT is a group of words that begins with a capital letter and ends with a period, but the group of words does not express a complete thought or contain a main clause.

Lesson 1 ✳ *Identifying Subordinate Clauses*

A main clause is a group of words with a subject and a verb. It is called a simple sentence when the first word is capitalized and it ends with a period, a question mark, or an exclamation point.

Example: (We) <u>enjoy</u> eating ice cream. (main clause or simple sentence)

A SUBORDINATE CLAUSE (or dependent clause) is a group of words with a subject and a verb that is introduced by a subordinator. It is not called a sentence; it makes an incomplete statement.

Example: (subordinator)
because (we) <u>enjoy</u> eating ice cream

EXERCISE 1A

If the group of words is a subordinate clause, put an X on the line at the right.

1. We listened to the debate.   _____

2. Before we listened to the debate   _____

3. As the chairman pounded his gavel on the table   _____

4. The chairman pounded his gavel on the table.   _____

Although the subordinate clauses you have just marked make incomplete statements, the subjects and verbs are not missing. What is missing is a main clause. To complete the statement in the subordinate clause, you must join it to a main clause. Then you will have a complete statement or, in other words, a sentence.

The following subordinate clause is incomplete by itself. It should not be followed by a period.

Example: While the band took a break

It leaves a question unanswered. You want to ask:

What happened while the band took a break?

It needs another clause, the main clause, to answer this question. You might complete the sentence as follows:

While the band took a break, I soaked my feet.

The difference between a main clause and a subordinate clause is often only the *addition* of one word at the beginning of the clause. If you add a subordinator to a main clause, you make a subordinate clause.

Example: the band took a break (main clause)
while the band took a break (subordinate clause)

EXERCISE 1B

Study the subordinators on the next page. Underline the subordinator in each of the following clauses. Then complete the sentence by adding a comma and a main clause.

1. After the band had been rehearsing for two hours _____

2. When the director told us to keep marching _____

3. Although everyone complained _____

4. Because we were going to march in the Rose Parade _____

5. Before we went home that day _____

> Remember, the subordinate clause can *never* stand alone as a sentence. When it stands alone and is punctuated like a sentence, it is called a SENTENCE FRAGMENT.

Subordinators	
Place:	where, wherever
Time:	after, before, when, whenever, as, since, until, as soon as, while, as long as
Cause or Purpose:	so that, in order that, as, because, since, that, why
Condition:	if, unless, when, whether
Contrast:	although, even though, while, whereas
Concession:	as if, though, although
Comparison:	than
Identification:	that, who, what, whom, whose, which

Some of the words listed above function as subordinators in some sentences and as prepositions in other sentences.

The <u>subordinator</u> is followed by a subject and a verb.

Example: before (Tyrone) <u>goes</u> to work = subordinate clause

The <u>preposition</u> is followed by a noun and its modifiers.

Example: before work = prepositional phrase
(Prep) (N)

Notice that like is not a subordinator. Therefore, it is incorrect to say, "Like I said, . . ." The word <u>like</u> is used <u>only</u> as a preposition.

EXERCISE 1C

Referring to the subordinators listed above, change the following main clauses to subordinate clauses by adding a subordinator to the beginning of the clause. Do not use the same subordinator twice.

1. _____ the rain became heavy

2. _____ the players left the field

3. _____ the groundskeepers covered the infield

4. _____ the crowd ran for protection under the covering

5. _____ some people had brought umbrellas

Copyright © 1999 by Addison-Wesley Educational Publishers Inc.

	EXERCISE 1D	

Write a complete sentence by adding a main clause to each subordinate clause you have written in Exercise 1C. The first sentence is completed for you as an example.

1. My friend and I knew they would delay the game <u>after the rain became heavy</u>.

2. _____

3. _____

4. _____

5. _____

> A COMPLEX SENTENCE has a main clause and one or more subordinate clauses.

	EXERCISE 1E	

In the paragraph on page 236, write the appropriate subordinators in the blanks, choosing each from the list of subordinators in the box following the paragraph.

Example: (Although) many older Japanese have had an aversion to buying used merchandise, many young people now make weekly trips to their favorite "recycle shops" (where) they buy secondhand bargains.

The Japanese, _____ were enthusiastic buyers of expensive imported goods _____ times were good, have turned to "recycle shops," _____ offer used luxury items at reduced prices. _____ a young Japanese woman may have less money to spend during these years of recession, she hasn't lost her desire for a Gucci hand-bag _____ original price may have been $800. Their grandmothers, concerned with cleanliness and the possibility _____ the spirit of the former owners remained with their possessions, avoided second-hand objects, but these young women seem undisturbed by such concerns. The stores _____ they shop formerly were pawn shops _____ were located in back alleys. _____ they hope to attract an entirely different clientele, owners of these stores have redecorated them and restocked them with used luxury brand names. _____ many young Japanese women live at home, they can spend up to 90% of their income on luxuries. Consequently, they shop _____ they can find a $200 dress or accessory at the discount price of $30.

Subordinators				
because	when	although	whose	that
where	which	wherever	who	since

Note: "That" is used more than once in the paragraph.

Sentences with More Than One Subordinate Clause

The following sentence has one subordinate clause. It begins with the word "When."

When the Aztecs designed their cities, each street was half roadway and half canal.

The next sentence has two subordinate clauses. They begin with the words, "which" and "that."

The Aztecs used canoes to transport their crops, which were grown along the banks of the lake in small terraced plots that climbed the mountain slopes.

EXERCISE 1F

In the following complex sentences, underline the subordinate clauses and put parentheses around the subordinators. Begin by circling the subjects and underlining the verbs.

1. When the Aztecs arrived in the Valley of Mexico in 1325, they became farmers who had to create their farmland artificially.

2. They settled on an island that was in the middle of Lake Texcoco, and after they dredged mud from the bottom of the lake, they piled it along the shores to create "floating" gardens.

3. Since water continuously seeped up through the mud, the soil was kept moist, allowing plants to grow and protecting the crops from drought before the rainy season began.

4. As the Aztec population expanded, the "floating" gardens were used for urban development, while food production was moved to the southern end of the valley.

5. The Aztecs' settlement developed into a city of thousands of small islands which were divided by canals that formed the basis of their transportation system.

● ● ● ● ● ● ● ● ● ● ● ● ● ● ● ● ●
GROUP ACTIVITY
● ● ● ● ● ● ● ● ● ● ● ● ● ● ● ● ●

Place parentheses around subordinators and underline all subordinate clauses. Then get together with two of your classmates and, as a group, write a paragraph about a fruit that you find in your local grocery store. Try to follow the pattern of sentences in this paragraph. Use complex sentences. Place parentheses around the subordinators and underline the subordinate clauses. Exchange your work with that of another group in your class to check your sentences.

<u>Do</u> you know (what) <u>a kiwi is?</u> It is a plum-sized fruit that has become popular all over America. When you look at the outside, you see a dull brown, fuzzy exterior. When you cut it open, the fruit is bright green and fragrant. While some people who have tasted it think that it tastes like a banana, others find the flavor hard to describe. It is considered nutritious because it contains more vitamin C than an orange does. Kiwi growers also say that the juice can be sprinkled on tough meat as a tenderizer. Although it was first cultivated in China about 300 years ago, it was not known in the western hemisphere until the twentieth century. Now, most kiwis come from New Zealand where they grow all year round. If you have not tasted a kiwi yet, you may be in for a surprise. They are, however, quite expensive, so they may strain your budget while they tingle your tastebuds.

Lesson 2 ✳ *Using Subordinate Clauses*

Subordination, the use of subordinate clauses, gives writers another option for adding ideas to their sentences and variety to their writing. In addition, the subordinator shows the precise relationship between the subordinate clause and the main clause of the sentence.

Examples: 1. (Mario) <u>was</u> in Rome. A (thief) <u>stole</u> his wallet.
                  (main clause)   (main clause)

         2. (When) (Mario) <u>was</u> in Rome, a (thief) <u>stole</u> his wallet.
              (subordinate clause)   (main clause)

By using subordination in sentence 2, the writer makes the time and place of the theft exact and emphasizes one idea — the theft of the wallet. Combining these two main clauses into one complex sentence also improves the style.

         3. The (people) on the bus <u>had</u> <u>offered</u> to help him, and

            (Mario) <u>thanked</u> them. (two main clauses)

         4. (Mario) <u>thanked</u> the people on the bus ((who)) <u>had</u>

            <u>offered</u> to help him. (one main clause and one subor-

            dinate clause)

Sentence 4 improves an awkward sentence by subordinating the first clause in sentence 3 to the second clause. The subordinate clause clarifies the situation by restricting the word <u>people</u> to those who helped Mario.

In previous chapters, we often combined ideas by coordinating them— that is, by linking them with the words <u>and</u>, <u>but</u>, or <u>or</u>. Coordination works well when the parts are of equal importance, but when the ideas are not of equal importance, it's better to subordinate one idea to another.

EXERCISE 2A

In the following paragraph, the writer uses many subordinate clauses. These complex sentences help the writer condense ideas and present them clearly. As you read the paragraph, choose the subordinator that best fits the sentence from the box at the end of the paragraph. Then answer the questions at the end of the paragraph.

_____ Blanche attended a lab technician's convention in Vancouver, British Columbia, she was delighted. _____ she came from a small town in Missouri, she had never seen such a big city with so many tall buildings. The city was surrounded on all sides by water, _____ caused the sunlight to sparkle as it bounced off the surface of the waves in the harbor. The glass and steel skyscrapers shimmered _____ they reflected the dazzling sunlight. She enjoyed a visit to the Anthropology Museum at the University of British Columbia, _____ enormous totem poles overwhelmed the large gallery rooms and stood in an outdoor courtyard, memorials of the ancient Indians _____ had carved them. She then ate a picnic lunch on the grass outside the museum with her friends _____ enjoyed the view of Vancouver framed by the mountains. _____ she drove to Queen Elizabeth Park, she went to the Bloedel Conservatory to see the many different plants and colorful little birds that flew around inside the domed garden. In the evening she went to Stanley Park _____ she wanted to eat at the Teahouse Restaurant, _____ she sat outdoors and admired the sunset over the harbor. The next day she took a sea-bus across the water _____ she could look back at the city's skyline from the shore of North Vancouver. _____ she left Vancouver, she

drove to Granville Island to shop at the outdoor markets for souvenirs,

_____ she brought back to her family in Missouri.

> **List of Subordinators**
>
> Notice that some subordinators are used twice in the paragraph.
>
> | | | | |
> |---|---|---|---|
> | after | so that | before | because |
> | when | who | where | which |

Write your answers in complete sentences. Practice using subordinate
clauses in the sentences you write.

Example: Where did Blanche come from? Blanche came from a
small town in Missouri where she had never seen a city as
big as Vancouver.

1. Why did Blanche go to Vancouver? _____

2. What did she especially like about the city? _____

3. Why did she go to Stanley Park? _____

4. What did she do when she took the sea-bus? _____

5. Why did she go shopping on Granville Island? _____

Using Subordination to Correct Comma Splices and Run-on Sentences

Subordination gives you another way to correct COMMA SPLICES and
RUN-ON SENTENCES by placing one idea in a subordinate clause and
the other in a main clause.

Example: (because) According to legend, Navajos are fine weavers,
the Spider Woman taught a young Navajo girl the art of
weaving. (comma splice)

Correction: According to legend, Navajos are fine weavers because the
Spider Woman taught a young Navajo girl the art of weav-
ing.

EXERCISE 2B

Correct the following comma splices and run-on sentences. Join the ideas in the main clauses into a complex sentence by changing one main clause to a subordinate clause. Use the subordinator in the parentheses. On the line at the right, identify the error as CS (comma splice) or RO (run-on). Punctuate the sentence correctly.

1. (although) Spiders are of great benefit to our environment many people, unfortunately, dislike and fear them. _____

   _____

2. (while) Several species are quite poisonous these represent a very small fraction of the 30,000 species of spiders in the world. _____

   _____

3. (since) Spiders are invaluable to us, they devour more insects than all other insectivores together. _____

   _____

4. (because) According to many scientists, spiders keep the balance of nature, without spiders, these insect pests would eliminate man by destroying his food supply. _____

   _____

5. (when) Spiders, in general, appear in a favorable light they appear in folk tales, myths, and legends throughout the world. _____

   _____

Punctuation

> **A. Use commas after introductory subordinate clauses.**

At the beginning of a sentence, use a comma <u>after</u> a subordinate clause.

Example: When schools add computer-aided instruction, teachers are able to send their students to the lab for individualized tutoring.

See Chapter 9 for a more detailed discussion of this use of the comma.

EXERCISE 2C

Insert commas where they are needed. Some sentences do not need commas added.

1. Although many people might laugh at the idea of computers belonging in every classroom others will accept the reality.

2. While some critics prefer an excellent teacher many would vote for an excellent multimedia computer system.

3. Generations of pupils who have learned from textbooks are protesting against the expense of electronic installations.

4. If you really want to improve the quality of education in America keep computers out of the classroom.

5. That slogan has been adopted by those parents whose children need more textbooks, teachers, and traditional values.

> **B. Use commas to set off nonessential clauses.**

Use commas to enclose a clause containing nonessential material. The information may add some details, but the reader could understand the main idea of the sentence without the clause.

Example: Stan, who arrived late, had to sit in the last row.

Omit the words enclosed by commas, and the sentence reads:

Stan had to sit in the last row.

The main idea of the sentence is unchanged.

> Do not use commas to enclose clauses that are essential to the meaning of the sentence.

Example: The people <u>who arrived early</u> had the best seats.

If the subordinate clause is omitted, the main idea of the sentence is lost: The people had the best seats. The subordinate clause is needed to identify the people—those who arrived early.

When "that" or "which" introduces a subordinate clause, follow the same rule for enclosing nonessential material.

Examples: The seat that Stan preferred was in the first row.

Stan's seat, which was most unsatisfactory, was in the last row.

Blanche wanted to see the little birds that flew around inside the domed garden.

Blanche wanted to shop at the outdoor markets for souvenirs, which she brought back to her family in Missouri.

EXERCISE 2D

Insert commas where necessary. Some sentences do not need commas added.

1. The sled dog race that is run between Whitehorse, Canada, and Fairbanks, Alaska, should not be confused with the more widely publicized Iditarod.

2. The Iditarod Trail Sled Dog Race which is a 1,150-mile race in Alaska from Anchorage to Nome began in 1973.

3. The race that is known as the Yukon Quest International Sled Dog Race made its first appearance in 1983 and covers about 1,060 miles.

4. The fifteen mushers who complete the race share a purse of $125,000.

5. Promoters of the Yukon Quest which shares many similarities with the Iditarod maintain that their race is more challenging and less commercial than its competitor.

6. Both races are endurance contests in the subarctic wilderness which test both human and canine ability to face the extreme hardships and isolation imposed by the courses.

 EXERCISE 2E

Combine the following sentences into complex sentences.
a. Form a subordinate clause by placing the subordinator in parentheses in the position indicated by the caret (∧).
b. Make any necessary changes in the punctuation and in the capitalization.

Example: ∧ Ty Cobb, nicknamed "The Georgia Peach," was one of the greatest of all baseball players. He was a bitter, angry man. (Use <u>although</u>.)

<u>Although</u> Ty Cobb, nicknamed "The Georgia Peach," was one of the greatest of all baseball players, he was a bitter, angry man.

1. His lifetime batting record ∧ was 4,191 hits in 24 seasons. It remained unbroken until the summer of 1985. (Use <u>which</u>, omit <u>It</u>.)

_____

_____

_____

2. Cobb ∧ was a multimillionaire. He gave financial help to young college students, endowed a hospital in his hometown, and gave anonymous aid to indigent ballplayers. (Use <u>who</u>, omit <u>He</u>.)

_____

_____

_____

3. He remained a public idol to many. ∧ Most of his fans were ignorant of his violent disposition. (Use <u>since</u>.)

_____

_____

_____

4. ∧ He was sick and old. Cobb welcomed a fight. (Use <u>although</u>.)

_____

_____

_____

5. Cobb threatened to use a loaded handgun. ∧ He carried it with him. (Use <u>that</u>, omit <u>it</u>.)

_____

_____

_____

6. His health actually suffered. ∧ He hated doctors and refused to follow their instructions. (Use <u>because</u>.)

_____

_____

_____

7. He increased his consumption of alcohol. ∧ Doctors warned him not to drink. (Use <u>after</u>.)

_____

_____

_____

8. The baseball star mistreated his fellow players, his friends, and his family. ∧ He alienated everyone close to him. (Use <u>until</u>.)

_____

_____

9. During his last years, ∧ he faced pain and death. He was virtually alone. (Use <u>as</u>.)

_____

_____

_____

Lesson 3 ✳ *Sentence Fragments*

A sentence FRAGMENT is a group of words that begins with a capital letter and ends with appropriate punctuation such as a period, but the group of words does not express a complete thought or contain a complete main clause.

Some professional writers use fragments in magazines and books. We hear sentence fragments used in conversation, as in the following example:

> "Did you leave school early yesterday?"
> "Yes, after my music class."

Although the last bit of dialogue begins with a capital letter and ends with a period, it is not a complete sentence. It is a sentence fragment. When used in formal writing, fragments can confuse the reader.

Four Types of Sentence Fragments

It will be easier for you to correct fragments in your own writing if you learn to recognize these four types of fragments:

1. punctuating subordinate clauses as sentences
2. missing subjects or missing verbs

3. using verbals instead of verbs or using participles without auxiliary verbs
4. using lists and examples not connected to a subject and verb

1. Punctuating Subordinate Clauses as Sentences

Identifying the Error: When Jean came home.

This is the most common form of fragment. This subordinate clause is punctuated like a sentence.

Correcting the Error: When Jean came home, she turned on the stereo.

1. You can, of course, simply remove the subordinator, and you will have a complete sentence:
2. More than likely, however, the fragment will appear among the sentences of a paragraph you are writing. Therefore, you should connect the fragment to a sentence that is before or after the subordinate clause and change the punctuation.

(Error) We had just finished dinner. When Jean came home. (fragment)
(Correct) We had just finished dinner when Jean came home.

(Error) When Jean came home. (fragment) She turned on the stereo.
(Correct) When Jean came home, she turned on the stereo.

Note

When a subordinate clause is at the beginning of a sentence, place a comma after it.

EXERCISE 3A

If the following sentence fragments were complete sentences, they could be connected to form a paragraph about Tina Turner. You can turn these fragments into sentences by adding a main clause to each one. Place a comma after the subordinate clause if necessary. Correct the punctuation and change the capital letters to lower case as needed.

1. _____ Because Tina Turner has made a great comeback.

2. While she is loved by rock 'n' roll fans._____

3. If she can also sing rhythm and blues. _____

4. Although Tina worked to escape her past. _____

5. _____ After they were married.

6. _____ Since she has great talent.

7. _____ Who is very popular.

8. Before she became a star. _____

9. _____ As much as she could.

10. _____ That Tina Turner's story was true.

2. Missing Subjects or Missing Verbs

Identifying the Error: Swims for an hour in the pool.

Swims for an hour in the pool. <u>Swims</u> is a verb, but both nouns (<u>hour</u> and <u>pool</u>) are objects of the prepositions <u>for</u> and <u>in</u>. So this is a fragment because there is no subject.

Correcting the Error: Add a subject to make a sentence.

> s
> (Correct) Carla <u>swims</u> for an hour in the pool.

EXERCISE 3B

Change the following fragments into sentences. Write your sentences on the lines. Do not leave out any words in the phrases and change the punctuation as necessary.

1. And transferred to the university this fall. _____

   _____

2. A dorm on campus or a room in town. _____

   _____

3. Enrolling in classes._____ _____

    _____

4. To make an appointment with a counselor. _____

    _____

5. Michelle has almost completed all the courses required for her major.

    Except for English 101, Psychology 2, and History 17._____

    _____

6. The instructor reviewed the material to be covered in the chapter test.

    Especially calling our attention to the last three pages._____

    _____

3. Using Verbals Instead of Verbs

Identifying the Error: Riding our bicycles on the bike path.

In this case, the writer mistakes the verbal for a main verb and also leaves out the subject.

Correcting the Error

1. Supply an auxiliary verb and, if necessary, a subject.

    (We) were riding our bicycles.

2. Attach the fragment to the sentence preceding it or to the one following it.

    (verbal phrase)
    (We) enjoyed ourselves, riding our bicycles on the bike path.

    (verbal phrase)
    Riding our bicycles on the bike path, (we) stopped to talk to several friends.

3. Supply a verb and a completer or an object. The verbal phrase <u>riding our bicycles</u> serves as the subject of the sentence.

(Riding our bicycles) on the bike path <u>is</u> good exercise.

4. Using Lists and Examples Not Connected to a Subject and Verb

Identifying the Error: 1. The pattern, pinking shears, straight pins, and the material.

                      2. For example, my College Algebra final last semester.

A fragment is frequently a list or an example explaining some thought that the writer has just expressed. As in the error identified in 2, this kind of fragment often begins with one of the following words:

also	especially	except
first	for example	including
such as		

Correcting the Error

You could turn this fragment into a sentence by supplying its own subject and verb. (My College Algebra final last semester was too long.) In most cases, however, you should connect the fragment to the sentence preceding it.

1. First assemble the items you will need to cut out your skirt<u>:</u> the pattern, pinking shears, straight pins, and the material.
2. Some examinations are not fair<u>,</u> for example, my College Algebra final last semester.

EXERCISE 3C

Mark F for sentence fragment or S for sentence on the lines at the right. Then correct the fragments on the lines on page 252.

1. Kim's sister wants to move to Chicago. _____

2. Concerned with the view from her apartment. _____

3. She needs to be near the central business district.   _____

4. Whenever she does the shopping.   _____

5. And will come home every weekend.   _____

6. First by cutting down on unnecessary purchases.   _____

7. She is studying the newspaper advertisements.   _____

8. The location that she wanted.   _____

9. Wondering what she would do until moving day.   _____

10. Because she would not be able to find a parking space.   _____

_____

_____

_____

_____

_____

_____

_____

_____

GROUP ACTIVITY

Underline and correct the seven sentence fragments in the following paragraph. Answer the questions at the end of the paragraph in complete sentences.

Then get together with two or three classmates and check each other's work. As a group, write a paragraph about the changing views of how pirates operated. What do you think is the truth about their methods? Exchange your paragraph with that of another group to proofread for complete sentences. If you find any sentence fragments, underline and correct them. Discuss your work in class.

Pirates are often pictured as inhuman. Quick to kill someone in pursuit of treasure. In movies and novels, they often sank helpless ships. Forcing prisoners to walk the plank. But scholars in recent years have said that most of the mythology is wrong or misleading. They were less cruel and more democratic than previously thought. They carefully divided up the distribution among crew members. Including rare jewelry from the African gold trade. From recent finds on pirate ships located on the ocean bottom, scientists have learned that real pirates had no time for such ceremonies. As sending victims walking down the plank. They imprisoned some sailors and even treated them well. Also, pirates were not exclusively European. Perhaps as many as 30% of them were black slaves who had escaped from captivity. Or been freed by pirate gangs to join in the attacks on organized trade. These crews had established democratic principles aboard ship. Even the most feared captain, the famous Captain Blackbeard, shared equally with the members of the crew. As he could not receive a larger portion of the booty. Blackbeard's ship has now been located off the coast of Beaufort, N. C. Where it has lain since 1718. When the divers search that ship, they hope to find further proof of the lack of accuracy in the typical portrayal of pirates.

1. How are pirates usually pictured in movies and novels?

2. How did they actually treat prisoners?

3. How do movies depict the racial characteristics of the crew of a pirate ship?

4. What was the actual makeup of the crew?

5. Why was the captain of the pirate ship not entitled to the largest portion of the booty?

Summary of Chapter 7

Choose words from the box on the next page to complete these sentences.

1. A subordinate clause is a group of words with a subject and a verb that cannot stand alone as a _____ because it makes an incomplete statement.

2. A sentence that has a main clause and at least one subordinate clause is called a _____ sentence.

3. You can correct comma splices and run-on sentences by making one of the clauses a _____ clause.

4. You learned four ways to correct sentence fragments in your writing.

    First, you can remove the _____ to change a subordinate clause to a main clause.

5. A second way to correct sentence fragments is to _____ the fragment to a sentence that is before or after the subordinate clause and change the punctuation.

6. A third way to correct a sentence fragment is to supply the missing
_____ or verb.

7. A fourth way to correct a sentence fragment is to supply an
_____ verb and, if necessary, a subject.

complex	subordinator	subject
sentence	attach	auxiliary
subordinate		

Sentence Combining

Using subordinate clauses will enable you to add variety to your sentences. You can make your writing more interesting and effective by learning how to subordinate one idea to another, as demonstrated here.

Example: Use a verbal phrase, a prepositional phrase, and a subordinate clause.

1. I have attached two pictures to my paper.
2. The pictures bring back memories.
3. Some of the memories are good.
4. Some of the memories are bad.
5. The memories are of Fort Benning, Georgia.
6. At Fort Benning, Georgia, I trained to be a parachutist.

Combined Sentence

The attached two pictures bring back some good and some bad memories of Fort Benning, Georgia, where I trained to be a parachutist.

We have combined the six sentences into one by subordinating one of the main clauses and reducing the number of verbs. This technique allows the writer to express the six ideas more concisely.

In the following exercise, combine the short sentences into longer ones by following the suggestions given.

a goal? If you know someone who has successfully completed a marathon, try to arrange an interview.

Step 1: Begin by listing, freewriting, or making a cluster to generate your ideas. After you have finished, talk about the subject with several of your classmates.

Step 2: State your position in a topic sentence. You may want to revise the sentence later, but knowing the direction you want to take will help you plan your paragraph.

Step 3: When you talked to your classmates, you may have found that you didn't have enough support to defend your point of view. Go back over your notes. Write down two or three main reasons and develop examples and details to support each one.

Step 4: Making a simple outline before you write your rough draft will help you decide on the order in which to present each supporting point. (See the discussion of outlining on pages 9–10 of Chapter 1.)

Step 5: When you have completed the rough draft, check it carefully and correct any fragments, comma splices, and run-on sentences you find before writing the final copy.

ALTERNATE WRITING ASSIGNMENT

President Clinton said in his 1997 State of the Union address that all schools should have access to the Internet by the twenty-first century. His belief that every schoolchild should be familiar with the information that is available through the use of computers and modems is shared by many people. However, many others believe it would be better to spend the money on basic textbooks and excellent teachers. What is your view of this subject? Do you agree that the future of our society depends on wiring every classroom to the World Wide Web? Consult other people in your class as to their views. What is the response of the majority of the members of your class? Include your survey results in your paragraph as well as your own opinions on the influence of computers in the classroom. Follow the steps outlined above in your prewriting activities.

✎ Chapter 7 Practice Test: Subordinate Clauses

Name _____

Date _____ Class Time _____

Instructor _____

I. Put parentheses around the subordinator. Then underline the sub-ordinate clause.

1. The driver who changed lanes abruptly in front of Mr. Barr caused the accident.

2. Although Mr. Barr tried to stop in time, his brakes were not working properly.

3. Fortunately he was wearing a seat belt since he always remembered to "buckle up."

4. When he saw the damage to his car, he knew he would have to call a tow truck.

5. Both drivers, who had only minor bruises, were not seriously hurt.

II. A. Change the following main clauses into subordinate clauses by adding a subordinator to the beginning of the clause. Do not use the same subordinator twice.

1. _____ we went to the community center to hear the candidates

2. _____ Mr. Wayne was the moderator of the meeting

3. _____ my friend asked a question

4. _____ the candidate refused to recognize him

5. _____ some reporters for the local newspaper covered the meeting

✍ Chapter 7 Practice Test: Subordinate Clauses (cont.)

II. B. Make a complete sentence by adding a main clause to each subordinate clause you have made in Part II. A. Your sentence must include both clauses.

1. _____

2. _____

3. _____

4. _____

5. _____

III. Write three sentences that have one main clause and at least one subordinate clause. Place parentheses around the subordinator.

1. _____

2. _____

3. _____

IV. Identify the following comma splices (CS) and run-on sentences (RO) on the lines at the right. Then, join the ideas in the main clauses into a complex sentence by changing one main clause to a subordinate clause. Use the subordinator in the parentheses.

1. (if)   Morgan's TV reception is poor he may have to install a satellite TV antenna.   _____

_____

2. (that, omit "it")   The Picasso painting is valued at $10 million, it was bought by a Japanese investor.   _____

_____

3. (so that)   Megan bought a new car, she can have reliable transportation.   _____

_____

Chapter 7 Practice Test: Subordinate Clauses (cont.)

4. (as long as)   We may as well buy a new dishwasher we are
                   remodeling the kitchen.   _____

   _____

5. (who, omit "they")   Many listeners enjoy listening to National
                         Public Radio they show their appreciation
                         by giving financial support to their local
                         stations.   _____

   _____

V. A. There are five incomplete sentences in the following paragraph.
        Indicate on the lines on page 262 whether a sentence is com-
        plete (S) or a fragment (F).

1. Muzak is difficult to escape unless city dwellers stay out of many public places.   2. Such as shopping malls, supermarkets, offices, restaurants, and elevators.   3. Even if they do, Muzak invades their homes via the telephone.   4. When they are put "on hold" while waiting for the completion of a call.   5. Although most people hear canned music almost daily.   6. Few of them actually listen to it.   7. The sound of Muzak has changed little in 60 years.   8. The musical selections have always been carefully chosen to blend into the background of any activity.   9. By playing well-known tunes that would appeal to a mass audience.   10. This music is intended to make people feel good.   11. In the belief that they will then be productive workers and willing buyers.   12. Many people, however, regard Muzak as another form of noise pollution.

Chapter 7 Practice Test: Subordinate Clauses (cont.)

1. _____

2. _____

3. _____

4. _____

5. _____

6. _____

7. _____

8. _____

9. _____

10. _____

11. _____

12. _____

V. B. On the lines below, rewrite the incomplete sentences that you have just identified as sentence fragments. Rewrite each one by combining it with another sentence next to it.

1. _____

2. _____

3. _____

4. _____

5. _____

Chapter 7 Answer Key

Exercise 1A

1. _____

2. _____X_____

3. _____X_____

4. _____

Exercise 1B
1. after
2. when
3. although
4. because
5. before
Your instructor will check your sentences.

Exercises 1C and 1D
Your instructor will check your answers.

Exercise 1E

The Japanese, <u>who</u> were enthusiastic buyers of expensive imported goods <u>when</u> times were good, have turned to "recycle shops," <u>which</u> offer used luxury items at reduced prices. <u>Although</u> a young Japanese woman may have less money to spend during these years of recession, she hasn't lost her desire for a Gucci handbag <u>whose</u> original price may have been $800. Their grandmothers, concerned with cleanliness and the possibility <u>that</u> the spirit of the former owners remained with their possessions, avoided second-hand objects, but these young women seem undisturbed by such concerns. The stores <u>where</u> they shop formerly were pawn shops <u>that</u> were located in back alleys. <u>Because</u> they hope to attract an entirely different clientele, owners of these stores have redecorated them and restocked them with used luxury brand names. <u>Since</u> many young Japanese women live at home, they can spend up to 90% of their income on luxuries. Consequently, they shop <u>wherever</u> they can find a $200 dress or accessory at the discount price of $30.

Exercise 1F

1. (When) the ⟨Aztecs⟩ <u>arrived</u> in the Valley of Mexico in 1325, ⟨they⟩ <u>became</u> farmers ⟨who⟩ <u>had to</u> create their farmland artificially.

2. ⟨They⟩ <u>settled</u> on an island ⟨that⟩ <u>was</u> in the middle of Lake Texcoco, and (after) ⟨they⟩ <u>dredged</u> mud from the bottom of the lake, ⟨they⟩ <u>piled</u> it along the shores to create "floating" gardens.

3. (Since) ⟨water⟩ continuously <u>seeped</u> up through the mud, the ⟨soil⟩ <u>was kept</u> moist, allowing plants to grow and protecting the crops from drought (before) the rainy ⟨season⟩ <u>began</u>.

4. (As) the Aztec ⟨population⟩ <u>expanded</u>, the "floating" ⟨gardens⟩ <u>were used</u> for urban development, (while) food ⟨production⟩ <u>was moved</u> to the southern end of the valley.

5. The Aztecs' ⟨settlement⟩ <u>developed</u> into a city of thousands of small islands ⟨which⟩ <u>were divided</u> by canals ⟨that⟩ <u>formed</u> the basis of their transportation system.

Exercise 2A

1. (When) Blanche attended a lab technician's convention in Vancouver, British Columbia
2. (Because) she came from a small town in Missouri
3. (which) caused the sunlight to sparkle
4. (when) they reflected the dazzling sunlight
5. (where) enormous totem poles overwhelmed the large . . .
6. (who) had carved them
7. (who) enjoyed the view of Vancouver framed by the mountains
8. (After) she drove to Queen Elizabeth Park
9. (because) she wanted to eat at the Teahouse Restaurant
10. (where) she sat outdoors . . .
11. (so that) she could look back at the city's skyline . . .
12. (Before) she left Vancouver
13. (which) she brought back to her family in Missouri.

Your instructor will check your sentences.

Exercise 2B

1. Although spiders are of great benefit to our environment, many people, unfortunately, dislike and fear them. _RO_

2. While several species are quite poisonous, these represent.,. _RO_

3. Spiders are invaluable to us since they devour… _CS_

4. According to many scientists, spiders keep the balance of nature because, without spiders, these… _CS_

5. Spiders, in general, appear in a favorable light when they appear… _RO_

Other sentences may also be correct. Check with your instructor.

Exercise 2C

1. Although many people might laugh at the idea of computers belonging in every classroom, others will accept the reality.
2. While some critics prefer an excellent teacher, many would vote for an excellent multimedia computer system.
3. Generations of pupils who have learned from textbooks are protesting against the expense of electronic installations. (no comma needed)
4. If you really want to improve the quality of education in America, keep computers out of the classroom.
5. That slogan has been adopted by those parents whose children need more textbooks, teachers, and traditional values. (no comma needed)

Exercise 2D

1. The sled dog race that is run between Whitehorse, Canada, and Fairbanks, Alaska, should not be confused with the more widely publicized Iditarod. (no comma needed)
2. The Iditarod Trail Sled Dog Race, which is a 1,150-mile race in Alaska from Anchorage to Nome, began in 1973.
3. The race that is known as the Yukon Quest International Sled Dog Race made its first appearance in 1983 and covers about 1,060 miles. (no comma needed)
4. The fifteen mushers who complete the race share a purse of $125,000. (no comma needed)
5. Promoters of the Yukon Quest, which shares many similarities with the Iditarod, maintain that their race is more challenging and less commercial than its competitor.
6. Both races are endurance contests in the subarctic wilderness, which test both human and canine ability to face the extreme hardships and isolation imposed by the courses.

The subject and the verb must agree in number.

A singular subject (one person or thing) takes a singular verb.

The bird sings.
The wheel turns.
The student reads.

A plural subject (more than one person or thing) takes a plural verb.

The birds sing.
The wheels turn.
The students read.

In the examples above, you can see that the singular verb in the present tense ends in **-s** when the subject is he, she, or it or a singular noun that can be replaced by he, she, or it. A subject and a verb agree if you match the form of the verb in number and person with the subject.

Examples:

1. Bill walks to work. He walks to work.
2. Sarah runs on the track. She runs on the track.
3. This pencil needs to be sharpened. It needs to be sharpened.
4. The tennis players run after the balls. They run after the balls.

Which sentences have singular subjects and verbs? _____

Which sentence has a plural subject and verb? _____

Are the verbs ending in **-s** singular or plural? _____

Check your answers with your instructor.

❋   *EXERCISE 1A*   ❋

Write five sentences using the verbs in the parentheses. Use a singular common noun as the subject and the present tense of the verb.

                                        s
Example: (fly)   The airplane <u>flies</u> nonstop to Chicago.

1. (make) ______________________________

2. (turn) ______________________________

3. (use) ______________________________

4. (lend) ______________________________

5. (play) ______________________________

EXERCISE 1B

Now rewrite the sentences that you just completed. Change each subject from singular to plural. Make sure the verb agrees with the subject.

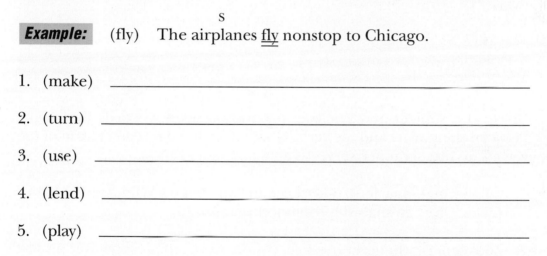

Example: (fly) The airplanes <u>fly</u> (S) nonstop to Chicago.

1. (make) ______________________________

2. (turn) ______________________________

3. (use) ______________________________

4. (lend) ______________________________

5. (play) ______________________________

Lesson 2 *Subjects and Verbs— Four Difficult Patterns*

A. Words That Come Between the Subject and the Verb

Words that come between the subject and the verb do *not* change subject-verb agreement.

Examples:

1. Today the purpose of many zoos in large cities is not the same as in the past.

The subject "purpose" is singular, so the verb "is" is singular.

The words "of many zoos in large cities" that come between the subject and the verb do not affect the agreement.

2. Until this century, the people visiting the zoo were the first consideration, not the animals.

The subject _____ is plural, so the verb _____ is plural. The words "visiting the zoo," that come between the subject and the verb do not affect the agreement. (The subject is "people" and the verb is "were.")

EXERCISE 2A

Circle the subject and enclose in parentheses any words that come between the subject and the verb. Then underline the correct form of the verb. The first sentence serves as an example to follow.

1. Open-range (quarters), (like those in San Diego's Wild Animal Park), (gives, _give_) animals the room to live naturally.

2. Zookeepers, whenever possible, (works, work) to preserve and protect exotic species.

3. Endangered species, such as the condor, (is, are) bred in the zoo and later set free.

4. These fully grown animals, released into their natural habitats, (seems, seem) to have a good chance of survival.

5. Obviously not all zoos in the country (plays, play) this important role.

6. Making these changes in an old zoo (takes, take) money, space, and time.

EXERCISE 2B

Circle the word that is the subject. Underline the verb that best completes each sentence.

1. The effects of the long cold wave (lingers, linger) on.

2. The fruit trees, which were just beginning to flower, (has, have) withered.

3. The flowers that had appeared (is, are) turning brown.

4. The farmers, who could lose millions of dollars, (is, are) using several methods to protect the crops.

5. The hope of everyone concerned (is, are) for the early arrival of spring weather.

B. Reversed Word Order

A verb agrees with the subject even when the subject comes *after* the verb.

Here <u>are</u> some (reasons) for testing the air in your home.

The plural subject <u>reasons</u> comes after the verb.

In general when sentences begin with <u>there</u>, <u>here</u>, and <u>where</u>, the subject follows the verb. Rearrange the sentence to find the subject:

> Here <u>are</u> some reasons for testing the air in your home.
> (becomes)
> Some reasons for testing the air in your home <u>are</u> here.

EXERCISE 2C

In the following sentences, circle the subject. Underline the correct form of the verb in each sentence. Some of the sentences have the subject before the verb, and some have the subject after the verb.

1. There (is, are) disagreement on the seriousness of indoor air pollution.

2. Some researchers say that there (is, are) much to be learned about controlling indoor air quality.

3. Experts agree that there (is, are) greater chances of problems developing in older homes.

4. The first clue that a home may have a problem (is, are) often increased humidity.

5. Increased humidity in an insulated home (signals, signal) that the rate of air change is low and other air pollutants may be building up.

6. There (is, are) devices that can eliminate the problem.

7. One widely used device in new homes (is, are) the air-to-air heat exchanger.

8. A problem that can occur with heat exchangers (is, are) condensation.

9. Here (is, are) the best way to lower indoor pollution.

10. Electric appliances (is, are) best to prevent pollution from developing inside a home.

EXERCISE 2D

Write six sentences, two beginning with Here is/are, two with There is/are, and two with Where is/are. When you have completed this exercise, get together with two or three classmates to check each other's work.

1. (Here is) _____

2. (Here are) _____

3. (There is) _____

4. (There are) _____

5. (Where is) _____

6. (Where are) _____

C. Compound Subjects Joined by <u>and</u>

Compound subjects joined by <u>and</u> usually take a <u>plural</u> verb.

Example: Both the clock radio and the toaster need to be returned today before the warranties expire.

The subjects in the main clause are "clock radio and toaster." They are joined by "and," so the verb "need" is plural.

EXERCISE 2E

Write six complete sentences, using the words given at the left as the subjects of your sentences. Use the present tense of the verb. In this exercise write about Marla and Jack's efforts in a large department store to return the toaster and the clock radio.

Example: (housewares department and electronics department)
The housewares department and the electronics department are located at opposite ends of the third floor.

1. Marla and Jack _____

2. The toaster and the clock radio _____

3. Standing in line and waiting _____

4. Jack and the department manager _____

5. The receipts and the warranties _____

6. The time and the effort _____

D. Compound Subjects Joined by <u>or</u>, <u>Neither . . . nor</u>, or <u>Either . . . or</u>

When subjects are joined by these connectives, the verb agrees with the subject *closer* to the verb.

Example: Neither the tenants nor the landlord <u>expects</u> the door bell to be fixed today.

The nearer subject, "landlord," is singular, so the verb "expects" is used to agree with it.

EXERCISE 2F

Insert the form of the verb <u>have</u> that best completes each sentence. Choose either <u>has</u> or <u>have</u>.

1. The telephone and the front door bell in an apartment _____ not been working.

2. The tenants and the landlord _____ tried unsuccessfully to solve the problem.

3. The electrician and the telephone repairman _____ been trying to make an appointment to fix the bell and the telephone.

4. Neither the landlord nor the tenants _____ been able to hear the knock on the door.

5. Because the workers cannot get into the apartment, neither the telephone nor the front door bell _____ been fixed.

6. Either the tenants or the landlord _____ to stay outside to wait for the repairmen.

EXERCISE 2G

Write sentences using the following words as the subjects of your sentences. Use a verb in the present tense.

1. The library that was built recently _____

2. The books on the shelf in the library _____

3. Magazines and newspapers _____

4. Neither the librarian nor the clerks _____

5. Students and instructors _____

Lesson 3 ❊ *Subjects and Verbs— Special Problems*

A. Subjects That Are Singular

When used as subjects, the words below take singular verbs.

any	every	no	some	other words
anybody	everybody	nobody	somebody	each
anyone	everyone	no one	someone	either
anything	everything	nothing	something	neither

EXERCISE 3A

Circle the subjects. Underline the correct form of the verb in the parentheses.

Examples: (Is, Are) everyone going to work during summer vacation?

Each of us (has, have) a job.

No one who is a college student today (need, needs) to read a survey to know that the cost of a college education has risen. Almost everyone I know at school (work, works) during the school year, and nobody (take, takes) the summer off. Neither of my two closest friends (receive, receives) any financial support from home. In addition to working, each (depend, depends) on student loans to help cover the increased costs of tuition, lodging, and books. If either (plan, plans) to attend graduate school, she must expect to make monthly student loan payments for some years following graduation.

5. How important is the shelf where you store your photos?
    Use "Any" as the subject of your sentence.

    Any _____

6. What is the best method of identifying your photos?
    Use "All" as the subject of your sentence.

    All _____

7. Do you have any damaged photos?
    Choose either "None" or "Some" as the subject of your sentence.

    None_____ or

    Some _____

8. What can you do to restore your damaged photographs?
    Use "Any" as the subject of your sentence.

    Any _____

C. Collective Nouns

Collective nouns represent a collection of persons, places, things, ideas, or activities.

audience	college	crowd	band
committee	family	class	company
government	group	jury	management
number	school	society	team

It is often difficult to decide whether a collective noun is singular or plural. Most of the time, use a singular verb or rewrite the sentence to make the subject clearer. Instead of saying: "The band are tuning their instruments," you could say, "The band members are tuning their instruments."

Examples: 1. The number of courses offered this semester is small.
               2. My favorite musical group is playing at the club all
                   week.

D. Nouns Ending in -s That Are Not Plural

Some nouns, such as physics, economics, mathematics, measles, mumps, and news are considered singular even though they end in **-s,** and they take singular verbs.

Example: (Measles) is caused by a virus and usually occurs during childhood.

<table><tr><td>✳</td><td>EXERCISE 3C</td><td>✳</td></tr></table>

Underline the correct verb.

1. Mathematics (is, are) required for all engineering students.

2. Politics (was, were) viewed as the motive for the senator's vote against the tax bill.

3. Gymnastics (has, have) become a popular event in the Olympics.

4. The news of a recent archaeological discovery (was, were) announced by the university today.

5. Physics (include, includes) the study of optics.

> Consult your dictionary whenever you are in doubt about whether a particular word is singular or plural.

E. Time, Money, and Weight

Words that specify *time, money,* or *weight* require a singular verb when they are considered as a unit even if they are plural in form.

Examples: 1. Two (semesters) <u>is</u> really a short time.

2. Five (dollars) <u>is</u> a modest fee for an entrance exam.

F. Titles

Titles of songs, plays, movies, novels, or magazine articles require singular verbs even if the titles are plural.

Example: *The Carpetbaggers* was both a novel and a movie.

G. Names of Organizations and Businesses

The names of organizations and businesses that are plural in form but singular in meaning require a singular verb. Substitute a pronoun for the proper noun to determine which verb to use.

Examples: Vons advertises in the newspaper every Thursday.
(It advertises ...)

The House of Representatives is in session today.
(It is in session today.)

EXERCISE 3D

Write five sentences on the lines below, using the words at the left as subjects. Use the present tense of the verb.

1. *The Stone Diaries* ________________________________
2. The League of Women Voters ________________________________
3. Five pounds of bananas ________________________________
4. Twenty dollars a month ________________________________
5. *Underground Voices,* a short film about black poets, ________________
6. TLR Office Systems ________________________________

H. Special Problems of Agreement

***Who, That,* and *Which* as Subjects** *Who, that,* and *which* used as subjects take singular verbs if the words they refer to are singular. They take plural verbs if the words they refer to are plural.

Examples:

1. Mark taped the tennis matches (that) were on Channel 4 while he watched the baseball game on Channel 9 Saturday afternoon. (The verb "were" is plural because it agrees with its subject "that." "That" is plural because it refers to the plural noun "matches.")

2. Mark's friend (who) works every Saturday came over to watch the tape that night. (The verb "works" is singular because it agrees with its subject "who." "Who" is singular because it refers to "friend," a singular noun.)

EXERCISE 3E

Write the noun that <u>who</u>, <u>which</u>, or <u>that</u> refers to on the line at the right. Then underline the correct form of the verb in parentheses.

Example: Businesses that (sell, sells) products for leisure activities compete with television.   <u>businesses</u>

1. The television set has become a home-entertainment center for Americans who (seeks, seek) recreation during their leisure time.   _____

2. The family of four that usually (goes, go) to a movie theater once or twice a week can now save money, watching cable television at home.   _____

3. People with videotape cassette recorders, which (plugs, plug) into the television set, schedule their favorite programs at hours most convenient for the family.   _____

4. Instead of going to a video-game arcade, many consumers play video games that (hooks, hook) up to their own televisions.   _____

5. And, of course, commercial television, which (has, have) been keeping Americans at home for years, continues to consume one billion hours of their time each day.   _____

G R O U P   A C T I V I T Y

Read the following paragraph. Circle each "who," "which," and "that" used as the subject of a clause, and underline the verb in the clause. Bracket the words to which these subjects refer. When you have finished, you should have circled "who" three times, "which" five times, and "that" twice. Then answer the questions and follow the directions on page 283.

The blossoming of the cherry [trees] (that) surround the Jefferson Memorial on the Tidal Basin is one of the loveliest signs of spring in the nation's capital. The 3,700 trees of several varieties, which were a gift of Japan in 1912, grow in two parks in Washington, D. C. Most of the trees, which are the Yoshino variety, produce a white, cloud-like blossom, while the Akebonos, fewer in number, contribute a delicate pink to the sea of color, appearing briefly for two weeks each year. A weeklong Cherry Blossom Festival, which opens with the lighting of a 300-year-old, 8-½-foot Japanese stone lantern, includes a parade and many other activities. The blossoms, as might be expected, do not appear on schedule every year on a specific day; the time ranges somewhere between March 15, the earliest date, and April 18, the latest one recorded. The hundreds of thousands of tourists, who arrive in expectation of the event, will be disappointed if the trees do not flower during their visit. Moreover, the festival plans, which await completion, depend upon the estimated blossoming time.

The question that arises for most of us concerns how the date can be predicted with a high degree of accuracy. Fortunately, the National Park Service horticulturist, who seems to use a combination of art and science to make his prediction, is equal to the task. Beginning in late February, when the small red buds begin to appear, he makes daily visits to observe the trees, watching for the change in the buds from a tight red to a putty white. He also considers two factors which affect the blooming time, daylight and temperature. In general, the length of daylight tells plants when to blossom, and there are some biologists who feel daylight is a more reliable factor than temperature. He has learned, however, that local temperature plays a special role in regard to cherry trees. Warm days with no snow on the ground will bring an earlier bloom than the same temperature accompanied by snow on the ground. He suggests that the trees are, in effect, standing with their "feet" in ice water although the days are warm. In this way, he estimates the week of peak bloom quite accurately to the satisfaction of the festival personnel and a great many people from out of town.

1. Where are the cherry trees growing? Use a complex sentence with "that" or "which" as the subject of the subordinate clause.

2. Why is it important to predict the peak blooming period? Use a complex sentence with "that" or "which" as the subject of the subordinate clause.

3. Who forecasts the blooming time? Use a complex sentence with "who" as the subject of the subordinate clause.

4. What factors does he consider in making his prediction? In your answer use a complex sentence with "that," "which," or "who" as the subject of the subordinate clause.

Compare your answers and your sentences with those of several of your classmates. If you have any questions, consult your instructor.

Together with your classmates, write a paragraph discussing some other indication of the arrival of spring. If you prefer, write about one of the other three seasons instead of spring. Be sure to check your sentences carefully for subject-verb agreement before you exchange paragraphs with another group in your class.

Lesson 4 ※ *Agreement of Pronoun and Antecedent*

An ANTECEDENT (A) is the noun, pronoun, or noun phrase to which a PRONOUN (P) refers. The pronoun agrees in number, person, and gender with the antecedent.

Example: Christopher (A) showed Erika <u>his</u> (P) art collection.

The possessive pronoun "his" refers to the noun "Christopher."

You make few errors in pronoun-antecedent agreement in most of the sentences you write; however, the following sentence patterns may give you trouble.

A. Words That Separate Antecedent and Pronoun

Be sure that the pronoun agrees with the antecedent and not with another noun that may be placed closer to the pronoun than the antecedent is.

Example: One (A) of the players injured in the game sprained <u>his</u> (P) ankle.

"One" is the singular antecedent of the pronoun "his," not the plural noun "players."

B. Compound Antecedents

Compound antecedents usually require a plural pronoun.

Example: Christopher (A) and Erika (A) exhibited <u>their</u> (P) oil paintings in the student art show.

However, if the two antecedents are joined by or, neither . . . nor, or either . . . or, the pronoun agrees with the antecedent closer to the pronoun.

When one antecedent is plural and the other singular, place the plural antecedent second to avoid writing an awkward sentence.

Example: (awkward)   Neither my parents nor my brother would admit that he couldn't solve my sister's algebra problems.

(rewritten)   Neither my brother nor my parents would admit that they couldn't solve my sister's algebra problems.

EXERCISE 4A

Fill in the correct pronoun on the lines in these sentences. Write the word or words that are the antecedents on the line at the right.

Example: The student artist who sold me these paintings signed his name in the corner.   _____artist_____

1. Both Matt and Richard are exhibiting _____ paintings in the student art show.   _____

2. Jaime, one of the students in our photography class,

    produced _____ pictures with the aid of a computer.   _____

3. Neither Jan nor Theresa has ever entered _____ photographs in a competition before today.   _____

4. Mr. and Mrs. Asano, who are local artists, have given us

    _____ help in judging the entries in the exhibition.   _____

5. Has either the photographer or the journalism

    students completed _____ work on the publicity for the show?   _____

ALTERNATE WRITING ASSIGNMENT

The toy industry has a few surprises for shoppers. According to one observer: "The major trend is electronic toys, and the craze has reached hysterical proportions. If the current toy trends continue, next year's assortment might include electronic versions of tag, hop-scotch, jump rope, and tree climbing."

Toys obviously have changed quite a bit in the last ten years. Are electronic toys more fun or more satisfying than those you played with when you were growing up? If you believe that toys were more fun before the age of computers, tell about some of the toys popular with children when you were young. Describe a favorite toy and explain what made it special to you. You may also write about some of the new electronic toys. Describe one or two in detail and explain their appeal.

Chapter 8 Practice Test: Agreement

Name _____

Date _____ Class Time _____

Instructor _____

I.   Underline the correct form of the verb.

1.   According to a survey, a large group of listeners (object, objects) to the program's talk-show format.

2.   On the last page of the report (was, were) listed the preferences of these listeners.

3.   There (has, have) been some changes made now in the original program.

4.   This past week, news and music (has, have) replaced the talk-show format.

5.   The new format, according to the station manager, (seem, seems) to please the audience.

II.   Underline the correct verb.

1.   Economics (is, are) not a difficult subject for Alan.

2.   The audience (were, was) delighted by the speaker's sense of humor.

3.   Each of the students (learn, learns) at a different rate.

4.   My new scissors never (need, needs) sharpening.

5.   Neither of the players (seem, seems) to be worried about the outcome of the game.

III.   Underline the correct pronoun in the following sentences.

1.   Both Allison and Meredith said (she, they) would come to the study session.

2.   Neither Allison nor Meredith remembered to bring (their, her) class notes to the study session.

Chapter 8 Practice Test: Agreement (cont.)

3. The economic crisis will present the new government with (its, their) greatest challenge.

4. The basketball team has won all (their, its) home games.

5. Many states, like California, allow some of (its, their) traffic violators to attend traffic schools instead of paying fines.

IV. Rewrite these sentences by giving unclear pronouns specific antecedents or by replacing the underlined pronouns with nouns.

1. Marsha called her mother once a week when <u>she</u> was out of town.

   _____

2. The doctor returned his patient's call before <u>he</u> went to lunch.

   _____

3. <u>They</u> should make pedestrians and roller skaters stay off the bike path.

   _____

4. The city council argued for hours before passing the new ordinance restricting parking on certain residential streets. <u>This</u> angered the citizens who attended the meeting.

   _____

5. Daniel turned in a late research paper <u>which</u> annoyed his history instructor.

   _____

V. Write your own sentences according to instructions.

1. Use <u>either James or Laura</u> as the subject. Use a verb in the present tense.

   _____

Chapter 8 Practice Test: Agreement (cont.)

2. Write a sentence beginning with <u>Here is.</u>

    _____

3. Write a sentence with the word <u>news</u> as the subject. Use a verb in the present tense.

    _____

4. Write a sentence using the word <u>anyone</u> as the subject. Use a verb in the present tense.

    _____

Chapter 8 Answer Key

Exercise 1A and Exercise 1B
Your instructor will check your sentences.

Exercise 2A

	Subjects	Aux. Verbs and Main Verbs	Words Between Subject and Verb
1.	quarters	give	(like those in San Diego's Wild Animal Park)
2.	Zookeepers	work	(whenever possible)
3.	species	are bred	(such as the condor)
4.	animals	seem	(released into their natural habitats)
5.	zoos	play	(in the country)
6.	Making these changes	takes	(in an old zoo)

Exercise 2B

	Subject	Verb
1.	effects	linger
2.	trees	have
3.	flowers	are
4.	farmers	are
5.	hope	is

Exercise 2C

	Subject	Verb
1.	disagreement	is
2.	much	is
3.	chances	are
4.	clue	is
5.	humidity	signals
6.	devices	are
7.	device	is
8.	problem	is
9.	way	is
10.	appliances	are

Exercise 2D
Your instructor will check your sentences.

Exercises 2E
Your instructor will check your answers.

Exercise 2F
1. have   2. have   3. have   4. have   5. has   6. has

Exercise 2G
Your instructor will check your sentences.

Exercise 3A
Subjects: 1. No one   2. everyone   3. nobody   4. Neither   5. each   6. either
Verbs: 1. needs   2. works   3. takes   4. receives   5. depends   6. plans

Exercise 3B

Your instructor will check your sentences.

Exercise 3C

1. is   2. was   3. has   4. was   5. includes

Exercise 3D

Your instructor will check your sentences.

Exercise 3E

	Antecedents	**Verbs**
1.	Americans	seek
2.	family	goes
3.	recorders	plug
4.	video games	hook
5.	television	has

Exercise 4A

	Pronouns	**Antecedents**
1.	their	Matt and Richard
2.	his	Jaime
3.	her	Neither Jan nor Theresa
4.	their	Mr. and Mrs. Asano
5.	their	students

Exercise 4B

1. its   2. its   3. its   4. their   5. its

Exercise 4C

	Pronouns	**Antecedents**	**Possible Revisions**
1.	his or her	Someone	Someone left those books on the desk.
2.	his or her	anyone	Has anyone brought a camera?
3.	her	each	
4.	his or her	Nobody	Nobody has received the final grades in the mail yet.
5.	his or her	Everyone	All employees must show their badges to the guard at the gate.

Your instructor will check your sentences.

Exercise 4D

1. who   2. that   3. who   4. that   5. that

Exercise 4E

1. Jacquie said to Tess, "I have lost my pen."
2. There are so many automobile accidents because drivers are careless.
3. Charles Brocard is a marine archaeologist. Marine archaeology is a new and challenging profession.
4. Before taking a test, Roberto studies and gets a good night's sleep. Rest is important.
5. Juan told Bob, "Your car needs repainting."
6. In some parts of Canada the people speak French.

Summary of Chapter 8

1. subject   2. pronoun   3. follows   4. plural   5. singular   6. singular   7. singular
8. antecedents

 Commas

Definitions of Terms

In Chapter 9 you will study these ten rules for using COMMAS:

1. Use a comma between two main clauses connected by a coordinating connective.
2. Use commas to separate three or more items in a series.
3. Use a comma after introductory words and phrases.
4. Use a comma after introductory subordinate clauses.
5. Use commas to separate two or more adjectives before a noun.
6. Use commas to enclose words that interrupt.
7. Use commas to set off words in direct address.
8. Use commas to set off nonessential words, phrases, and clauses.
9. Use commas to set off direct quotations.
10. Use a comma after each item in geographical names, dates, and addresses.

Lesson 1 ❈ *Coordinating Connectives Between Main Clauses; Items in a Series; Introductory Phrases and Clauses*

Many writers are confused about when to use commas. Perhaps someone told you to read the sentence aloud and put a comma in wherever you pause. Although it is true that commas generally do mark a break or a pause, it is *not* a good idea to rely on your ear in this way. It is much better to learn the uses of commas. Studying the ten rules in this chapter should help you understand the use of commas.

1. Use a Comma Between Two Main Clauses Connected by a Coordinating Connective

Place a comma before a coordinating connective (and, but, for, or, nor, so, and yet) when it joins two main clauses.

Example: The outfielder dropped the fly ball, and the runner on third base scored.

Unnecessary Commas The following sentence does not have a comma before the connective. In this sentence, and connects the two parts of a compound verb, not two main clauses.

Example: The outfielder dropped the ball and committed an error.

EXERCISE 1A

Insert commas where necessary.

It is not true that flamingos are pink only because they eat pink shellfish. The pinkness of flamingos is determined by food but it is not determined by pink shellfish. The factors in the flamingo's diet that ensure pinkness are carotenoid pigments and these pigments are found in plankton, diatoms, and blue-green algae. The flamingos eat the plankton and algae. Then they process the yellow carotene into a red compound and that substance is stored in their legs and their feathers. Flamingos must get enough of the right pigment or they will lose their color when they molt. The pink color is very important as flamingos do not seem to breed successfully without it. In captivity they were once fed ground-up carrots and red pepper to keep them in the pink but now the zoo keepers try to reproduce their natural diet.

| | **EXERCISE 1B** | |

Circle the unnecessary commas. Do not circle the commas that separate main clauses.

The government has spent billions of dollars to protect our shorelines from the destruction of storms, but coastal geologists maintain that these efforts only accelerate the damage. Engineers build structures such as jetties, or breakwaters, yet fail to stop the erosion. Geologists say that this policy is based on a misunderstanding, for all the engineers' good intentions. Beaches do not need these barriers, and actually provide protection for the continent. Sand builds up in sand dunes when the ocean is calm, and waves move this sand out to the sea bottom during a storm. Beaches then become flatter, so waves break earlier, and cause less erosion. Beaches that have neither seawalls, nor bulkheads to interrupt the natural cycle rebuild their defenses as calmer waters carry the sand back to the shore. Miles of east-coast beaches have disappeared after 70 years of engineered beach construction, and the loss can only continue if the advice of geologists is ignored.

2. Use Commas to Separate Items in a Series

Use commas to separate *three or more items* in a series. The items may be single words, phrases, or clauses. A comma before the last item is optional if there are exactly three items in the series. In the following examples, you may omit the comma before *and* in sentences 2 and 3 if you wish.

Examples: 1. Marty is taking courses in economics, typing, accounting, and statistics this semester. (words)
2. I went to the bank, did some shopping, and returned home by eleven. (phrases)
3. Leroy cut the grass, Cathy pulled the weeds in the flower beds, and Pat trimmed the hedges. (main clauses)

Unnecessary Commas No commas are necessary in the following sentence because there are only two items in the series.

Example: Tennis and swimming are her favorite sports.

EXERCISE 1C

Write a sentence using each of the following series or pairs. Use commas where needed.

1. Melissa   Adrian   John   Diane

   _____

   _____

2. listened attentively   took notes   reviewed chapter summaries

   _____

   _____

3. watched TV   listened to CDs

   _____

   _____

4. writing   telephoning   faxing

   _____

   _____

5. made a list   drew a cluster   prepared an outline

   _____

   _____

If the circled comma is necessary, write *Yes* on the line at the right. If the circled comma is unnecessary, write *No* on the line at the right.

1. Gordon Parks is a noted photographer, poet, author, filmmaker ⊙ and composer.   _____

2. He once attributed his early determination to become a photographer to three influences: some 1930s Farm Security Administration photographs ⊙ an art show in a Chicago museum, and a newsreel of a World War II Japanese bombing raid.   _____

3. He began his career on the Seattle waterfront with an inexpensive camera that was secondhand ⊙ but in excellent condition.   _____

4. The young Midwesterner, who spent his early years in Kansas ⊙ Minnesota, and Washington, had his first photo exhibit in the storefront window of the Eastman Kodak Company in Minneapolis.   _____

5. He was a staff photographer at *Life* magazine ⊙ for 20 years, where he developed an expertise that ranged widely from photojournalism to fashion photography.   _____

6. Parks achieved an international reputation as one of several African-American photographers whose pictures of African Americans revealed the close family ties ⊙ and rich community life in the midst of a segregated, restrictive society.   _____

7. His photographs, such as his famous "American Gothic," recorded the black experience, but he actually was less interested in color ⊙ or race than in the injustices suffered by the defenseless everywhere.   _____

3. Use a Comma After Introductory Words and Phrases

At the beginning of a sentence, use a comma after a long phrase.

Examples: 1. *By the end of the second week of school,* Ken began making plans for Thanksgiving weekend.
2. *Looking at his calendar,* Ken realized that he had weeks to wait for the holiday.

The comma after a single introductory word or an introductory short phrase is optional. Although many writers use the comma after these expressions, others do not.

Examples: 1. *During the recent heat wave,* we hoped a rainstorm would bring relief. Finally, one arrived, but the humidity only increased.
2. *In that heat* no one could work outdoors comfortably. (comma optional)
3. *Later* we went to a movie to cool off before eating dinner. (comma optional)

If there is any question about the meaning of the sentence, use a comma after a single word or a short phrase of introduction.

1. Inside, the theater was cool and dark.
2. While ordering, my friends and I drank iced tea at the restaurant.

Try reading these two sentences without commas, and you will see why the comma in each case is essential to understanding the meaning.

EXERCISE 1E

Insert commas where necessary. In some sentences the comma is optional.

1. Among the staples of southwestern cooking the chile is probably the most essential.

2. By the way New Mexicans spell "chile" with a final "e" not an "i."

3. In addition the chile is not actually a pepper as Columbus believed when he "discovered" it on one of his voyages.

4. In fact the capsicum (chile) is a distant cousin of the tomato and is classified by botanists as a fruit.

5. Ranging from mild to incredibly hot the chile's color depends on when it is harvested.

6. Produced by the same plant green chilies are picked early and red chilies late in the season after they have matured.

7. Moreover color is no guide to pungency; red or green sauce can be mild or hot depending on each specific batch.

8. While eating a food flavored with the chile you may suddenly need to put out the fire, but eat something sweet or creamy instead of reaching for a glass of ice water.

EXERCISE 1F

If the circled comma is necessary, write *Yes* on the line at the right. If the circled comma is unnecessary, write *No* on the line at the right.

1. As a matter of fact ⊙ few people would say that telling a lie is okay. _____

2. But ⊙ they would have to admit that they tell lies sometimes. _____

3. At work ⊙ they often say to another employee, "What a fine report you produced!" _____

4. In their own minds ⊙ they are probably thinking, "I could have done it better." _____

5. Lying ⊙ for all its possible social value, is almost never called by its real name. _____

6. For example ⊙ some politicians would only admit they told a lie by saying, "Mistakes were made." _____

4. Use a Comma After Introductory Subordinate Clauses

Use a comma after a subordinate clause at the beginning of a sentence.

Example: *When you move to your new office,* send us your address.

EXERCISE 1G

Insert commas where they are needed. Some sentences do not need commas added. Do not remove any commas from the paragraph.

Although a comet looks very beautiful as it sails across the sky it is not much more than a dirty snowball. A comet consists of about 25 percent dust and chunks of rocky or metallic material and about 75 percent ice. While the ice is mainly frozen water it also contains a mixture of methane, ammonia, and carbon dioxide molecules. When a comet passes close to the sun it loses some of its matter. Some of its ice turns to a gas form as a comet nears the sun. The gases spread out around the nucleus, forming a large, thin atmosphere called a "coma," which glows in the sunlight. If the supply of gases from the nucleus changes a comet can brighten and fade noticeably. As a comet approaches the sun a solar wind sweeps a comet's gases away from the sun. So a second tail consisting of dust particles may also appear. Although this dust tail is shorter than the gas tail it may also be visible from earth. In fact, some comets have been observed to have as many as nine tails.

| | EXERCISE 1H | |

If the sentence is punctuated correctly, write *Yes* on the line at the right. If the sentence is punctuated incorrectly, write *No* on the line.

1. Country music began several hundred years ago, when Scotch-Irish settlers came to the Appalachian region bringing their folk music with them. _____

2. Although the newcomers still played the "old" music, it began to change with their use of "new" homemade instruments such as the banjo, the guitar, and the zither. _____

3. This "fiddle music" or "Old Time Music" gained a wider audience during the 1920s after Victor Records arrived in the South to record these rural musicians. _____

4. In 1926 when Jimmie Rodgers, recognized today as the "Father of Country Music," and his hillbilly band moved to Asheville they began attracting enthusiastic audiences. _____

5. Since the music has borrowed extensively from spirituals, blues, jazz, and honky-tonk and added instruments such as drums and the electric guitar, it has evolved into a distinctively American music. _____

6. The lyrics tell stories about ordinary people and their continual struggle with the harsh facts of their lives. _____

7. Because "country" music has now become the music of our towns and cities it has been called the "folk music" of working people and a "native American art form." _____

GROUP ACTIVITY

Insert commas as needed in the following paragraph. These are commas between two main clauses joined by coordinating connectives, between items in a series, and following introductory phrases and clauses. Do *not* remove commas. Then answer the questions below the paragraph.

Geothermal heat may be a new source of energy for us but it is an ancient means of providing power by tapping a natural resource. Subsidized by federal grants and tax advantages developers have tripled the use of geothermal power. In many western states today communities are hoping to reduce their dependence on fossil fuels by utilizing this alternative energy source where it is available. Since geothermal heat is a fairly economical source of power it has a growing number of supporters. Boise, Idaho, has become well-known among proponents of this form of energy because this city has taken advantage of the hot wells underneath it. Boise has laid pipes beneath its streets to heat restaurants shops business offices and the state office buildings. This old-new source of power can supply only a small part of the nation's energy needs but it can provide a substantial savings to those regions possessing this natural advantage.

Together with two or three classmates check each other's insertion of commas in the paragraph. Then write sentences as directed below, and exchange your work with that of another group in your class. Check each other's sentences for the correct use of commas.

1. What is meant by geothermal heat? (Your answer should have at least two main clauses joined by a comma and a coordinating connective.)

2. Why has Boise, Idaho, chosen to use this method to heat businesses? (Your answer should have an introductory phrase followed by a comma.)

3. What changes has Boise made in its street design? (Your answer should have items in a series separated by commas.)

4. Why have developers shown an interest in using geothermal heat? (Your answer should have an introductory subordinate clause followed by a comma.)

Lesson 2 ✳ *Adjectives Before a Noun; Words That Interrupt; Direct Address*

5. Use Commas to Separate Adjectives Before a Noun

Use commas to separate two or more adjectives that modify the same noun if a coordinating connective such as *and* can be inserted between the adjectives. You can use two tests to tell whether or not to put a comma between modifiers before a noun.

1. Use a comma if and can be inserted between the adjectives.
2. Use a comma if you can reverse the order of the adjectives.

Example: Bob was the most aggressive, skillful player on the court.

Use a comma because you could say:

1. Bob was the most aggressive and skillful player on the court.
                                  or
2. Bob was the most skillful, aggressive player on the court.

Unnecessary Commas   Do *not* put a comma between adjectives if and cannot be placed between them or if you cannot reverse their order.

Example: He was the most aggressive, skillful basketball player on the court.

You would not write skillful and basketball player.

You cannot reverse the words—basketball skillful player.

Therefore, do not put a comma between skillful and basketball.

The adjectives placed before basketball player modify both words. Do not put a comma between the final modifier and the noun.

EXERCISE 2A

Insert additional commas as needed in the following sentences to separate adjectives before a noun.

1. In the early morning, the joggers run effortlessly along the deserted shell-strewn beach.

2. Even on gray foggy chilly mornings, they wear only tank tops and brief running shorts.

3. Bicycle riders on the nearby winding concrete bike path must be alert as jogging parents push their small children in vehicles especially constructed for this purpose.

4. Some cyclists are also accompanied by their youngsters riding in low plastic-curtained trailers attached to the back of the bikes.

5. When the morning overcast begins to burn off, the second shift appears: volleyball players head for the courts, and bikini-clad sunseekers lie down on their brightly colored beach towels for a serious tanning session.

EXERCISE 2B

If the sentence is punctuated correctly, write *Yes* on the line at the right. If the sentence is punctuated incorrectly, write *No* on the line.

1. Woodchucks are plump, low-slung animals. __________

2. They are not the largest, North American rodents; beavers are. __________

3. Most slow fat woodchucks hibernate in winter.   _____

4. Woodchucks are found in rural and suburban areas
    in the eastern United States.   _____

5. Woodchucks will eat any growing, green plants.   _____

6. Use Commas to Enclose Words That Interrupt

Use commas on *both* sides of a word (or a group of words) that interrupts
the flow of thought in a sentence.

Examples: 1. Airline pilots, by the way, are often cautious automo-
                     bile drivers.
                 2. The guests, it seems, are enjoying the party.
                 3. Several changes in the enrollment procedure,
                     however, are planned for the coming semester.

Do not use just one comma; enclose the interrupting word or words
between two commas.

Unnecessary Commas   Do not use commas to enclose prepositional
phrases that do not interrupt the flow of thought in a sentence.

Example: The dwarf lemon tree in the tub on the patio grew rapidly
                and produced fruit in no time at all.

This sentence does not require any commas.

EXERCISE 2C

Insert commas where necessary.

   Most experts agree despite conclusive evidence that the lemon tree

probably originated in southeast Asia in the vicinity of Burma thousands

of years ago. Although this evergreen tree is sensitive to freezing weather,

the fruit does best as a matter of fact exposed to the occasional cold snap that a hot, humid climate lacks. California growers as a result use wind machines and heaters in their groves to regulate temperature. Lemon trees under ideal conditions can bear buds, flowers, developing fruit, and mature fruit all at the same time. Citrus trees moreover require a fair amount of water; rain however can damage the fruit. Every part of the fruit we are told from seed to peel has a use from food preparation and general household use to medicinal and commercial applications. Most of us without a doubt use lemons most frequently as flavor intensifiers. In some cultures people indeed know the meaning of using the entire fruit: they eat the lemon as we would an apple, peel and all.

EXERCISE 2D

If the sentence is punctuated correctly, write *Yes* on the line at the right. If the sentence is punctuated incorrectly, write *No* on the line.

1. Mr. Toshida, arrived in San Francisco with his family, from a small town in Japan. _____

2. Dr. Okada, however, came to San Francisco from Tokyo. _____

3. Both men it would appear, had little trouble adjusting to life in America. _____

4. Mr. Toshida made his fortune, I believe, by manufacturing computer chips. _____

5. Dr. Okada in no time at all was successful as a dentist. _____

7. Use Commas to Set Off Words in Direct Address

Use commas to set off the names and titles of people spoken to directly.

Examples: 1. "Pat, will you please call Dr. Hodge for me?" Paul said.
2. "I called you, Dr. Hodge, to ask for some information," said Pat.
3. "How often should Paul take the medicine, Doctor?" asked Pat.

These three examples show words in direct address at the beginning, in the middle, and at the end of sentences. Notice the use of commas.

EXERCISE 2E

Insert commas where necessary.

1. "I don't entirely agree Jim with your position," said Ella.

2. "Ella you never agree with me," said Jim.

3. "I agree with you most of the time Jim," said Ella.

4. "Well then Ella why don't you agree with me now?" said Jim.

5. "Jim I cannot agree with you because you are wrong," said Ella.

6. "Ella tell me that you love me anyway," said Jim.

EXERCISE 2F

If the sentence is punctuated correctly, write *Yes* on the line at the right. If the sentence is punctuated incorrectly, write *No* on the line. Insert commas as needed in the sentences that are punctuated incorrectly.

1. Scott do you have time to review this proposal with me this afternoon?   _____

2. It is a pleasure to recommend you for promotion to Office Manager Mrs. Vasquez. _____

3. We are sending the information that you requested sir by second-day air letter. _____

4. Your request for a month's leave of absence, Alice, has been approved. _____

5. Thank you one and all for your work on this important project. _____

Lesson 3 ❋ *Nonessential Words, Phrases, and Clauses; Direct Quotations; Dates, Geographical Names, and Addresses*

8. Use Commas to Set Off Nonessential Words, Phrases, and Clauses

Use commas to enclose words, phrases, and clauses containing nonessential material. The information in these words may add some details, but the reader could understand the main idea of the sentence if they were left out.

Examples:
1. Marcie Evan, who is our pitcher, will be a sportscaster next fall.
2. *Cannery Row,* a novel by John Steinbeck, has been made into a movie.

Omit the words enclosed by commas, and the sentences above read:

1. Marcie Evan will be a sportscaster next fall.
2. *Cannery Row* has been made into a movie.

As you can see, the main ideas of both sentences are unchanged by omitting the nonessential words.

Unnecessary Commas   Do not use commas to enclose words, phrases, and clauses that are essential to the meaning of the sentence.

Example: Will the person <u>who parked in the loading zone</u> move his car?

If the subordinate clause <u>who parked in the loading zone</u> is omitted, the main idea of the sentence is lost. The person cannot be identified; you do not know who should move his car.

Example: The novel *Cannery Row* has been made into a movie.

In this sentence the title is necessary to identify the book; therefore, you do not use commas.

EXERCISE 3A

Insert commas where necessary. Some sentences may not need commas.

1. My friend Carla Caraway went to New York to get a job as a dancer.

2. A young woman alone in a strange city must learn how to take care of herself.

3. She auditioned for Judith Jamison the famous choreographer of the Alvin Ailey company.

4. Carla breathless and exhausted waited after the audition to hear the choreographer's opinion.

5. Carla joined the Ailey company one of the best dance companies in the world.

EXERCISE 3B

Insert commas where required to set off nonessential words, phrases, and clauses.

1. The talented American contralto Marian Anderson who had sung at the White House was barred from singing in Constitution Hall in Washington.

2. Instead Ms. Anderson sang at the Lincoln Memorial before 75,000 people who had gathered in support of her.

3. Three Aaron Copland ballets drawing upon American themes are *Billy the Kid, Rodeo,* and *Appalachian Spring*.

4. Copland wrote *Appalachian Spring* for Martha Graham choreographer and dancer.

5. Ernest Hemingway an American author began his first job as a newspaper reporter at the age of eighteen.

6. The novel *A Farewell to Arms* was based on Hemingway's experiences as an ambulance driver during World War I.

7. American heroes who had been neglected by standard history books were portrayed by Jacob Lawrence in his paintings.

8. Gilbert Stuart an early American painter is best known for his portraits of George Washington.

9. Frank Lloyd Wright one of the first architects to use glass and metal walls for office buildings achieved early recognition outside the United States.

10. The hotel that Wright designed in Tokyo after World War I showed inventiveness in its earthquake-resistant construction.

9. Use Commas to Set Off Direct Quotations

Use commas to set off direct quotations from the rest of the sentence.

Examples:

1. "Perhaps," my brother said to me, "you should study once in a while."
2. She asked, "Won't anybody help me?"
3. "I don't want to watch television tonight," Jan said.
4. "I'll be back in an hour," Jim answered, "so don't leave without me."

In sentence 3, although "I don't want to watch television tonight," is a main clause, do not use a period until the end of the complete statement. Note that commas are placed <u>inside</u> the quotation marks.

EXERCISE 3C

Insert commas where necessary.

1. "I can never do these homework assignments" Gary complained.

2. "Well" said his mother "you haven't even tried."

3. "I never learn anything in that class" he said "so what's the point?"

4. "Besides" he said to her "I have a date tonight."

5. "Gary, you should do your assignment before you go out" his mother advised.

6. "I have to leave in one hour" he told his mother.

7. "If you begin to work right now" she said "you will have plenty of time."

8. "I'll do it when I return" he said as he left the house.

9. "Gary, come right back here" she called "and finish your homework."

10. "You might as well relax, Mom" said Gary's sister. "He has already gone."

EXERCISE 3D

Insert commas where required to set off:
a. direct quotations
b. words of direct address
c. nonessential words or phrases

1. "Greg did you hear about the recent triathalon competition in Hawaii?" Diane asked.

2. "I hadn't realized" she continued "how popular the sport has become."

3. "The athlete who attempts the Ironman competition must be in top physical condition Diane" Greg replied.

4. "Most other triathalon competitions as a matter of fact are not as demanding as the Ironman" he pointed out.

5. "If your goal Greg is just to complete the triathalon" Diane said "you don't need to worry about speed."

6. The doctor said "Hypothermia can be a threat to the swimmers if the water is especially cold."

7. "One of the greatest dangers to the athletes during the marathon run" he added "is dehydration."

8. "For most triathalons, competitors are required to sign waivers releasing the promoters from responsibility for the athletes' safety" Greg said.

9. Diane remarked "The most successful athletes as I might have expected train under conditions similar to those of the competition."

10. "Competitors should train for at least three months" the doctor advised "in each of the three sports: swimming, running and cycling."

10. Use Commas in Dates, Geographical Names, and Addresses

Use commas after every item in dates, geographical names, and addresses as shown in the following examples:

Dates: Maria started a new job on Monday, June 15, 1998.

Geographical names: Miami, Florida, is the site of the Orange Bowl.

Addresses: James's address is 2208 N. McKnight Road, Philadelphia, PA 19103. (The zip code is not separated by a comma from the name of the state.)

Note: An address on an envelope is written as follows:

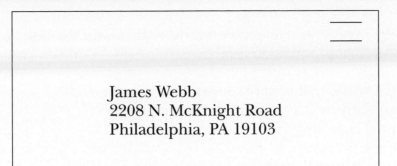

James Webb
2208 N. McKnight Road
Philadelphia, PA 19103

Unnecessary Commas   Commas may be omitted when the day of the month is not given or when the day of the month precedes the month.

Examples: Maria started a new job in June 1998.
Maria started a new job on Monday, 15 June 1998.

<table><tr><td>�֎</td><td>**EXERCISE 3E**</td><td>✷</td></tr></table>

Insert commas where necessary.

1. George will move to Las Vegas Nevada in January.

2. His address has been The Stanford Arms Hotel Apt. 10 536 W. 18th Street Rittman Indiana 46206 for the last six years.

3. We will forward his mail to his new address: The Pyramid Hotel Las Vegas Nevada 89501.

4. Bill Wilson is a salesperson for Fashion Clothing Co. 2473 White Plains Road Bronx New York 10111.

5. On 2 April 1999 Bill traveled from New York to Dallas Texas to attend a fashion show.

6. The fashion show was held at the Plaza Hotel 8 Fifth Street Dallas Texas.

EXERCISE 3F

If the sentence is punctuated correctly, write *Yes* on the line at the right. If the sentence is punctuated incorrectly, write *No* on the line.

1. Send Lynn's mail in care of Mrs. R. B. Singer, 1532 Stone Canyon Drive Santa Maria Arizona 85321 starting Tuesday July 28, 1998. _____

2. Dionne Warwick was born on December 12, 1941, in East Orange, New Jersey, according to the records. _____

3. Circle March 15 on your calendar as a reminder to file your income tax. _____

4. Return this form to the Department of Motor Vehicles, 128 S. Cadillac Ave., Newbury, Montana 59711, by Monday, March 2, 1998, to avoid paying a penalty. _____

5. Join the campaign against cigarette smoking by sending a contribution to GASP, P.O. Box 632, College Park, Maryland 20740. _____

6. Charles Lindbergh, flying the "Spirit of Saint Louis," left Mineola New York on May 20 1927 and arrived in Paris France on May 21, 1927. _____

7. Write to the Magicians' Guild of America at 20 West 40th Street, New York, New York 10018, for membership information. _____

GROUP ACTIVITY

Review of Lessons 1, 2, and 3

Insert commas where necessary.

Last summer Juan Romero a schoolteacher and his family drove across the country from Pueblo Colorado to Washington D.C. They left Pueblo on July 2 in their new brown tightly packed station wagon and they planned to return on August 31. Since they were going to be away a long time Mr. Romero had asked the post office to forward their mail to them at their friends' house 22654 Constitution Drive Washington D.C. After leaving Pueblo Mr. Romero and his wife Julia and their four children Alfredo Maria Pedro and Juan Jr. drove south to Santa Fe New Mexico. As the Romeros drove east along Route 40 they passed an Indian trading post. "Let's stop here" Alfredo shouted. When the car rolled to a stop Mr. and Mrs. Romero gave each child some money to spend in the trading post. In a short while they returned to the car carrying Indian arrowheads peace pipes pottery and a feather headdress. The family who were now even more crowded together in the car drove through Texas Arkansas and Tennessee. Mrs. Romero could tell that the children were bored so she persuaded her husband to stop in Nashville at Opryland USA. In a flash the four youngsters escaped from the back seat to buy autographed records a large plastic guitar a harmonica and a white cowboy hat. Once back on the road Mr. Romero said that he would not stop again until they had reached their destination. However before they had traveled much farther they had made several stops at parrot jungles alligator farms and other roadside tourist attractions even stopping at the beach in Norfolk Virginia. "On our trip back to Colorado" said Mrs. Romero "we'll have no room to sit if we stop at one more place." From then on therefore they just bought food which filled their stomachs but not the car. After seeing the sights in Washington D.C. they returned to Pueblo and the whole family agreed that they had had a memorable vacation.

Check your answers to the paragraph above with those of your group. As a group, plan a trip that you might take. Make an outline of the places you would like to go. Then using the Romero family's experience as a guide, write a paragraph describing the things you expect to see and do. Try to include the following items punctuated with the appropriate commas in your sentences.

1. Adjectives before a noun
2. Words that interrupt
3. Words of direct address
4. Nonessential words, phrases, or clauses
5. Direct quotations
6. Dates, geographical names, and addresses

Summary of Chapter 9

Choose words from the box on the next page to complete these sentences. There are ten rules for using commas that should help you to be certain about comma placement.

1. First, use commas between two _____ clauses connected by coordinating connectives.

2. Second, use commas to separate words, phrases, or clauses in a

   _____. There should be more than _____ items listed.

3. Third, place a comma after a long introductory _____ .

4. Fourth, place a comma after a _____ clause at the beginning of a sentence.

5. Fifth, use commas to separate _____ or more adjectives that modify the same noun.

6. Sixth, use commas on both sides of a word (or group of words) that

   _____ the flow of thought in a sentence.

7. Seventh, use commas to _____ the names and titles of people spoken to directly.

8. Eighth, use commas to enclose words, phrases, and clauses containing _____ material.

9. Ninth, use commas to set off _____ quotations from the rest of the sentence.

10. Tenth, use commas after every _____ in addresses or dates.

direct	subordinate	nonessential
interrupts	series	direct
main	three	two
item	set off	phrase

Sentence Combining

In this exercise you will be combining words, phrases, and clauses that you have been learning to punctuate correctly in this chapter. In the example that follows, the combined sentence opens with an introductory subordinate clause and two prepositional phrases. Notice the placement of the commas. Why are there no commas after *several* and *dozen*? Are the commas after *mountainside* and *lights* optional?

1. Astronomers meet on the darkest nights.
2. The nights are darkest during the week after the new moon.
3. These are amateur astronomers.

No one working with these students claims to know how to keep all students in school. Counselors, teachers, and administrators are in the front lines of what seems at times to be a losing battle. Actually, this problem should be everyone's concern since uneducated, unemployed citizens affect us all.

Write a composition discussing the reasons that students drop out of junior or senior high school. Suggest some strategies to keep these students in school. Your topic sentence should state your opinion and give your reader some idea of the strategies you will discuss. Give examples from your own observation and experience. Consider the community, the family, the school, and the students themselves as you plan your paragraphs. Refer to Chapter 1 as a guide to planning, organizing, and writing your paper. When you proofread your rough draft, check the use of commas. Are any missing, or are any unnecessary?

ALTERNATE WRITING ASSIGNMENT

Read the sentences in Exercise 1F over again. The subject of "social lying" is one that is familiar to almost everyone. Think back to the times you have had to lie to be socially tactful: "What a pretty dress!" or "What a great haircut you got!" You can probably supply many more examples of tiny white lies you have told or been told. Sometimes a person even masquerades as someone else to achieve a goal. Think, for example, of police who assume false identities to infiltrate drug rings or of civil rights advocates who pose as apartment applicants. Many philosophical and religious traditions condemn all lies and deceit. But where do you draw the line? Explain your personal reactions to telling little white lies.

Refer to Chapter 1 to guide you in planning your composition. Show your rough draft to a classmate and consider the suggestions offered before attempting to write a final draft.

Chapter 9 Practice Test: Commas

Name _____

Date _____ Class Time _____

Instructor _____

I. Insert commas where they are necessary. Some sentences may not require commas.

1. The senator in the meantime had difficulty raising money for a reelection campaign.

2. Orrin likes to watch movies that were made during the 40s.

3. No one in our tour group but Mr. Froloff spoke Russian.

4. Many schools have signed up for advertiser-supported classroom television in spite of criticism from teachers administrators and parents.

5. While painting the women talked about how to clean paintbrushes.

6. My new travel bag which collapses to fit under an airline seat carries all I need for a weeklong stay.

7. Spring officially began on March 21 at 4:19 P.M.

8. Clark calls himself a collector of valuable beverage containers but his family refers to him as a pack rat.

9. Wall Street a narrow street in lower Manhattan is one of the world's great financial districts.

10. Readers would you like to learn how to make $85,000 a year in the real estate market?

11. Everyone who has seen that film seems to think it will win an Oscar.

12. We sat on the pier and watched the surfers while we ate our picnic lunch.

13. "Housing affordability" Senator Bidwell asserted "is a national issue."

Chapter 9 Practice Test: Commas (cont.)

14. When the newspaper printed the correction it appeared in a brief paragraph buried on an inside page.

15. Jesse couldn't decide whether to buy a bicycle a surfboard a camera or a radio with his prize money.

16. Linda wrote to the Cherry Blossom Festival Committee P.O. Box 343324 Washington D.C. 20033 for information.

17. To establish a credit rating Wes began using charge accounts and credit cards for major purchases.

18. Most cats don't like to exercise and can gain weight quickly when they are overfed.

19. The Atlantic Computer Center at 1852 Kingsdale Avenue has computers for sale at reasonable prices.

20. The experienced district attorney asked the witness a series of tough probing questions.

II. Following the directions, write sentences of your own.

1. Write a sentence containing two main clauses joined by a coordinating connective. Punctuate the sentence correctly.

_____

_____

2. Write a sentence containing two or more adjectives that modify the same noun. Punctuate the sentence correctly.

_____

_____

Chapter 9 Practice Test: Commas (cont.)

3. Write a sentence that contains an introductory phrase or an introductory subordinate clause. Punctuate the sentence correctly.

_____

_____

4. Write a sentence that contains a complete address, including both the city and the state. Punctuate the sentence correctly.

_____

_____

Chapter 9 Answer Key

Exercise 1A
1. food, but
2. pigments, and
3. compound, and
4. pigment, or
5. pink, but

Exercise 1B
The unnecessary commas have been removed in this paragraph.

The government has spent billions of dollars to protect our shorelines from the destruction of storms, but coastal geologists maintain that these efforts only accelerate the damage. Engineers build structures such as jetties or breakwaters yet fail to stop the erosion. Geologists say that this policy is based on a misunderstanding for all the engineers' good intentions. Beaches do not need these barriers and actually provide protection for the continent. Sand builds up in sand dunes when the ocean is calm, and waves move this sand out to the sea bottom during a storm. Beaches then become flatter, so waves break earlier and cause less erosion. Beaches that have neither seawalls nor bulkheads to interrupt the natural cycle rebuild their defenses as calmer waters carry the sand back to the shore. Miles of east-coast beaches have disappeared after 70 years of engineered beach construction, and the loss can only continue if the advice of geologists is ignored.

Exercise 1C
Your instructor will check your sentences.

Exercise 1D
1. Yes   2. Yes   3. No   4. Yes   5. No   6. No   7. No

Exercise 1E
The commas in sentences 2, 3, 4, and 7 are optional.
1. Among the staples of southwestern cooking, the chile is probably the most essential.
2. By the way, New Mexicans spell "chile" with a final "e" not an "i."
3. In addition, the chile is not actually a pepper as Columbus believed when he "discovered" it on one of his voyages.
4. In fact, the capsicum (chile) is a distant cousin of the tomato and is classified by botanists as a fruit.
5. Ranging from mild to incredibly hot, the chile's color depends on when it is harvested.
6. Produced by the same plant, green chilies are picked early and red chilies late in the season after they have matured.
7. Moreover, color is no guide to pungency; red or green sauce can be mild or hot depending on each specific batch.
8. While eating a food flavored with the chile, you may suddenly need to put out the fire, but eat something sweet or creamy instead of reaching for a glass of ice water.

Exercise 1F
1. Yes   2. No   3. (comma optional)   4. Yes   5. Yes   6. (comma optional)

Exercise 1G

Although a comet looks very beautiful as it sails across the sky, it is not much more than a dirty snowball. A comet consists of about 25 percent dust and chunks of rocky or metallic material and about 75 percent ice. While the ice is mainly frozen water, it also contains a mixture of methane, ammonia, and carbon dioxide molecules. When a comet passes close to the sun, it loses some of its matter. Some of its ice turns to a gas form as a comet nears the sun. The gases spread out around the nucleus, forming a large, thin atmosphere called a "coma," which glows in the sunlight. If the supply of gases from the nucleus changes, a comet can brighten and fade noticeably. As a comet approaches the sun, a solar wind sweeps a comet's gases away from the sun. So a second tail consisting of dust particles may also appear. Although this dust tail is shorter than the gas tail, it may also be visible from earth. In fact, some comets have been observed to have as many as nine tails.

Exercise 1H

1. No   2. Yes   3. Yes   4. No   5. Yes   6. Yes   7. No

Exercise 2A

1. In the early morning, the joggers run effortlessly along the deserted, shell-strewn beach.
2. Even on gray, foggy, chilly mornings, they wear only tank tops and brief running shorts.
3. Bicycle riders on the nearby, winding concrete bike path must be alert as jogging parents push their small children in vehicles especially constructed for this purpose.
4. Some cyclists are also accompanied by their youngsters riding in low, plastic-curtained trailers attached to the back of the bikes.
5. When the morning overcast begins to burn off, the second shift appears: volleyball players head for the courts, and bikini-clad sunseekers lie down on their brightly colored beach towels for a serious tanning session.

Exercise 2B

1. Yes   2. No   3. No   4. Yes   5. Yes

Exercise 2C

Most experts agree, despite conclusive evidence, that the lemon tree probably originated in southeast Asia in the vicinity of Burma thousands of years ago. Although this evergreen tree is sensitive to freezing weather, the fruit does best, as a matter of fact, exposed to the occasional cold snap that a hot, humid climate lacks. California growers, as a result, use wind machines and heaters in their groves to regulate temperature. Lemon trees, under ideal conditions, can bear buds, flowers, developing fruit, and mature fruit all at the same time. Citrus trees, moreover, require a fair amount of water; rain, however, can damage the fruit. Every part of the fruit, we are told, from seed to peel has a use, from food preparation and general household use to medicinal and commercial applications. Most of us, without a doubt, use lemons most frequently as flavor intensifiers. In some cultures people, indeed, know the meaning of using the entire fruit: they eat the lemon as we would an apple, peel and all.

Exercise 2D

1. No   2. Yes   3. No   4. Yes   5. No

Exercise 2E
1. "I don't entirely agree, Jim, with your position," said Ella.
2. "Ella, you never agree with me," said Jim.
3. "I agree with you most of the time, Jim," said Ella.
4. "Well then, Ella, why don't you agree with me now?" said Jim.
5. "Jim, I cannot agree with you because you are wrong," said Ella.
6. "Ella, tell me that you love me anyway," said Jim.

Exercise 2F
1. No   2. No   3. No   4. Yes   5. No
1. Scott,   2. Manager, Mrs.   3. requested, sir,   5. you, one and all,

Exercise 3A
1. My friend Carla Caraway went to New York to get a job as a dancer. (No commas needed.)
2. A young woman, alone in a strange city, must learn how to take care of herself.
3. She auditioned for Judith Jamison, the famous choreographer of the Alvin Ailey company.
4. Carla, breathless and exhausted, waited after the audition to hear the choreographer's opinion.
5. Carla joined the Ailey company, one of the best dance companies in the world.

Exercise 3B
1. The talented American contralto, Marian Anderson, who had sung at the White House, was barred from singing in Constitution Hall in Washington.
2. Instead, Ms. Anderson sang at the Lincoln Memorial before 75,000 people who had gathered in support of her.
3. Three Aaron Copland ballets, drawing upon American themes, are *Billy the Kid, Rodeo,* and *Appalachian Spring.*
4. Copland wrote *Appalachian Spring* for Martha Graham, choreographer and dancer.
5. Ernest Hemingway, an American author, began his first job as a newspaper reporter at the age of eighteen.
6. no commas
7. no commas
8. Gilbert Stuart, an early American painter, is best known for his portraits of George Washington.
9. Frank Lloyd Wright, one of the first architects to use glass and metal walls for office buildings, achieved early recognition outside the United States.
10. no commas

Exercise 3C
1. "I can never do these homework assignments," Gary complained.
2. "Well," said his mother, "you haven't even tried."
3. "I never learn anything in that class," he said, "so what's the point?"
4. "Besides," he said to her, "I have a date tonight."
5. "Gary, you should do your assignment before you go out," his mother advised.
6. "I have to leave in one hour," he told his mother.
7. "If you begin to work right now," she said, "you will have plenty of time."
8. "I'll do it when I return," he said as he left the house.
9. "Gary, come right back here," she called, "and finish your homework."
10. "You might as well relax, Mom," said Gary's sister. "He has already gone."

Exercise 3D

1. "Greg, did you hear about the recent triathalon competition in Hawaii?" Diane asked.
2. "I hadn't realized," she continued, "how popular the sport has become."
3. "The athlete who attempts the Ironman competition must be in top physical condition, Diane," Greg replied.
4. "Most other triathalon competitions, as a matter of fact, are not as demanding as the Ironman," he pointed out.
5. "If your goal, Greg, is just to complete the triathalon," Diane said, "you don't need to worry about speed."
6. The doctor said, "Hypothermia can be a threat to the swimmers if the water is especially cold."
7. "One of the greatest dangers to the athletes during the marathon run," he added, "is dehydration."
8. "For most triathalons, competitors are required to sign waivers releasing the promoters from responsibility for the athletes' safety," Greg said.
9. Diane remarked, "The most successful athletes, as I might have expected, train under conditions similar to those of the competition."
10. "Competitors should train for at least three months," the doctor advised, "in each of the three sports: swimming, running, and cycling."

Exercise 3E

1. George will move to Las Vegas, Nevada, in January.
2. His address has been The Stanford Arms Hotel, Apt. 10, 536 W. 18th Street, Rittman, Indiana 46206, for the last six years.
3. We will forward his mail to his new address: The Pyramid Hotel, Las Vegas, Nevada 89501.
4. Bill Wilson is a salesperson for Fashion Clothing Co., 2473 White Plains Road, Bronx, New York 10111.
5. On 2 April 1999, Bill traveled from New York to Dallas, Texas, to attend a fashion show.
6. The fashion show was held at the Plaza Hotel, 8 Fifth Street, Dallas, Texas.

Exercise 3F

1. No   2. Yes   3. Yes   4. Yes   5. Yes   6. No   7. Yes

Summary of Chapter 9

1. main   2. series, three   3. phrase   4. subordinate   5. two   6. interrupts
7. set off   8. nonessential   9. direct   10. item

Punctuation, Capitalization, and Usage

Lesson 1 ✳ *Period, Question Mark, and Exclamation Point*

When you speak, you use pauses, gestures, and changes in the pitch of your voice to signal the units of thought. When you read, marks of punctuation provided by the writer guide you. When you write, you also must provide guideposts for your readers.

Period (.)

1. Use a period at the end of a sentence.

   Example: The Nguyen family planned their trip carefull**y.** They studied maps and travel books.

2. Use a period after an abbreviation.

   Examples: Mr. Jones   etc.
   Prof. Anderson   P.M.
   Dr. Brown   B.A.

3. Use a period after initials.

   Examples: K. C. Jones   Howard C. Smith

B. The semicolon is used before adverbial connectives like <u>however</u>, <u>nevertheless</u>, <u>consequently</u>, <u>therefore</u>, and <u>then</u> to join two main clauses.

Example: They want to travel through several states in a short time; therefore, they will join a tour group for this trip.

2. The semicolon is used as a separator. The semicolon is used between words or word groups in a series if the items in the series contain one or more commas.

Example: Their travel plans include Philadelphia, Pennsylvania; Boston, Massachusetts; and Washington, D.C.

Colon (:)

1. The colon is used at the end of a main clause to introduce a list.

Example: On their next trip, they would like to visit four other states: Arizona, Utah, Wyoming, and South Dakota.

2. The colon often comes after words like <u>the following</u> or <u>as follows</u>.

Example: On this tour they plan to see <u>the following</u> places: the Grand Canyon, Bryce Canyon National Park, Yellowstone National Park, and Mount Rushmore.

No colon is used between a verb and the objects or completers that follow it.

Examples: a. The tour bus carried the passengers, their guide, and
      their luggage.

      b. In Washington, D.C., the three places Ann especially
      enjoyed were Mt. Vernon, the Lincoln Memorial, and the
      Smithsonian.

3. The colon is used after a salutation in a business letter.

Example: Dear Mr. Wilkins:
Please consider me for the position of junior accountant in your firm.

4.   The colon separates the hours and minutes when you are writing the time.

> **Example:**   Our class meets daily at 10:30 A.M.

Do not use a colon if no minutes are given.

> **Example:**   Our class meets daily at 10 A.M.

EXERCISE 2A

Insert semicolons or colons where they are needed in the following sentences.

1.   Men of the Native American Hopi tribe don masks and costumes in their religious ceremonies to impersonate supernatural beings called kachinas these kachinas can represent both good and evil spirits.

2.   Hopi children believe in kachinas in much the same way other children believe in Santa Claus in fact, male relatives in their guise as kachinas sometimes bring gifts to the children.

3.   Hopi kachina dolls are small dolls made to resemble the kachinas they are carved from dried cottonwood roots and painted with poster paints.

4.   The names of many of these dolls are descriptive, such as cross-legged kachina, and they are often named for the following birds and mammals rooster, bear, eagle, and badger.

5.   Since Hopis are a farming people and rain is vital to their crops, dolls often show these symbols for rain and water lightning bolts on the head, a forehead band symbolizing a rainbow, feathers on the head standing for clouds, and the fringe of a sash representing rain.

6.   The dolls are not religious objects they hang upon the walls or from the rafters of the house where they serve the important educational purpose of familiarizing the child with the many different kachinas of the Hopi people.

GROUP ACTIVITY

Add colons, semicolons, periods, or question marks as needed in the following letter.

Mrs Stephanie Culp
Priority Management Systems, Inc
1379 Heather Lane
Baltimore, MD

Dear Mrs Culp

I recently read an article that explained how your company, Priority Management Systems, Inc , helps make business offices more efficient I would like your advice about the following problems I have a messy desk, an overflowing file cabinet, and a drawer full of unpaid bills

The article stated that you advise executives as follows set up a system of baskets on the desk to sort out the papers however I can never find the time to stop and rearrange my papers

Would you be willing to visit my office to help me get organized I would be very appreciative furthermore I would be willing to pay you well for your time

Please send me a copy of your book, *How to Get Organized When You Don't Have the Time,* as soon as possible

Sincerely yours,

Annette Harris

After completing the above exercise, get together with two or three classmates to check each other's work. Cut out an article that describes a service or an advertisement that offers one from a newspaper or magazine and bring it to class. As a group, choose one of the articles from among those you and the members of your group have brought to class and respond to it in a letter as the writer of the above letter did. Use the patterns below as a guide for your sentences.

1. Letter salutation: _____

2. Main clause: list. _____

3. Main clause; however, main clause. _____

4. Main clause; main clause. _____

Lesson 3 ✳ *Quotation Marks*

Direct Quotations

Quotation marks are used primarily in direct quotations. Put quotation marks around the exact words of the speaker.

Examples: 1. Pete called, "Anyone for tennis?"
2. "I would rather play golf," replied Tiger.

> Note the punctuation for direct quotations: Use a comma before the direct quotation. Use quotation marks around the speaker's exact words. Use a capital letter for the first word of the direct quotation.

Split Quotations

Examples: 1. "Come on, Monica," Steffi said. "Let's play tennis instead of watching TV."
2. "But, Steffi," Monica asked, "don't you want to see if Tiger wins this match on TV?"

Split Quotations

Note the punctuation for split quotations:

In 1, there are two sentences. The first one begins with Come and ends with said. Therefore, the L of Let's is capitalized as the first word of the second sentence.

In 2, the word don't begins with a small letter because the words on either side of Monica asked are the two parts of a single sentence.

End Punctuation in Quotations

Periods and commas are always placed <u>inside</u> quotation marks.

Examples: 1.   "Let's go shoot a few baskets, Michael."
2.   "I'm playing in a golf tournament today," answered Michael.

Question marks and exclamation points are placed *outside* quotation marks except when the quotation itself is a question or an exclamation.

Example: Did Andre say, "I want to play tennis"?

Exceptions: 1.   Pete called, "Anyone for tennis?" (The quotation is a question.)
2.   The fans shouted, "Touchdown! Touchdown!" (The quotation is an exclamation.)

Quotations Within Quotations

Single quotation marks are used to enclose quoted material within a direct quotation.

Example: He frequently says, "Remember President Kennedy's words: 'If a free society cannot help the many who are poor, it cannot save the few who are rich.' "

Unnecessary Quotation Marks   Do not enclose an indirect quotation in quotation marks. It is a report in different words of what a speaker or writer said. The word "that" usually indicates the following words are an indirect quotation.

Examples: Marcus said, "I'll never eat at Joe's Pizza Palace again." (direct quotation)
Marcus <u>said that</u> he would never eat at Joe's Pizza Palace <u>again</u>. (Indirect quotation, do *not* use quotation marks.)

Quotation Marks and Underlining in Titles

A. Use quotation marks for short works.

1. title of article
2. title of chapter

3. title of short story
4. title of song
5. title of poem

B. In handwritten or typed work, underline the words that would be italicized in printed material.

Examples: Warren saves all his <u>National Geographic</u> magazines.
Warren saves all his <u>*National Geographic*</u> magazines.

1. title of book
2. title of magazine
3. title of newspaper
4. title of play, movie, work of art
5. title of record album
6. foreign words
7. words used as words

Examples:

1. Have you read the article "Getting the Airmail off the Ground" in the May issue of <u>Smithsonian</u>? (title of an article and title of a magazine)

2. Stan never gets tired of watching *Star Wars* and *2001: A Space Odyssey*. (titles of movies)

3. The English instructor assigned two short stories for us to read: "Everyday Use" by Alice Walker and "A & P" by Eudora Welty. (titles of short stories)

4. Wynton Marsalis won a Pulitzer Prize in music for his jazz oratorio *Blood on the Fields*, which is a history of slavery and a love story. (title of a work of art)

5. "Guiding Children's Book Selection," a chapter in <u>Children & Books</u>, contains standards for evaluating books. (title of a chapter and title of a book)

6. The word <u>freedom</u> is difficult to define. (word used as a word)

C. Never use quotation marks around the title of your own composition.

EXERCISE 3A

Use quotation marks or underline as needed in the following sentences.

1. Have you seen The Tempest at the Old Globe Theater yet? he asked.

2. Ben said that he had just returned the book Beloved, by Toni Morrison, to the library.

3. Can you believe that Mr. Marquez said, Read the chapter called Causes of the Civil War by tomorrow?

4. The article A Private Solution to a Public Problem in this morning's NY Times offers one more proposal to ease the state's financial crisis.

5. When Rose was three years old, her favorite poem was The Owl and the Pussycat.

6. Oprah Winfrey, 20/20, and NYPD Blue are three television shows that Ron always watches.

EXERCISE 3B

Write your own sentences including the items in the parentheses.

1. (a split quotation) _____

_____

2. (a direct quotation that is a question) _____

_____

3. (an indirect quotation) _____

_____

4. (a chapter in a book) _____

_____

5. (titles of two songs) _____

_____

Lesson 4 ✻ *Other Marks of Punctuation— Hyphen and Dash*

Hyphen (-)

1. Use a hyphen to join two or more words that serve as a single adjective describing a noun.

    Example: My son and I had a heart-to-heart talk.

2. Use a hyphen to divide a word at the end of a line of writing or typing. If you are unsure about the correct syllable division, consult a dictionary.

    Example: Hazel and Hugh discussed their son's problems together.

Never divide a word of one syllable at the end of a line. Whenever possible, avoid dividing a word.

3. Use a hyphen with fractions, compound nouns, and compound numbers.

    Examples: thirty-five   forty-ninth   father-in-law
    self-improvement   one-half

Dash (—)

A dash signals an interruption in the sentence. Use dashes before and after interrupters.

Example: Some—but not all—of the problems were difficult.

Note: On a keyboard, strike the hyphen key twice to form the dash. Do not overuse the dash. It should not be used as a substitute for commas, semicolons, or colons just because you are unsure about which to use.

EXERCISE 4A

Insert hyphens where they are needed in the following sentences.

1. One half of my income goes for rent.
2. Adlai Stevenson was not a well known politician before he ran for the presidency.
3. President Franklin D. Roosevelt said in his second inaugural speech, "I see one third of a nation ill housed, ill clad, ill nourished."
4. Margot works as a freelance writer; she edits self help books.
5. Two thirds of the Senate voted for the proposed insurance bill cov ering high risk drivers.

Lesson 5 *Capital Letters*

EXERCISE 5A

Answer the following questions to see how many uses of capital letters you already know. Refer to an almanac or an encyclopedia if necessary.

1. Write the title and the first and last names of the sixteenth U.S. president.

   ____

2. In what state was he born?

   ____

3. Write the season of the year and the name of the month in which he was born.

   ____

4. What is the name of the holiday we observe in his honor?

   ____

5. What political party did he belong to?

        _____

6. What war was fought during his administration?

        _____

7. Give the title of a famous speech that he made honoring U.S. soldiers who fell in battle. Near what town and in what state did he make it?

        _____

8. What is the name of the proclamation he made?

        _____

9. Write the full name of the person who assassinated him.

        _____

10. In what building did the assassination take place?

        _____

11. In what city and state is he buried?

        _____

12. What is the name of the river near his Memorial?

        _____

13. Write the title of a college course in which you might learn more about this president.

        _____

14. Write the address of the present residence of U.S. presidents. Include the name of the street.

        _____

2. We visited the liberty bell in philadelphia last august.   _____

_____

_____

_____

3. i don't think that the senator should have traveled at government expense to the french riviera, Do you?   _____

_____

_____

_____

_____

_____

4. Paul likes to watch *good morning america* every morning before going to work at boeing aircraft co.   _____

_____

_____

_____

_____

_____

5. Chuck said, "let's go to a Rock Concert next saturday."   _____

_____

_____

_____

_____

Lesson 6 ✳ *Usage*

Words that sound alike or look alike can cause many problems in spelling. Study the following words and refer to these pages when you are writing your paragraphs.

A/An/And

1. Use a before words beginning with consonants or consonant sounds.

   Examples: a chair, a boy, a tree, a picture, a year

2. Use an before words beginning with vowels (a, e, i, o, u) or a silent *h*.

   Examples: an apple, an egg, an idea, an honor, an opal

3. And connects words, phrases, and clauses. It is a coordinating connective.

   Example: Dan plays both the guitar and the piano.

EXERCISE 6A

Use these words in sentences of your own.

1. (a)_____

2. (an)_____

3. (and)_____

Accept/Except

1. Accept is a verb. It means to receive gladly; to agree to.

   Example: Will Julie accept the job offer in Alaska?

2. Except is a preposition. It means excluding, but.

   Example: None of us has been to Alaska except Ward.

EXERCISE 6B

Fill in the blanks with the correct words:

1. Stan will _____ the award for our division at the luncheon.

2. Everyone attended the luncheon _____ Jerry.

Use these words in sentences of your own.

1. (accept)_____

2. (except)_____

Advice/Advise

1. Advice is a noun. It means an opinion, from one not immediately concerned, about what could or should be done about a problem.

   Example: We all depend on Sally for advice.

2. Advise is a verb. It means to offer advice; to counsel. Note: Pronounce the s like a z.

   Example: She advised me to petition for graduation soon.

EXERCISE 6C

Fill in the blanks with the correct words:

1. Can the counselor_____ me what courses to take next semester?

2. Will you follow her _____?

Use these words in sentences of your own.

1. (advice) _____

2. (advise) _____

Affect/Effect

1. <u>Affect</u> is usually used as a verb. It means to have an influence on; to touch or move the emotions of someone.

> ***Example:***   The drop in sales may <u>affect</u> the company's future plans.

2. <u>Effect</u> is usually used as a noun. It means the final result; the outcome.

> ***Example:***   All employees felt the <u>effect</u> of the budget cut.

EXERCISE 6D

Fill in the blanks with the correct words:

1. The recent cold weather may _____ the fruit crop.

2. The _____ of the freeze became quickly apparent in the rising price of produce.

Use these words in sentences of your own.

1. (affect) _____

2. (effect) _____

Already/All Ready

1. <u>Already</u> is an adverb. It means by this time; before; previously.

> ***Example:***   They had <u>already</u> bought their tickets.

2. <u>All ready</u> is an adjective. It is used to express complete readiness.

> ***Example:***   The tourists were <u>all ready</u> to board the plane.

EXERCISE 6E

Fill in the blanks with the correct words:

1. Is everyone _____ to go to the beach?

2. We have _____ packed a lunch to take with us.

Use these words in sentences of your own.

1. (already) _____

2. (all ready) _____

Mini Review 1

Underline the correct form of the word in parentheses.

1. The (affect, effect) of his (advice, advise) was greater than he had expected.

2. We were (all ready, already) to go (accept, except) for Denise.

3. The drive was pleasant (except, accept) for (an, a) unexpected detour.

4. The new ruling has (already, all ready) (affected, effected) office morale.

5. Would you (advice, advise) me to (accept, except) the position?

Dessert/Desert

1. Dessert is a noun. It means the last course of a lunch or a dinner.

    Example: His favorite dessert is apple pie.

2. Desert is used as a noun to mean barren land, an area of little rainfall.

    Example: The Sahara Desert is in Africa.

3. Desert is used as a verb to mean to leave or abandon.

    Example: The soldier deserted his post during the battle.

EXERCISE 6F

Fill in the blanks with the correct words:

1. Maria prepared fried bananas for _____.

2. Many flowers bloom in the _____ in the spring.

3. Brian's father _____ his family.

Use these words in sentences of your own.

1. (dessert) _____

2. (desert, n.) _____

3. (desert, v.) _____

Its/It's

1. It's is the contraction of it is or it has.

Example: It's time to feed the cat.

2. Its is the possessive form of the pronoun it.

Example: The cat doesn't like its food.

EXERCISE 6G

Fill in the blanks with the correct words:

1. _____ been raining all day.

2. The bear stayed in _____ cave during the storm.

Use these words in sentences of your own.

1. (its) _____

2. (it's) _____

Know/No

1. Know is a verb. It means to understand; to be familiar with; to be certain of.

Example: Who knows the way to the museum?

2. No is a negative. It means not any; not one.

Example: We have no map.

EXERCISE 6H

Fill in the blanks with the correct words:

1. Kathy _____ longer lives in Denver.

2. Dave _____ her new address in Portland.

Use these words in sentences of your own.

1. (know) _____

2. (no) _____

Lead/Led

1. Lead is a noun. It is pronounced like led. It means a soft, bluish white element used in pencils. If it is used as a verb, it is pronounced "leed." It means to show the way by going in advance; to conduct.

Examples: Lead is a dense metal.
The conductor will lead the orchestra.

2. Led is the past tense and the past participle of the verb lead.

Example: The guide led us through the forest.

EXERCISE 6I

Fill in the blanks with the correct words:

1. Early alchemists tried to make gold out of _____.

2. The sergeant _____ his men into battle.

Use these words in sentences of your own.

1. (lead) _____

2. (led) _____

Loose/Lose

1. <u>Loose</u> is an adjective. It means not tight fitting; too large; not fastened.

   Example: The string on that package was too <u>loose</u>.

2. <u>Lose</u> is a verb. Pronounce the <u>s</u> like a <u>z</u>. It means to misplace; to fail to win.

   Example: I hope the package won't <u>lose</u> its wrappings.

EXERCISE 6J

Fill in the blanks with the correct words:

1. I will _____ these keys if I don't buy a new key ring.

2. The key ring broke, and the _____ keys fell to the pavement.

Use these words in sentences of your own.

1. (loose) _____

2. (lose) _____

Mini Review 2

Underline the correct form of the word in parentheses.

1. The guide (lead, led) the hikers through the (desert, dessert).

2. We (no, know) a restaurant that serves the best (desserts, deserts) in town.

3. There is (no, know) (lead, led) in a pencil.

4. The dog (lead, led) (its, it's) puppies to the food.

5. Tighten that screw; (its, it's) (lose, loose) again.

6. I (no, know) that Bob will (lose, loose) our respect if he (desserts, deserts) the group now.

Past/Passed

1. Past is a noun. It means the time before the present. It can be used as an adjective to describe that which has already occurred.

   Example: Try not to think about the past.

2. Passed is the past tense and the past participle form of the verb pass. It means succeeded in, handed in, or went by.

   Example: Andrea waved and smiled as she passed by us.
   Larry passed in his term paper on time.

EXERCISE 6K

Fill in the blanks with the correct words:

1. Henry liked to tell us about his _____ experiences.

2. Tom _____ by our house last night about this time.

Use these words in sentences of your own.

1. (past) _____

2. (passed) _____

Personal/Personnel

1. Personal is an adjective. It means something private or one's own. Pronounce this word with the accent on the first syllable.

    Example: My diary is my personal property.

2. Personnel is a noun. It means the group of people employed by a business or a service. Pronounce this word with the accent on the last syllable. It may take either a singular or a plural verb.

    Example: The president of the company sent a memo to all of the personnel.

❋ **EXERCISE 6L** ❋

Fill in the blanks with the correct words:

1. Please don't ask so many _____ questions.

2. She was vice-president in charge of _____ in our company.

Use these words in sentences of your own.

1. (personal) _____

2. (personnel) _____

Principal/Principle

1. <u>Principal</u> is usually used as a noun. It means a person who is a leader, someone who is in charge. When it is used as an adjective, it means leading or chief.

Example: The <u>principal</u> of the high school spoke at the assembly.

2. <u>Principle</u> is a noun. It refers to basic truths, rules of human conduct, and fundamental laws.

Example: Our constitution is based on the <u>principles</u> of democracy.

EXERCISE 6M

Fill in the blanks with the correct words:

1. I know him to be a man of high _____.

2. The _____ partner in the law firm signed the contract.

Use these words in sentences of your own.

1. (principal) _____

2. (principle) _____

Quiet/Quite

1. <u>Quiet</u> means silent, free of noise.

Example: I need a <u>quiet</u> place to study.

2. <u>Quite</u> means entirely; really; rather.

Example: You have been <u>quite</u> busy all day.

EXERCISE 6N

Fill in the blanks with the correct words:

1. The Smith family lives on a very _____ street.

2. The street is not _____ as _____ as it used to be.

Use these words in sentences of your own.

1. (quiet) _____

2. (quite) _____

Suppose/Supposed

Suppose is a verb. It means to assume to be true; to guess; to think.

Example: Do you suppose it will rain today?

Note: The verb suppose is often used in the passive and is followed by *to*. Do not forget to add the **d** to the verb: supposed.
Supposed to, in this sense, means to expect or require.

Example: He is supposed to clean his room.

The example means that he is expected to clean his room.

EXERCISE 6O

Fill in the blanks with the correct words:

1. This is _____ to be one of the best restaurants in town.

2. I _____ we will arrive home by noon.

Use these words in sentences of your own.

1. (suppose) _____

2. (supposed) _____

Then/Than

1. Then is an adverb. It means at that time; next in time, space, or order.

Example: Tom and Rhonda had dinner, and then Rhonda watched TV.

2. Than is used in comparative statements to introduce the second item.

Example: Tom said he would rather wash the dinner dishes than watch TV.

EXERCISE 6P

Fill in the blanks with the correct words:

1. Mike gets up earlier ______ Jay does.
2. He prepares breakfast, and ______ he takes a shower.

Use these words in sentences of your own.

1. (then) ____________________
2. (than) ____________________

There/Their/They're

1. There shows direction. It means at that place. It is often used to introduce a thought, as in there is or there are.

Example: There are no tickets left for the World Series games.

2. Their is the possessive form of the pronoun they. It means belonging to them.

Example: Some of the fans have already received their tickets in the mail.

3. They're is a contraction of the two words they are.

Example: They're very happy people.

| ✳ | **EXERCISE 6Q** | ✳ |

Fill in the blanks with the correct words:

1. _____ is going to be a parade on St. Patrick's Day.

2. I hear that _____ giving a party in _____ home to celebrate the holiday.

Use these words in sentences of your own.

1. (there) _____

2. (their) _____

3. (they're) _____

Mini Review 3

Underline the correct form of the word in parentheses.

1. Hal's (principals, principles) would not let him charge (personnel, personal) expenses to his expense account.

2. I had (suppose, supposed) that he would rather fly (then, than) drive to the conference.

3. We were (quiet, quite) surprised by the changes in the company (personal, personnel).

4. Based on (passed, past) experience, the organizers were (supposed, suppose) to reserve a bigger ballroom for the meeting.

5. (They're, their, there) expecting a larger crowd (then, than) they had last year.

7. Are, Sugar Bowl, New Year's Day
8. In, I, Saturdays
9. Yellowstone National Park, United States
10. My, Hemingway, I

Exercise 5C
1. My son brushes with Crest toothpaste every morning.
2. We visited the Liberty Bell in Philadelphia last August.
3. I don't think that the senator should have traveled at government expense to the French Riviera, do you?
4. Paul likes to watch *Good Morning America* every morning before going to work at Boeing Aircraft Co.
5. Chuck said, "Let's go to a rock concert next Saturday."

Exercises 6A-6W
Your instructor will check your sentences.

Exercise 6B
1. accept   2. except

Exercise 6C
1. advise   2. advice

Exercise 6D
1. affected   2. effect

Exercise 6E
1. all ready   2. already

Exercise 6F
1. dessert   2. desert   3. deserted

Exercise 6G
1. It's   2. its

Exercise 6H
1. no   2. knows

Exercise 6I
1. lead   2. led

Exercise 6J
1. lose   2. loose

Exercise 6K
1. past   2. passed

Exercise 6L
1. personal   2. personnel

Exercise 6M
1. principles   2. principal

Exercise 6N
1. quiet   2. quite, quiet

Exercise 6O
1. supposed   2. suppose

Exercise 6P
1. than   2. then

Exercise 6Q
1. There   2. they're, their

Exercise 6R
1. Though   2. thought, through

Exercise 6S
1. two   2. too, to

Exercise 6T
1. used   2. used

Exercise 6U
1. weather   2. whether

Exercise 6V
1. Who's   2. whose

Exercise 6W
1. You're   2. your

Mini Review 1
1. effect, advice   2. all ready, except   3. except, an   4. already affected
5. advise, accept

Mini Review 2
1. led, desert   2. know, desserts   3. no, lead   4. led, its   5. it's, loose
6. know, lose, deserts

Mini Review 3
1. principles, personal   2. supposed, than   3. quite, personnel   4. past, supposed
5. They're, than

Mini Review 4
1. Who's, your   2. thought, used   3. whether, your, weather   4. Whose, two
5. too, who's

Summary of Chapter 10
1. period   2. question mark   3. semicolon   4. colon   5. quotation marks
6. comma   7. hyphen   8. dash   9. capital   10. underlining

✳ *Additional Topics for Writing Assignments*

1. Imagine that you are applying to participate in a student work-study program. If you are accepted, you will live in a foreign country for the summer. Describe yourself, your interests, your family, and your life in the United States. Explain why you want to go to that country to study. Do you have any special links to the country through your family? Are you interested in its language, art, history, geography, or neighboring countries? How would you benefit by the experience?

2. You will need a partner for this assignment. Choose a person in the class who is new to you rather than someone you already know. Interview that person so you can introduce your new friend to members of the class. Ask questions about family, schoolwork, goals, and ambitions. Take notes as you listen to the answers to your questions. Then write a paragraph introducing that person. When you both have finished writing your paragraphs, form a group with two other students and take turns reading your paragraphs of introduction aloud.

3. Describe how you would spend a perfect day in the summer. Describe in detail what places you would go, what you would do there, what (or whom) you would take along, and what you especially like about summer. If you prefer another season, you might write about a perfect day in the spring, winter, or fall.

4. Explain what you liked or disliked about <u>one</u> of the following topics:
    a. A movie that you saw recently.
    b. A TV show that you watched recently.
    c. A book that you read recently.

5. What is music to your ears? Write about the music you listen to regularly. When and where do you listen? Do you listen to the radio at home, in the car, or on headphones while you exercise? Do you have a collection of videos, tapes, or CDs? Do you have a favorite instrumental group or a singer that you especially like to hear perform this music? How does this music make you feel? Explain in specific detail why this particular kind of music appeals to you.

6. Imagine that you are going to take a trip.
    a. Describe your destination, transportation, clothes, restaurants, nightclubs, souvenirs, parties, or anything else that you believe would contribute to an enjoyable vacation.

b. Explain why you chose this particular place.

c. What do you think are the benefits of taking a trip?

7. Tell about a past experience that you remember especially well. Perhaps it was the funniest, the most frightening, or the happiest experience you can remember.

OR

Describe some event that might be called the "big event" in your life.

8. Do you (or did you ever) belong to a group or an organization? Perhaps you work in a group on the job that functions as a team.

a. Describe its purpose and its activities.

b. Explain why you joined it. What do you contribute to it? To what do you attribute the high or low morale that may exist?

c. Discuss your experiences as a member of a group. What do individual members of a group gain by their participation in it?

9. Let's assume that you now have your college degree and that you are applying for your first full-time job. Aside from salary, what working conditions and benefits are most important to you? Rank them in order of importance, and, in each instance, explain specifically its importance. Remember: do not write about salary. When your instructor returns your work, meet with three classmates and discuss your papers, comparing the points you listed. Choose the best paper from each group to read aloud to the class.

10. Discuss the advantages and disadvantages of going to school while holding a job.

OR

Write about how to succeed in school after being away for three years or more.

OR

Write about how you deal with pressure on your job or at school.

11. Write about a profession or an occupation you would choose to enter if you could.

a. Describe the kind of work you would be doing.

b. Explain why this work appeals to you.

c. Do you see any disadvantages in this profession or occupation?

12. Many people object to the amount of time and money adolescents spend on video games in electronic amusement centers. Some people have attempted to have laws passed limiting the number of hours that young people can spend in these centers, and others want to bar anyone under age eighteen from playing the games. On the other hand, others believe that this is a matter for parents to decide, not one for the law.

Give your opinion on this controversial subject. Are the games harmful to adolescents when they play in an amusement center? If your answer is yes, in what ways are they harmful? Should limits be imposed? If so, by whom and what should they be? What are the problems in enforcing a law restricting this activity?

OR

Suppose you were a parent whose children were spending most of their leisure time in amusement centers. Would you favor action against the operators of these centers? If so, what would you suggest? Or would you be concerned only with keeping your own children from spending their time and money there? What other activities might you suggest to replace the games they enjoy there?

13. Why did you decide to attend this college? Explain why and possibly how you chose this college. Describe your first impressions of the campus. How could the college be improved? You might discuss registration procedures, the cafeteria, counseling, class schedules, course offerings, or anything else you would like to see improved.

14. Go to a shopping mall or a park. Find a comfortable place to sit for a while in order to observe people carefully. Select one person and give a complete description of this person's appearance and behavior. If possible, take notes to refer to when you complete this assignment at home.

15. Recall the details of how you learned a specific skill such as swimming, skating, typing, driving a car, riding a bicycle or a surfboard, playing a musical instrument, or playing baseball or some other sport. Remember to describe the steps in your learning process.

16. Car Mechanic

Describe the ideal car mechanic. What characteristics does a good mechanic have? Give examples of good service and explain how important the knowledge of the mechanic about your particular make and model of car is. Have you ever had exceptionally good work done by a mechanic? Describe the circumstances.

OR

Coach of a Sports Team

Describe the ideal coach. How much influence does the coach have on the players' lives on and off the field? Can the coach make a poor player better, or a good player even better? How does the coach's ability to inspire confidence in the players affect the outcome of the game? Relate some experience you may have had with an outstanding coach.

OR

Bus Drivers or Taxi Drivers

Describe the characteristics of the ideal driver of a bus or a taxi. Tell how the driver handles traffic problems encountered in the course of a day. How does the driver deal with these problems and difficult people? Describe a memorable ride you may have taken with a bus or taxi driver that illustrates the characteristics you mentioned were essential for a successful driver.

17. Go to the campus career counseling center to inquire about a career that interests you. Who spoke with you? What information did you obtain that will be helpful to you? Tell why you felt encouraged or discouraged about seriously planning for that career. Explain why you do or do not feel that the center provides a worthwhile service. Do not copy from any written material you may receive at the center.

18. Write a letter to the editor of your campus newspaper, commenting on an article. Express your agreement or disagreement with the writer. Offer your opinion based on your experience and observations on the subject. Support your point of view with specific examples. Don't just write in general terms. Attach a copy of the article that provoked your comments.

19. Mentoring is not a new idea, but it has been given impetus by President Clinton's goal of finding a "caring adult or mentor for every at-risk child in the country." Many organizations already operate nonprofit agencies that match adult volunteers with disadvantaged teenagers, and other groups now have promised to recruit two million mentors by the year 2000. Supporters of the programs believe that mentors are an effective way of helping these young people, and they have success stories that demonstrate this positive influence. Critics of the program, however, say that the mentor program can create more problems than it solves, and they offer examples of disappointment and resentment. Several factors seem to be essential in determining the success or failure of this approach to a serious social problem: the screening and the training of the volunteers, the matching of mentor and teenager, and the dedication and responsibility of the mentors themselves. Explain whether you favor or oppose mentoring. Would you be willing to devote two years to being a mentor? What personal qualities do you think are most important for a successful mentor? Do you think that better ways exist within the family or the neighborhood to guide young people? Are there any risks in having an adult from "outside" attempt to guide a young person whose early years have been so difficult?

20. Explain how to market a new product such as jogging shoes, cosmetics, a food processor, detergent, toothpaste, a camera, or any other small item that you are familiar with. Consider strategies for attracting the consumer's attention. For instance, decide on a name for the product and explain why you think the name will help to sell it. How will you determine the price? Do customers respond to product demonstrations in stores? Can you give away samples of your prod-

uct or send coupons through the mail? What can you do to make the customer want to try your product?

OR

Explain why you are willing to try a new product. How does the manufacturer persuade you to buy something that you may not even need? Do you pay attention to advertisements in newspapers and magazines and on radio and television? If so, what kind of approach appeals to you? Do you respond favorably to coupons, samples, and store demonstrations? Do you ever buy a new product because a friend or an acquaintance recommends it? Write about specific products that you have actually used.

21. Write a letter to a personnel manager of a company requesting an interview for a job. Tell the reasons why you are qualified for the job. Describe your past experience, if any, and relate your education to the requirements of the position. Use your actual present experience, education, and qualifications.

   Write at least 150 words in the body of the letter. Head your paper correctly and follow the business letter format shown below. Single-space letter headings.

Your address
Your city and state
The date

Mr. John Smith
Personnel Director
Star Enterprises
6132 Wilshire Boulevard
Los Angeles, CA 90036

Dear Mr. Smith:

Indent for paragraph. _____

_____

Sincerely yours,

Your name

22. Many American college freshmen are having difficulty doing college work. In fact, a concerned faculty committee at one university has addressed a letter to the parents of all eighth graders in the state, warning them that it is not too soon to begin preparing these students

for college. With this idea in mind, write a composition on one of the following topics:

a. Assume that you are the parent of an eighth grader. What steps will you take to see that your child is prepared for college? What recommendations will you make to your child?

b. Think back to your own years in junior high school and high school. Were you adequately prepared for college? What do you wish your parents, your teachers, and you had done differently? In what ways was your preparation good?

23. Women are often discouraged from entering certain occupations and professions. Do you think, for example, that women should be discouraged from becoming scientists, doctors, dentists, firefighters, police officers, heavy-equipment operators, or electricians? Are there any valid reasons for discrimination against women in these and other fields? If you believe that women should be encouraged to enter these fields, what, in your opinion, are the best ways to overcome the objections of others? Or do you believe that there are some occupations that only men should pursue and some that only women should pursue?

Present the reasons for your point of view. Focus on one occupation or profession (for example, military service) to write about in specific detail instead of writing about several in general terms.

24. Evaluate this writing class. Explain why you like or dislike the workbook, tests, writing assignments, and classroom activities. Please include any suggestions you may have to improve this course.

25. An activity like climbing Mt. Everest is expensive, dangerous, and physically and psychologically stressful. In your opinion, what are the benefits? Why do you think people subject themselves to such hardships? If you had your choice, would you go on such an expedition? Why or why not? If you did go, what steps would you take to prepare yourself for such an ordeal physically and psychologically? Use the questions as a guide to discuss your views about undertaking a difficult or dangerous adventure. Give specific reasons for attempting such a challenge and explain exactly how you would prepare yourself.

26. Disputes sometimes arise over the use of public lands or the allocation of public funds. Each side offers what appears to be a reasonable argument. Here are some samples of recent debates.

a. Should funds from the federal gas tax (less than 1 percent) be spent on bicycle projects such as bike lanes, trails, and parking facilities? Opponents say we can't afford such luxuries because we don't have enough money to repair highways and bridges needed to ensure public safety. Cyclists say that riding a bike is not a luxury; streets must be safe for all those who bike to work, and thus reduce pollution, traffic, and wear on the roads.

b. Environmentalists want to remove the automobile from Yosemite National Park to preserve the natural beauty by limiting the number of people in the park at a given time. Opponents counter that shuttles, day-use reservations, and higher fees will keep out ordinary American families to benefit elitist hikers and solitude lovers.

c. A similar argument has arisen in regard to the Grand Canyon. One group would ban or severely limit flights of small planes and helicopters over the park, charging that they contribute to the smog problem and disturb the tranquillity of visitors who have come to enjoy the natural beauty. The defenders of these flights maintain that people should have the opportunity to enjoy the grandeur of the canyon in this unique way.

Explain where you stand on one of these issues. You may not want to take either side, but, instead, propose a compromise. If you know of a similar debate in your area, you may, of course, write about that problem.

27. Every year a few top collegiate and professional athletes receive awards in recognition of their outstanding performances. What makes the "superstar" stand out from his or her extremely talented fellow athletes? Consider talent, coaching, discipline, motivation, and any other factors that may explain this athletic excellence. Or you may choose to write about the "superstar" in one of the performing arts.

28. Have you ever received a gift that you liked so much that you still remember how you felt when you opened the package? Describe the gift and explain what you particularly liked about it. When did you get it? Was the gift special, in part, because of your relationship with the giver? Was the gift a complete surprise, or was it something you had been wanting for a long time? Do you still have the gift? What is its condition today? If you no longer have it, what happened to it?
OR
Write about the pleasure you had planning and giving a gift to someone. Consider some of the questions above.

29. The traditional roles of both women and men have been changing during the last 40 years or so. These roles are not so clearly defined today as they were in the past. Changes may be seen, for instance, in clothing, hairstyles, professions, occupations, and interests. Psychologists, in fact, use the term *androgynous* (from the Greek roots for "man" and "woman") to suggest that members of both sexes combine "male" and "female" psychological traits in different degrees. Explain how the changing role of women may be seen as a "liberation" of American men as well. What pressures and responsibilities do women share with men in their new roles? Support your ideas with specific details and examples from your reading, your own experience, and your observations.

30. As you may already know, being sick can be expensive. If you have had to visit a doctor or an emergency room lately, you know how expensive it is. The situation is especially critical for those people who are at the poverty level, those who are called "the working poor." The "working poor" are those people who have an income below $15,000, and they frequently do not have the means to pay medical bills. In responding to the following questions, consider their problems. How do you think that medical bills should be paid? Should the patient have to pay all or part of the bill? Should either the state or the federal government pick up the bill? What should be the role of insurance companies? Discuss your opinions about the ways to pay for medical care by jotting down your ideas as they occur to you. Then select the two or three ideas you feel qualified to develop with specific support. You may want to inquire about the current methods of payment available in your state. Or, if you work, you may want to interview a person in the insurance department who can help answer some of these questions before you begin writing.
OR
If you prefer, write about one of the following subjects:
    1. Your own situation
    2. Uninsured children
    3. Unemployed people
    4. Elderly retired low-income people
Use the questions above as a guide in developing your paper.

31. Family lifestyles are changing. With the dramatic increase in single-parent and dual-career households, family life isn't as simple as it once was. Long commutes to and from work, community and school functions in the evenings, and involvement in health club programs, social clubs, hobbies, and other leisure activities all occupy more family time. How have these factors affected family life today?

32. Many colleges have spent millions of dollars on wiring for "smart" classrooms (Internet-connected lecture halls) in the belief that technology will transform the way we learn. Some professors plan to change the way they teach their courses. For example, students can view film clips, hear speeches, and rearrange the material, write about it, and share it with someone in another location. If you have had an opportunity to access the Internet, do you agree or disagree with using this method to teach college courses? Give specific examples of how a student can benefit from access to the Internet. If you disagree with using the Internet to teach courses, give specific reasons for your opinions.
OR
A possible topic for ESL students:
How would conducting business in your culture differ from doing business in the American culture? For example, in a Japanese busi-

ness meeting, if you try to deviate from the prearranged agenda and force consideration of a new topic, you might make the business people very uncomfortable. The emphasis on conformity in the Japanese culture discourages individual initiative. Further, when Westerners speak, the Japanese will often say, "Hai" (yes). This "hai" means, "Yes, I understand you," not "Yes, I agree with you." Because the Japanese person will attempt to tell a Westerner what he wants to hear, the American may think the other person is agreeing with him, when in fact, they do not agree at all.

If you identify with a different culture, explain how that culture's attitudes, speech patterns, and interpersonal behavior patterns would affect the way business is conducted. Compare and contrast those interactions with those in the United States.

33. What should be done to make your community a better place in which to live? **or** What should be done to improve your school environment?

Step 1. Start by jotting down all the improvements you would like to see in your community, neighborhood, or school.

Step 2. List the ways you think each improvement could be made.

Step 3. Decide who should be responsible for making the changes. If you are writing about the community, for example, decide whether it should be individuals, citizen groups, or government agencies. Can the media play a role? If you are writing about improving your school, you might consider participation in student government, peer counseling opportunities, availability of tutors, library and instructional facilities, financial aid, and student contributions to curricula planning.

Step 4. By now you probably have quite a list. You can't write about all of the items in a brief paper. Will you write, for instance, in the case of the community, about inadequate street lighting, smog, trash collection, houses that need painting, street cleaning, street repairs, or police protection? Narrow your topic to one or two improvements you would like to see made. You may want to write about your immediate neighborhood rather than the community as a whole if you live in a large city.

As You Write: First, state the problem. Give the reader, for example, a clear picture in a detailed description of the situation in your community. Consider some of the following questions:

Is the problem dangerous to the public now or will it be dangerous in the future?

Is the problem merely annoying or unsightly?

Are you the only one concerned, or do you hear similar objections from others?

Have any attempts been made to solve the problem?

Finally, describe in specific terms the improvements you recommend and give some concrete suggestions on how to bring them about.

34. Advertisers, as you know, use a variety of approaches to sell their products to us. Cut out an advertisement from a magazine or a newspaper and analyze the primary appeal it makes to the reader. As you study the ad, jot down your ideas in answer to the following questions. Include as many examples as you can find.

    a. If there is a picture, how is it part of the appeal? Did it attract you to the ad? How?

    b. Are the words persuasive?

    c. You have learned the importance of having the reader in mind when you write. Does the advertiser seem to be addressing a specific customer?

    d. Does the ad make any promises? Are there any facts?

    e. Does the ad appeal to any specific emotion or emotions?

    f. How successful is the advertisement? Would it persuade you to buy the product?

    Bring your advertisement and your notes to class. Form a group with three classmates to discuss your work in preparation for writing your rough draft. If your instructor approves, meet again to help each other with your rough drafts.

    You could meet with your group before you look for an ad and decide upon a single class of advertisements for all the members of your group to work on; for example, travel, cosmetics, pharmaceuticals, dental products, computers, insurance, or any number of others.

35. The Census Bureau recently released a survey on schools and homework. Among elementary and high school students, the median time spent doing homework is five-and-a-half hours a week. In private high schools, it is fourteen hours a week. Do you believe that homework encourages learning? From your experience in school, do you believe that students should receive more, less, or no homework? Argue for one of these proposals. Give specific examples to support your argument.

36. Do you exercise to keep fit as many other people do? Describe the best way you have found to keep in shape.

    Step 1. Make a list of the different exercises you do. Your list might include:

    a. aerobics

    b. walking

    c. jogging

    d. swimming

e. skiing

f. team sports

Try clustering or outlining techniques here. See Chapter 1.

Step 2.   Write a topic sentence that gives your opinion on why you believe it is important to exercise regularly.

Step 3.   Supply specific details about the equipment needed, any problems you have encountered, successes you have had, or any other details to interest your reader in your experiences.

Step 4.   Write a rough draft from your list and your notes. Concentrate on one or two methods of keeping fit. Illustrate your successes or your failures by telling your reader exactly how you progressed at each step of training.

Step 5.   Read your rough draft aloud or have someone in your class read it to you. Revise it according to the suggestions of your audience. Do you have a topic sentence and several supporting illustrations?

Step 6.   Recopy your paper before you submit it.

You might prefer to write about why you do not believe in keeping fit. If you do not exercise, write about your reasons for your choice and follow the steps outlined above.

Guide to Revision of Writing Assignments

Symbol	Error
Pl	Plural
Pos	Possessive
P Shift	Pronoun Shift in Person
Case	Pronoun Case
Vb	Verb
V Shift	Sequence of Tenses
V Tense	Incorrect Use of Tenses
SS	Faulty Sentence Structure
VF	Incorrect Verbal Form
CS	Comma Splice
Frag	Fragment
C	Comma
P	Other Marks of Punctuation
Cap	Capital
No Cap	No Capital
Adj	Adjective
Adv	Adverb
S-V Agr	Agreement of Subject and Verb
P-A Agr	Agreement of Pronoun and Antecedent
Ref	Pronoun Reference
RO	Run-On Sentence
MM	Misplaced Modifier
Sp	Spelling
W	Wordiness
WW	Wrong Word
^	Omission of Word
¶	Paragraph

# Glossary

Action verb   Tells what the subject does, did, or will do.

Adjective   Modifies a noun or pronoun. Answers one of the following questions: What kind? How many? Which one? Whose?

Adverb   Modifies a verb, adjective, or other adverb. Answers one of the following questions: When? Why? How? Where?

Adverbial connective (for example, however, nevertheless, or then)   Used with a semicolon and a comma to join main clauses. Also called an *adverbial conjunction* or a *conjunctive adverb*.

Agreement   The matching in number, gender, and person between subjects and verbs or pronouns and antecedents.

Antecedent   The noun, pronoun, or noun phrase to which a pronoun refers.

Auxiliary verb   The helping verb used with a main verb to form a verb phrase.

Base form of the verb   The present form of the verb with no *-s* at the end.

Collective noun (for example, family)   Refers to a collection of persons, places, things, ideas, or activities.

Comma splice   Grammatical error made when main clauses are joined with only a comma and no connective.

Common noun   Names people, places, things, ideas, or activities in general.

Comparative   A form of the adjective or adverb used to compare two people, places, ideas, things, or actions.

Completer   Follows a linking verb to describe or rename the subject.

Complex sentence   Composed of a main clause and one or more subordinate clauses.

Compound antecedent   Two or more antecedents joined by a coordinating connective.

Compound object   Two or more objects joined by a coordinating connective.

Compound sentence   Two or more main clauses joined by a connective and appropriate punctuation.

Compound subject   Two or more subjects joined by a coordinating connective.

Compound verb   Two or more verbs joined by a coordinating connective.

Contraction   A word formed by combining two words with an apostrophe to substitute for the omission of letters.

Coordinating connective (and, but, or, for, nor, so, yet)   Used with a comma to join words, phrases, and main clauses. Also called a *coordinating conjunction*.

Dangling modifier   An adjective or adverb that does not modify any word in the sentence.

Gender   Refers to the masculine, feminine, or neuter forms of third person pronouns.

Indefinite pronoun (for example, anyone or someone) Refers to people, things, or ideas in general rather than to specific antecedents.

Irregular verb   Does not follow any spelling rules to form the past tense.

Linking verb   Shows a relationship between the subject and the completer.

Main clause (independent clause)   A group of related words with a subject and a verb that can stand alone as a sentence if the first word is capitalized and the clause ends with a mark of punctuation such as a period or a question mark.

Misplaced modifier An adjective or adverb that has been placed next to a word it does not modify.

Modifier Describes, limits, or makes specific another word in the sentence.

Noun marker (for example, a, an, the) An adjective that points to the noun that follows it.

Noun Names a person, place, thing, idea, or activity.

Number Indicates the singular and plural forms of pronouns. Singular means one person or thing. Plural means more than one person or thing.

Object The noun or pronoun that answers the question "What?" or "Whom?" after an action verb. Objects also follow prepositions.

Parallel structure The placing of similar items in similar grammatical form.

Participle A verb form that may function as part of a verb phrase (was winning) or as an adjective (the winning team).

Past participle Formed by adding *-d* or *-ed* to the base form of a regular verb.

Perfect tenses Formed by using a form of the auxiliary verb *have* and the past participle of the main verb.

Person Indicates the person speaking, the person spoken to, or the person or thing spoken about.

Phrase Group of words without a subject and a verb. Examples are noun phrases, verbal phrases, verb phrases, and prepositional phrases.

Possessive noun Changes spelling to indicate a belonging-to relationship.

Preposition Used to show position, direction, or relationship.

Present participle Formed by adding *-ing* to the base form of a verb.

Pronoun Takes the place of a noun or refers to a noun. A personal pronoun shows person, number, and gender.

Proper noun Names a specific person, place, thing, idea, or activity.

Regular verb Adds *-d* or *-ed* to form the past tense.

Run-on sentence A grammatical error made when main clauses are joined with no punctuation or connective between them.

Sentence fragment Begins with a capital letter and ends with a period but does not express a complete thought or contain a main clause.

Sentence Has at least one subject and one verb and expresses a complete thought.

Simple sentence Composed of one main clause.

Subject The person or thing the verb is asking or telling about.

Subject of a command Understood to be "you."

Subordinate clause (dependent clause) A group of related words with a subject and a verb introduced by a subordinator. Makes an incomplete statement, so it must be attached to a main clause to be a complete sentence.

Subordinator (for example, because, that, although) Used to introduce a subordinate clause.

Superlative A form of the adjective or adverb used to compare three or more items.

Tense The change of verb form to indicate when the action occurred.

Verb A word or group of words indicating action or a state of being.

Verb phrase The combination of an auxiliary verb and one of the principal forms of a verb.

Verbal phrase A group of words that includes a verbal, a noun, and/or a prepositional phrase.

Verbal Formed from a verb but cannot function as a main verb. Used as a noun, adjective, or adverb.

Index

Titles
capitalization of, 352
quotation marks, 347–348
underlining, 347–348
Topic sentence, 12–16
Transitional devices, 26–30

Unity, 21–24
Usage (words that sound or look alike),
    355–372
a/an/and, 355
accept/except, 355–356
advice/advise, 356
affect/effect, 357
already/all ready, 357–358
dessert/desert, 358–359
its/it's, 359
know/no, 360
lead/led, 360–361
loose/lose, 361
past/passed, 362–363
personal/personnel, 363
principal/principle, 364
quiet/quite, 364–365
suppose/supposed, 365
then/than, 366

there/their/they're, 366–367
through/though/thought, 368
to/two/too, 368–369
use/used, 369–370
weather/whether, 370
whose/who's, 371
you/you're, 371–372

Verbal phrases
adding details with, 178–181
definition of, 178
punctuating, 121
Verbs
action, 72
auxiliary, 85–91
characteristics of, 72
compound, 36–39
irregular, 76–81
linking, 72, 73, 132–136
main, 85–86
object of, 125–129
principal forms of, 82–85
regular, 72–76
tense, 74
will/would, 95–97